MW01285232

Dedication

In memory of my father, Stanley Lester Cohen, 1923-1995, World War II veteran and concentration camp survivor, who instilled in me an understanding of justice and fairness, the belief that all people are equal, and the patriotic and religious ethics that make me want to leave the world a better place than it was when I arrived.

Author's Note

Where in our Constitution does it give the states the authority to regulate marriage? The concept of the marriage license is so ingrained in our culture that we assume it has always been there. Certainly, as a practicing family attorney for more than 25 years, I never doubted it. My job was to know the law, not to question it. Yet, when attended Washington University School of Law in St. Louis back in the mid-1980s, there was something about it that struck me as odd. Contract and tort law went back hundreds of years, but family law began at the turn of the 20th Century. After all, marriage has been around for thousands of years. So, why is marriage and divorce law so recent? As my career turned to writing, I began to dig deeper.

I asked myself, what is the source of the state's authority to regulate marriage? A license, by definition, is permission. Marriage is a right.[1] So why must we obtain the state's approval in order to marry? True, the state has the inherent police power it provide for the safety of its citizens. We must get the state's permission to work in certain professions in order to protect consumers, i.e., medicine, law, etc. As well, states issue driver's licenses only if a person meets the qualifications of being a safe driver. But what does marriage have to do with public safety?

In my 2015 book, *America Solved: A New Family for the 21st Century,* I explain how, for the past half a century, our federal government's inane policies have all but destroyed the family unit. In that book, I focused on proposed policies that would resurrect the nuclear family. In my research for that book, I read Harvard history professor Nancy Cott's 2000 publication, *Public Vows*,[2] where she tells us that at the founding of our nation, couples would "self-marry" and "self-divorce" at will, without any state intervention. Up until 2015, the Supreme Court had always said marriage was left to the states to regulate.[3] Three months after I published *America Solved*, the Supreme Court did as I predicted in that book, and extended the right to marry to same-sex couples.[4] Yet, buried in that decision, was a dramatic change in the Court's view of state regulation of marriage and divorce. The Supreme Court adopted Cott's finding that marriage in America began as a purely private affair, and has since evolved.

State regulation of marriage suddenly, with a stroke of a pen, came into doubt, for, if states did not have the authority to regulate marriage at our founding, how then could they acquire that power without a constitutional amendment? The answer not only casts doubt on state regulation of marriage, but also calls into question all of our assumptions about the common law rights and duties of husbands and wives. My discovery began when reading Georgetown Law School professor Randy Barnett's 2016 book, *Our Republican Constitution: Securing the Liberty and Sovereignty of We the People.*[5] In that book, Barnett explains that the Supreme Court's entire thinking of state control over personal rights changed dramatically within fifty years of our founding.

According to Barnett, at the beginning of our nation's history, the prevailing wisdom was that *We the People* was the people as individuals in the collective. In other words, the Constitution stood as an obstacle to the will of the majority abusing the minority. Then, with the election of Andrew Jackson, Barnett describes the ascent of the belief in what he calls the democratic view of the Constitution, one where *We the People* was the majority, not a collection of individuals. That view, with certain ebbs and flows, continued with all its infamy in Supreme Court decisions, i.e., The Dred Scott case,[6] *Plessy v. Ferguson*,[7] and Jim Crow laws,[8] until it began to wane slightly in 1954 with *Brown v. Board of Education*.[9]

In *Public Vows,* Nancy Cott explains how, in the 19th Century, states began to set down rules as to who can marry and who can divorce in accordance with Christian principles because, as I explain in *America Solved*, our nation had become a union of state theocracies. In *Our Republican Constitution*, Randy Barnett places that development in the context of majority rule, something that not even the passage of the Thirteenth [10] and Fourteenth[11] Amendments would stop. Barnett explains that the Supreme Court initially gave the post-Civil War Amendments strict readings, and continued to defer to the will of the majority and their elected representatives well into the 21st Century. Thus, when the subject of state regulation of marriage came before the Court for the first time in 1888 in the case of *Maynard v. Hill*, it was more than willing to subjugate all citizens to the whims of the Christian majority.*12* While that decision would not survive 21st Century scrutiny, it was, and continues to be, the primary legal authority for state regulation of marriage, as well as for the adoption of common law marital rights and duties on which all relevant federal and state laws are based.[13] Yet, as this book will explain, these common law rights and duties did not apply to all citizens because in fact they were contractual obligations enforceable only if the parties had married with the blessing of the Anglican Church.

This book, using both historical and legal analysis, will put forth the best argument for ending state regulation of marriage and divorce In Part I, it will set up the argument with explorations into the competing interests of state sovereignty and dig deep into the evolution of the right to marry, and then find the best plaintiffs to present a test case in federal court. In Parts II and III, it will set forth the arguments in support of that hypothetical claim, leaving no doubt that, not only is state regulation of marriage unconstitutional, but that its original purpose is no longer applicable. Finally, I will explain, as I first set out in *America Solved*, that the only way to restore marriage in America is to return it to what it was at our founding, a private contract between individuals and their private religious beliefs.

I.

SETTING UP
THE ARGUMENT

A. The State as Sovereign and Majoritarian Rule: Tracing the States' Legal Basis for Regulation of Marriage

In 1888, in *Maynard v. Hill*, the Supreme Court expressed the majority view of marriage in America:

> **Marriage**, as creating the most important relation in life, as having more to do with the morals and civilization of a people than any other institution, **has always been subject to the control of the legislature.** That body prescribes the age at which parties may contract to marry, the procedure or form essential to constitute marriage, the duties and obligations it creates, its effects upon the property rights of both, present and prospective, and the acts which may constitute grounds for its dissolution. [*Emphasis added*].[14]

As demonstrated in its 2015 opinion of *Obergefell v. Hodges*, the majority of the justices in the current Supreme Court believe marriage in the United States evolved from a private contract into what it is today. Even Mr. Justice Roberts, in his dissent in *Obergefell*, agreed with that premise.[15] Yet, Roberts holds on to the view that the majority has the right to dictate to the minority as to who can marry.

In 2013, in *U.S. v. Windsor,* the United States Supreme Court struck down a fateful attempt of Congress to define marriage as being between one man and one woman.[16] The act known under its acronym, DOMA, was originally signed into law during the Clinton administration, a rare exercise in cooperation between Democrats and Republicans. Now known as a precursor to the same-sex marriage cases that would follow two years later, *Windsor* speaks to the source of power of the State over its inhabitants:

> In order to assess the validity of that intervention it is necessary to discuss the extent of the state power and authority over marriage as a matter of history and tradition. State laws defining and regulating marriage, of course, must respect the constitutional rights of persons, [citations omitted] but, subject to those guarantees, "regulation of domestic relations" is "an area that has long been regarded as a virtually exclusive province of the States." [17]

Of course, the *Windsor* court was doing its due diligence and using its power under Article III of the United States Constitution to review an act of Congress to determine whether DOMA was valid. Yet, instead of determining whether Article II permitted Congress the authority to pass the Act in question, the Court seemed to focus on a history of federal deference:

> The recognition of civil marriages is central to state domestic relations law applicable to its residents and

citizens. *See Williams v. North Carolina*, 317 U.S. 287, 298, 63 S.Ct. 207, 87 L.Ed 279 (1942). "**Each state as a sovereign** has a rightful and legitimate concern in the marital status of persons domiciled within its borders"). The definition of marriage is the foundation of the State's broader authority to regulate the subject of domestic relations with respect to the "[p]rotection of offspring, property interests, and the enforcement of marital responsibilities." *Ibid.* "[T]he states, at the time of the adoption of the Constitution, possessed full power over the subject of marriage and divorce ... [and] the Constitution delegated no authority to the Government of the United States on the subject of marriage and divorce." [*Citations omitted*]. "The whole subject of the domestic relations of husband and wife, parent and child, belongs to the laws of the States and not to the laws of the United States."[*Emphasis added.*]

But is a state really a sovereign? Georgetown law professor Randy Barnett explains in *Our Republican Constitution*, that the modern concept of state sovereignty is a legal fiction. Sovereign refers to the king, and the Founders deposed the monarchy and replaced it with a republic. Barnett theorizes that approximately fifty years later, our republic began to morph into a democracy. As benign as that might sound, Barnett would beg to differ. A republic is a nation of the people, not as a majority, but as a group of individuals. A democracy is majority rule. But, most important, in Barnett's view, if the state refers to the people of the state and not the state itself, the state cannot be sovereign because the state serves the people, and not the other way around.[18] Barnett further argues that the very existence of the Eleventh Amendment[19] proves that the Founders never intended the states to be sovereign in the democratic view. In fact, the very existence of the amendment was to overrule the Supreme Court's 1793 decision in *Chisholm v. Georgia*[20] and its finding that a citizen of one state had the right to sue another state in federal court. In fact, even that amendment does not use the phrase "sovereign immunity." The Eleventh Amendment does not grant any rights, rather, it is specifically geared to limit judicial powers set forth in Article III of the Constitution.

In fact, it was this broad over reading of the Eleventh Amendment that was at the root of what Barnett calls the Democratic Constitution. If the state is nothing more than a collection of its individual citizens, then its authority is limited to what its citizens specifically grants to it. Since all citizens, as is said in the Declaration of Independence, are endowed with inalienable rights, it cannot be said that its citizens could transfer to their elected representatives the authority to violate those rights. The Constitution is a transfer of state authority to the federal government, but like title to property, one cannot transfer any authority one does not actually own. Rather, elected government, in John Locke's view, is not people transferring power to the state, but only delegating limited authority to elected representatives.[21]

As the Supreme Court said in *Chisholm v. Georgia*: "The United States are sovereign as to all the powers of Government actually surrendered: Each State in the Union is sovereign as to all the powers reserved."[22] But since the people could not transfer inalienable rights to the state, the State is not the King of the people. It is not even the will of the people. It serves the people, not as the will of the majority, but to everyone individually.[23]

Yet, the democratic view of state sovereignty permitted state courts to act as if the state had the power of a monarchy. In an 1824 opinion of the Maine Supreme Court that would be cited as authority in *Maynard v. Hill*, the State saw itself as the King, at least as far as the state of matrimony was concerned:

> When the contracting parties have entered into the married state, they have not so much entered into a contract as into a new relation, the rights, duties, and obligations of which rest not upon their agreement, but upon the general law of the State, statutory or common, which defines and prescribes those rights, duties, and obligations. They are of law, not of contract. It was of contract that the relation should be established, but, being established, the power of the parties as to its extent or duration is at an end. **Their rights under it are determined by the will of the sovereign, as evidenced by law.** *[Emphasis added.]*[24]

Therefore, according to the Supreme Court of Maine, at least in 1824, just as the King of England was the religious leader of his subjects, as was the state when it came to the right to marry. Campbell University law professor E. Gregory Wallace disagrees, saying that:

> The colonial and founding generations took seriously the unique character and claims of religion. For the most part, those who participated in constitutional achievement of religious freedom were themselves deeply religious persons: their worldview was Christian and their arguments and audience were almost exclusively Christian. They believed that religion is unique because it entails duties owed to God. Their principal justifications for religious freedom rested upon the theological premise that **God exists and is sovereign** over both human government and the individual citizen. (*Emphasis added*).[25]

In Wallace's view, the Supreme Court of Maine had it backwards. Under our Constitution, government had no say in religious affairs; rather, government was subject to the will of God. In *Public Vows,* Nancy Cott notes that, under Colonial rule, the Anglican Church, acting for the King, was the arbiter of marriage and divorce. Prior to the establishment of the Anglican Church, England was Catholic giving the Pope sole authority over marriage and divorce. When the Pope refused to grant King Henry his divorce from Catherine of Aragon so he could marry Anne Boleyn, the King chose to establish his own church rather than to obey. Thus, it was accepted that the King, as head of the Anglican

Church, was as the Pope, the sole arbiter of marriage and divorce. No marriage was valid unless the King decided it was and no divorce could occur without the approval of the sovereign (and eventually Parliament).[26]

The Puritans, the Pilgrims, and others, left England for America in search of religious freedom and to escape the very rules that the State of Maine was imposing. Cott tells us that, in early America, people would "self-marry" and "self-divorce." Couples would choose each other, and hold themselves out as being married with or without a religious ceremony. If the marriage did not take, Cott suggests that, when the couple split up and went their separate ways, the community generally accepted it, showing that marital behavior, as with all social behavior, depends on the mores of the community, not on an edict from the sovereign.

The idea of self-marriage and self-divorce is consistent with Barnett's theory of the Republican Constitution. The crux of his argument is that *We the People* have fundamental rights as individuals. *We the People* confer very limited powers as our chosen representatives to manage the affairs of state *We the People* empower the judiciary to review and strike down any act of the legislative branch that violate the inalienable rights of the individual. Barnett tells us that the *republican* vision of the Constitution was the majority view of justices of the early Supreme Court. The minority view, the view of a single justice, was that the Constitution was not a fixed document, but one that was subject to change depending on the views of the majority.

This Democratic Constitution would soon become the excuse to continue, and even extend the practice of slavery. According to Barnett, the Founders struggled with the language of the Constitution because it must define those born as slaves as non-persons. Most believed that slavery would die out on its own as technology would render it useless. The Founders couldn't have been more wrong. Rather than dying out, the South, ever fearful and paranoid of Northern power, pushed harder and harder. The Dred Scott decision was the penultimate fate of the conflict between the Bill of Rights and slavery. How, using the Constitution, could the Supreme Court find that a black man who earns his freedom in a Northern state could be considered a slave when he enters into a slave state? Certainly not using the Republican theory that Barnett describes: the theory that first comes rights, then comes government, and that chosen representatives, as servants of the people, were bound not to violate those rights.

Advocates of the Democratic Constitution justified the Dred Scott decision, just as it would justify Jim Crow fifty years later. Viewing *We the People* as the majority permitted any matter of limiting the rights of the minority. As Benjamin Franklin once said, democracy is two wolves and a sheep voting on what to have for supper. A republic protects the individual. A democracy does not care about the individual, but only the state. In a republic, the individual citizens select representatives and give them limited power to govern, with that limitation being the fundamental rights

15

that exist in the Bill of Rights, including *unenumerated* rights that are discussed in the Ninth[27] and Tenth [28]Amendments (as well as the Thirteenth and Fourteenth Amendments that would follow). Under the Democratic Constitution, Congress could justify the Kansas-Nebraska Act of 1854,[29] permitting the majority of the new states to vote on whether they prefer to be a slave state or a free state. As Barnett explains, only with this viewpoint could the majority get to decide whether a minority should be enslaved.

According to Barnett, when Republicans gained control of government after the Civil War, it passed the Fourteenth Amendment to reverse the Democratic Constitution in favor of the Republican Constitution in force at the time of our founding. The justices of the Supreme Court, however, schooled in Jacksonian Democracy, chose to minimize its effect, and when the subject of state regulation of marriage came before the Court in *Maynard v. Hill* in 1888, they ignored individual liberties in favor of Christian majoritarian control with the weakest of justifications:

> Thus, in *Cronise v. Cronise*, 54 Penn. St. 255, 261, the Supreme Court of Pennsylvania said: "Special divorce laws are legislative acts. This power has been exercised from the earliest period by the legislature of the province, and by that of the State, under the constitutions of 1776 and 1790... . The continued exercise of the power, after the adoption of the constitution of 1790, **cannot be accounted for except on the ground that all men, learned and unlearned,**

believed it to be a legitimate exercise of the legislative power. This belief is further strengthened by the fact that no judicial decision has been made against it. *Communis error facit jus* would be sufficient to support it, but it stands upon the higher ground of contemporaneous and **continued construction of the people** of their own instrument." [*Emphasis added.*]

Simply put, the law is valid because the majority says it is, and because the judiciary had not said it's not. As to marriage and divorce, the supreme courts of Pennsylvania and Maine justified their respective statutes because it was the will of the majority, and the majority had the right, in its view, to determine the rights of the individual. The opinions of these former colonies reach back to pre-Colonial times in a judicially dishonest effort to find authority on which to base their rulings. Just because it had not been challenged does not make the law valid. Since all law is based on authority, tradition is irrelevant, especially so if that tradition was under English rule and predated the Constitution.[30] Yet, with the endorsement of the Supreme Court in *Maynard v. Hill* in 1888, state regulation of marriage would become not just a tradition, but a longstanding one, one that still stands almost 130 years later.

B. The Evolution of the Right to Marry

1. Our Founding: The Search for "Perfect Freedom"

In 2015, in *Obergefell v. Hodges*, the Supreme Court found that same-sex couples had the same fundamental right to marry as different sex couples, and found that states' refusal to grant marriage licenses to same-sex couples would violate their Due Process and Equal Protection rights under the Fourteenth Amendment to the United States Constitution. The ruling created a celebration in the Progressive community and a funeral service for Christian Conservatives. Randy Barnett sees it differently. He sees the Court having historically abandoned its Article III responsibility to strike down unconstitutional laws in deference to the political process. According to Barnett, the Supreme Court picks and chooses which of the fundamental rights it wishes to uphold depending on political circumstances rather than the Constitution. Therefore, if same-sex marriage had not grown into general acceptance, the Court would not have used what is known as substantive due process to overturn a state statute prohibiting it.

The Republican Constitution was based on the preservation of freedom, as a libertarian essay explains in 2013:

> It was this conception of freedom that led to John Locke's claim that the purpose of law is to "preserve and enlarge freedom," not to abolish or diminish it. A social relationship is described as "free" if all parties in that

relationship can exercise their equal and reciprocal rights without coercive interference by others. According to this approach, it is possible, in theory, to have a political state of "perfect freedom." This would consist of a society whose government is strictly limited to the protection and enforcement of individual rights. To the extent that the powers of government are limited in this fashion, we are said to have a "free society." … Freedom, properly conceived, *should* mean the freedom to do whatever one wishes to do without the coercive interference of others.[31]

In our nation's first fifty years, Barnett tells us, the Republican constitution was the law of the land. Regarding Bill of Rights, Supreme Court Justice Hugo Black explained in 1947, was simply a restatement of that fact:

The first ten amendments were proposed and adopted largely because of fear that Government might unduly interfere with prized individual liberties. The people wanted and demanded a Bill of Rights written into their Constitution. The amendments embodying the Bill of Rights were intended to curb all branches of the Federal Government in the fields touched by the amendments — Legislative, Executive, and Judicial. The Fifth, Sixth, and Eighth Amendments were pointedly aimed at confining exercise of power by courts and judges within precise boundaries, particularly in the procedure used for the trial of criminal cases. Past history provided strong reasons for the apprehensions which brought these procedural amendments into being and attest the wisdom of their adoption. For the fears of arbitrary court action sprang largely from the past use of courts in the imposition of criminal punishments to suppress speech, press, and religion. Hence the constitutional limitations of courts' powers were, in the view of the Founders, essential supplements to the First Amendment, which was itself designed to protect the widest scope for all people to believe and to express the most divergent political, religious, and other views.[32]

2. **The Democratic Constitution:** *Baron* **as the Demarcation from Freedom.**

It all changed with the era of Jacksonian Democracy. In 1833, in the case of *Baron ex rel. Tierman v. Mayor of Baltimore*,[33] the Supreme Court declared that the Bill of Rights did not apply to the states, but only to actions of the federal government. As Mr. Justice Samuel Alito explained in 2010 in *McDonald v. City of Chicago*, the enormity of this four-page opinion cannot be understated.[34] In *Marbury v. Madison*, Chief Justice John Marshall painted the Court's authority with a broad brush, with no limitations of state actions, when he wrote:

This theory is essentially attached to a written constitution, and, is consequently, to be considered, by this court, as one of the fundamental principles of our society. It is not therefore to be lost sight of in the further consideration of this subject.

If an act of the legislature, repugnant to the constitution, is void, does it, notwithstanding its invalidity, bind the courts, and oblige them to give it effect? Or, in other words, though it be not law, does it constitute a rule as operative as if it was a law? This would be to overthrow in fact what was established in theory; and would seem, at first view, an absurdity too gross to be insisted on. It shall, however, receive a more attentive consideration.

It is emphatically the province and duty of the judicial department to say what the law is. Those who apply the rule to particular cases, must of necessity expound and interpret that rule. If two laws conflict with each other, the courts must decide on the operation of each. (*Emphasis added*.)[35]

Marbury v. Madison was 27 pages long. Yet, in *Baron*, in just four pages, and with little analysis, Marshall all but extinguished the personal rights that the people had demanded, for what real contact did ordinary people have with the federal government? But why did Marshall do it?

In his work, *Philosophy of History*, German philosopher Georg Wilhelm Friedrich Hegel, the father of modern historical thought, tells us that history is not merely ascertained as a fact, but understood by apprehending the reasons why the facts happened as they did.[36] So it is with John Marshall and his decision in *Baron*. Marshall understood how delicate our nation was, and treaded lightly. In 1803, with *Marbury v. Madison*, Marshall had adeptly expanded the authority of the Court in setting a foothold of the power in creating the power of judicial review, something that was not clearly set out in the Constitution.[37] Yet, by deciding in favor of the government and its authority to fire public employees, Marshall was able to grab that power without upsetting executive branch. His survival skills would soon be put to a test.

As Randy Barnett tells us in *Our Republican Constitution*, the Founders were certain that slavery would die of its own weight, and tabled the matter in order to gain support for the Revolution. They couldn't have been more wrong in their prediction. In 1794, Eli Whitney patented the cotton gin, a device that dramatically reduced the cost of producing cotton, causing Georgia, Mississippi, Alabama and Louisiana to drastically alter their agricultural philosophies, necessitating the need for more slave labor as the plant was extremely delicate and its cultivation was labor intensive.[38] With the Louisiana Purchase, leaders of the slave states were acutely aware how they might be outnumbered unless they could spread slavery into the western territories. At the same time, Northern states were acutely aware that slavery was seeping into the territories north of the Ohio River. Thus, when Missouri applied for statehood in 1919, in order to preserve the union, Kentucky's Henry Clay orchestrated the Missouri Compromise to temporarily prevent the South from succeeding.

The compromise, which please very few on either side, called for Missouri to be admitted as a slave state and Maine a free state, but most important, that slavery would not spread north of Missouri's southern border.[39]   The compromise fueled the birth of the Democrat party as a means to thwart any opposition to slavery, and General Andrew Jackson, flush from his victory at the Battle of New Orleans in 1815, was the perfect popular hero to lead the fight. After all, the South was powerful in the House of Representatives because a key compromise in the Constitution permitted them to count their slaves as 3/5 of a person against the total population of the state.

At the same time, the Christian revival historians call The Second Great Awakening was spreading across America, and that movement would bring a sense of Christian superiority that would be fodder for the birth of what Barnett calls the Democratic Constitution. It would also spawn the Abolitionist Movement and continue its righteous indignation through Reconstruction that would give birth to Carrie Nation and bring upon Prohibition and government controlled morality that would lead to a ban on contraceptives, homosexuality and polygamy, and continues to linger in the background today. When the abolitionists took control of Parliament in 1832, it was inevitable that they would abolish slavery, which they promptly did in July 1833, something that not only fueled the movement in America, but struck fear with Jackson and the Democrats.

Up until 1824, America had five presidents, four from Virginia and one from Massachusetts. John Quincy Adams, Secretary of State under James Monroe, was poised to continue. The presidential election of 1824, however, saw prim and proper Adams, who spend much of his life abroad, first with his father in France during the revolution, and then in the ambassador core, take on his principal rival, the backwoods, uneducated Jackson. Jackson won the most votes, but, as was the case with Thomas Jefferson and his alleged running mate Aaron Burr, no candidate would obtain the necessary majority of electoral votes throwing it to the House of Representatives and squarely at the feet of Henry Clay, the fourth place finisher and Speaker of the House. In what Jacksonians would call "The Corrupt Bargain," Clay, who despised Jackson, put together a coalition to give the presidency to Adams, while giving Clay the position of Secretary of State, then seen as the stepping stone to the presidency.[40]

Jackson, and his allies, were furious to say the least, and the ensuing wrath ruined any chance of Adams having a successful presidency.[41] Willful, self-confident, easily offended, he had a strong sense of personal honor and a violent temper, Jackson was the consummate soldier, but there was no middle ground. You were either with him or against him.[42] And, God help you if you were against him. Yet, his personal ambition also knew no quarter, as he openly defied President James Monroe and especially the Secretary of War, John C. Calhoun. Before the campaign in Florida, Jackson ordered that his officers to refuse any order that came through him. After the campaign, Calhoun demanded that a public rebuke for Jackson, but ironically, it was John Quincy Adams who saw the advantage of Jackson's illegal actions to obtain Florida from a crumbling Spanish Empire, an empire that, along with France, was a vital ally in our war for independence.

The election of 1828 set a standard of nastiness that dwarfs even the election of Donald Trump in 2016. During the election, an ally of Adams attacked Jackson's wife Rachel as a bigamist, claiming that her divorce from her prior husband was not final when she married Jackson. When Rachel died later that year, Jackson, who had won an overwhelming victory at the polls, blamed Adams and all of his allies. The wrath of Jackson was just beginning, and John Marshall found himself in the crosshairs. The issue was the independence of the Cherokee, and the treaty that had given them sovereignty over land in the state of Georgia. The Supreme Court ruling of *The Cherokee Nation v. The State of Georgia* [43] was one of several where Marshall attempted to find compromise to appease both sides, leading an ally of Jackson to utter the famous phrase: "Marshall has made his decision, now let him enforce it." [44] It is hard to grasp the sheer terror that Marshall must have felt as this tyrant defied a judgment of the Supreme Court that led to The Trail of Tears. It appeared that the nation was deeply divided, and Henry Clay stood at the forefront of a raging storm of populism that was sweeping away the civility of the Founders.

As Clay pushed the Cherokee issue before the populace, Jacksonians did not believe the Supreme Court was a fair arbiter. [45]

Therefore, when Jackson defeated Clay in a landslide in the 1832 election, Marshall decided not to test fate again and succumbed to political pressure. Since its inception, the Union was constantly on the brink of dissolution, and Marshall, ever the survivor, had to be concerned that defying Jackson's view of State's Rights, a position necessary to extend slavery, might bring down the Republic. Jackson was as close to Napoleon Bonaparte as our nation had ever seen, and the bloody conflict had just ended at Waterloo in 1815. So with *Baron*, in retrospect, Marshall could have been buying time. Further, Marshall also believed the preservation of the judiciary was paramount as at that time separation of powers was anything but determined.[46] The Jacksonians were the majority, and his decision in *Baron* was a simple reflection of that new reality. Marshall's goal of the independent judiciary would surpass all expectations, but the independence of the individual judges would not, each falling in line with Marshall's fears of political insurrection. At the end of his career, reflecting on his career, Marshall ever the politician said that he "never sought to enlarge judicial power beyond its intended bounds, nor feared to carry it to the fullest extent required." [47]

Yet, in preserving the fledgling Court, Marshall sacrificed the personal rights as stated in in the Declaration. According to Barnett, the Declaration tells us our fundamental rights are inalienable, and thus the people could not willingly transfer those rights to their elected representatives. To that end, the Bill of

Rights was simply an exclamation point. *We the People* ruled, and our representatives serve the people. But that was not the thinking of the Jacksonians. In their minds, the state, being the majority, ruled the people. For the Bill of Rights, however, *Baron* would be the demarcation point for the power struggle that would frame constitutional jurisprudence through today.

3. *The Republic Strikes Back: The Battle to Nullify* Baron

After the Civil War, the Republican majority (who Barnett calls Republican Constitutionalists) forced their viewpoint on the Democrats with the passage of the Thirteenth, Fourteenth and Fifteenth[48] Amendments Despite the fact that legislative history of the Fourteenth Amendment clearly showed it was intended to nullify *Baron*, the Supreme Court would have none of it, limiting the Fourteenth Amendment to anti-slavery amendment intended to reverse the Dred Scott decision, saying:

> The constitutional provision there alluded to did not create those rights, which it called privileges and immunities of citizens of the States. It threw around them in that clause no security for the citizen of the State in which they were claimed or exercised. Nor did it profess to control the power of the State governments over the rights of its own citizens.[49]

In his dissent in *Adamson*, Mr. Justice Black excoriated the Court's refusal to abide by the law:

My study of the historical events that culminated in the Fourteenth Amendment, and the expressions of those who sponsored and favored, as well as those who opposed its submission and passage, persuades me that one of the chief objects that the provisions of the Amendment's first section, separately, and as a whole, were intended to accomplish was to make the Bill of Rights, applicable to the states. With full knowledge of the import of the *Barron* decision, the framers and backers of the Fourteenth Amendment proclaimed its purpose to be to overturn the constitutional rule that case had announced. This historical purpose has never received full consideration or exposition in any opinion of this Court interpreting the Amendment. [50]

In 1947, Justice Black painted the history of jurisprudence as one that "contracted the effectiveness of the Fourteenth Amendment as a protection from state infringement of individual liberties enumerated in the Bill of Rights ... and represented a failure to carry out the avowed purpose of the Amendment's sponsors."[51]

In 1888, the Court was still enthralled with Jacksonian Democracy and majoritarian rule. This was especially true with the Court's blind acceptance of state regulation of marriage in *Maynard v. Hill*. From the time of *Maynard* until 1967, states enjoyed the legal authority to tell its citizens who could marry and who could not, especially when the marriage would be interracial. It was not until 1967, in *Loving v. Virginia*, that the Supreme Court

28

would strike down that particular state regulation.[52] In doing so, the Court overturned an 1883 Supreme Court decision that permitted racial desegregation, saying:

> The State finds support for its "equal application" theory in the decision of the Court in *Pace v. Alabama*, 106 U.S. 583 (1883). In that case, the Court upheld a conviction under an Alabama statute forbidding adultery or fornication between a white person and a Negro which imposed a greater penalty than that of a statute proscribing similar conduct by members of the same race. The Court reasoned that the statute could not be said to discriminate against Negroes because the punishment for each participant in the offense was the same.[53]

Separate But Equal and a limited role for the Fourteenth Amendment (other than the Right to Contract) would last almost one hundred years. As the Warren Court began to re-recognize, one at a time, certain fundamental rights that were enumerated in the Bill of Rights (or not), certain segments of the public began to complain of an activist judiciary legislating from the bench, just as it did in the same-sex marriage cases. The Warren Court, however, was not breaking new ground. It had as its precedent a case from 1923, *Meyer v. Nebraska*.[54] Decided amongst the surge in Fourteenth Amendment litigation, a period historians refer to of Economic Due Process, *Meyer v. Nebraska* marked a turning point in noneconomic rights. The case involved a Nebraska law prohibiting the teaching of a foreign language prior to the 8th grade. In striking down the law as a violation of the state's police power, the Court, referring to the Fourteenth Amendment, stated the issue as follows:

> The problem for our determination is whether the statute as construed and applied unreasonably infringes the liberty guaranteed to the plaintiff in error by the Fourteenth Amendment. "No State shall . . . deprive any person of life, liberty, or property, without due process of law." …
>
> While this Court has not attempted to define with exactness the liberty thus guaranteed, the term has received much consideration and some of the included things have been definitely stated. Without doubt, it denotes not merely freedom from bodily restraint but also the right of the individual to contract, to engage in any of the common occupations of life, to acquire useful knowledge, **to marry, establish a home and bring up children, to worship God according to the dictates of his own conscience**, and generally to enjoy those privileges long recognized at common law as essential to the orderly pursuit of happiness by free men.[55] *[Emphasis added.]*

Although it found that regulating the education of its populace was an important state interest, the *Meyer* Court found the Nebraska statute violated the basic fundamental rights of its citizens:

That the State may do much, go very far, indeed, in order to improve the quality of its citizens, physically, mentally and morally, is clear; but the individual has certain fundamental rights which must be respected. The protection of the Constitution extends to all, to those who speak other languages as well as to those born with English on the tongue. Perhaps it would be highly advantageous if all had ready understanding of our ordinary speech, but this cannot be coerced by methods which conflict with the Constitution — a desirable end cannot be promoted by prohibited means. ...

For the welfare of his Ideal Commonwealth, Plato suggested a law which should provide: "That the wives of our guardians are to be common, and their children are to be common, and no parent is to know his own child, nor any child his parent. . . . The proper officers will take the offspring of the good parents to the pen or fold, and there they will deposit them with certain nurses who dwell in a separate quarter; but the offspring of the inferior, or of the better when they chance to be deformed, will be put away in some mysterious, unknown place, as they should be." [*Citation omitted*.] In order to submerge the individual and develop ideal citizens, Sparta assembled the males at seven into barracks and [e]ntrusted their subsequent education and training to official guardians. Although such measures have been deliberately approved by men of great genius, **their ideas touching the relation between individual and State were wholly different from those upon which our institutions rest; and it hardly will be affirmed that any legislature could impose such restrictions upon the people of a State without doing violence to both letter and spirit of the Constitution.**[56] [*Emphasis added.*].

In what was certainly the pinnacle of the short rebirth of the Republican Constitution, the *Meyer* Court marks a turning point in our nation's history, the foundation for the end of majoritarian rule, specifically the doctrine of Separate But Equal in 1954 with *Brown v. Board of Education, supra.* Yet, *Meyer v. Nebraska* was not just a case about substantive due process. It was a complete acknowledgement of a plethora of individual liberties guaranteed under the Constitution that had long been "guaranteed to free men," including a right to privacy. Most important, the *Meyer* court found no need to search for a fundamental right in the language of the first eight amendments to the United States Constitution. Rather, without citing the Ninth Amendment, it instructed us of the "spirit" of the Constitution listing many rights not specifically enumerated.

After *Brown v. Board*, the Court continued to use substantive due process to push back against the will of the majority. Mr.

Justice Frankfurter explained the methodology in 1960's *Gomillion v. Lightfoot*:[57]

> When a State exercises power wholly within the domain of state interest, it is insulated from federal judicial review. But such insulation is not carried over when state power is used as an instrument for circumventing a federally protected right. This principle has had many applications. It has long been recognized in cases which have prohibited a State from exploiting a power acknowledged to be absolute in an isolated context to justify the imposition of an "unconstitutional condition." What the Court has said in those cases is equally applicable here, *viz.*, that "Acts generally lawful may become unlawful when done to accomplish an unlawful end, [*citation omitted*] and a constitutional power cannot be used by way of condition to attain an unconstitutional result." [*Citation omitted*.] [58]

Yet, the Supreme Court has never been a consistent force in protecting individual rights. Rather, since the birth of the Democratic Constitution, it has been in a constant struggle in search of a balance between the rights of the people and the power of their elected officials. This was certainly true in the 1950s and 1960s after President Dwight D. Eisenhower appointed Earl Warren as Chief Justice. Many conservatives still bemoan Ike's choice as a dreadful mistake. However, Barnett explains that Earl Warren and his contemporaries on the Court were just creatures of their times. The growth of substantive due process under the Warren Court was based, not necessarily on the Bill of Rights, but on the rights that were generally accepted in the political world just as it was with the Dred Scott decision a century earlier.[59] In *Loving v. Virginia*, for example, in 1967, the Court was willing to take on the subject of interracial marriage because of the passage of the Civil Rights Act of 1964 and the Voting Rights Act of 1965, where the majority of the people's representatives struck down racial discrimination at both the federal and state levels. In *Loving*, therefore, the Court felt political cover in dismissing out of hand the state of Virginia's reliance on the 1883 interpretation of the Fourteenth Amendment in *Pace v. Alabama* that permitted racial discrimination if the statute affected both white and blacks:

> However, as recently as the 1964 Term, in rejecting the reasoning of that case, we stated "*Pace* represents a limited view of the Equal Protection Clause which has not withstood analysis in the subsequent decisions of this Court."

Scotus watchers of today recognize this in terms of whether the Court is willing to take on an important issue of the day, as it did with racial discrimination, gender discrimination, the rights of out-of-wedlock children,[60] the right to privacy,[61] anti-sodomy laws,[62] the abortion question,[63] the right to travel,[64] the death penalty,[65] the right to counsel,[66] illegal searches,[67] the array of First Amendment[68] rights, Second Amendment rights,[69] etc., until the penultimate same-sex marriage case in 2015. According to

Barnett, each of these decisions were politically motivated. Instead, the Court should have adopted a blanket rule as in *Meyer v. Nebraska* where the Court listed many unalienable rights not enumerated in the first eight amendments, and in so doing recognizing the importance of catch all language of the Ninth Amendment. The lone exception is Mr. Justice Arthur Goldberg and his concurring opinion in *Griswold v. Connecticut*.[70]

4. *Griswold*: The New Demarcation Point for Political Discourse

The vote in *Griswold* was 4-3-2, with seven voting to overturn Connecticut's ban on contraceptives. Writing for a plurality of four, Mr. Justice William O. Douglas set off decades of controversy and created tons of fodder for originalists when he determined without precedent, that:

> The association of people is not mentioned in the Constitution nor in the Bill of Rights. The right to educate a child in a school of the parents' choice— whether public or private or parochial—is also not mentioned. Nor is the right to study any particular subject or any foreign language. **Yet the First Amendment has been construed to include certain of those rights.**[71] [*Emphasis added.*]

Politically speaking, one can only assume that Douglas and three of his colleagues believed the public would accept a right to privacy if it was part of the First Amendment, as if it were more important that the others. Rejecting Douglas' reasoning, Justice

Goldberg, with Chief Justice Warren and Associate Justice Willian J. Brennan joining, attempted to revitalize the Republican Constitution:

> The language and history of the Ninth Amendment reveal that the Framers of the Constitution believed that there are additional fundamental rights, protected from governmental infringement, which exist alongside those fundamental rights specifically mentioned in the first eight constitutional amendments.
>
> The Ninth Amendment reads, "The enumeration in the Constitution, of certain rights, shall not be construed to deny or disparage others retained by the people." The Amendment is almost entirely the work of James Madison. It was introduced in Congress by him and passed the House and Senate with little or no debate and virtually no change in language. It was proffered to quiet expressed fears that a bill of specifically enumerated rights could not be sufficiently broad to cover all essential rights and that the specific mention of certain rights would be interpreted as a denial that others were protected.[72]

In his dissent, Justice Byron White outwardly rejected Justice Goldberg's reliance on the Ninth Amendment, wishing to rely only on those specifically enumerated.[73] Thus, he also rejected the view of the plurality of justices that a right to privacy could be inferred from the First Amendment. Rather, he stood with former

Chief Justice Oliver Wendell Holmes and his firm conviction stated in 1919's *Schenk v. United States* that the Court should overturn the will of the majority only when it is arbitrary and unreasonable. [74] Justice White echoes Holmes in writing:

> Surely it has to be admitted that no provision of the Constitution specifically gives such blanket power to courts to exercise such a supervisory veto over the wisdom and value of legislative policies and to hold unconstitutional those laws which they believe unwise or dangerous. I readily admit that no legislative body, state or national, should pass laws that can justly be given any of the invidious labels invoked as constitutional excuses to strike down state laws. But perhaps it is not too much to say that no legislative body ever does pass laws without believing that they will accomplish a sane, rational, wise and justifiable purpose.[75]

In 2000, Justice Antonin Scalia presented the view of the Originalists that distinguish between the rights enumerated in the first eight amendments and those that he acknowledged where in the Ninth Amendment in the case of *Troxel v. Granville*. With regard to the Right to Parent, he said in his dissent:

> In my view, a right of parents to direct the upbringing of their children is among the "unalienable Rights" with which the Declaration of Independence proclaims "all

men . . . are endowed by their Creator." And in my view that right is also among the "othe[r] [rights] retained by the people" which the Ninth Amendment says the Constitution's enumeration of rights "shall not be construed to deny or disparage." The Declaration of Independence, however, is not a legal prescription conferring powers upon the courts; and the Constitution's refusal to "deny or disparage" other rights is far removed from affirming any one of them, and even further removed from authorizing judges to identify what they might be, and to enforce the judges' list against laws duly enacted by the people. Consequently, **while I would think it entirely compatible with the commitment to representative democracy set forth in the founding documents to argue, in legislative chambers or in electoral campaigns, that the State has *no power* to interfere with parents' authority over the rearing of their children, I do not believe that the power which the Constitution confers upon me *as a judge* entitles me to deny legal effect to laws that (in my view) infringe upon what is (in my view) that unenumerated right**. (*Emphasis added*.)[76]

In a recent interview, aired just after Justice Scalia's death in 2016, Justice Clarence Thomas, who sided with plurality in *Troxel*, argued that the Constitution must be read with the Declaration, but limited his inquiry as to personal rights to the first eight amendments, thus ignoring the Ninth Amendment. Yet, the Constitution does not clearly set out Originalists seem to ignore the echo Chief Justice Marshall's thought process in *Marbury v. Madison*, *supra* that it was the duty of the judiciary to strike down any law that violated the Constitution. If Scalia and the Originalists are correct, are they saying that judicial review, and landmark of all their jurisprudence, is unconstitutional? Surely not. So, therefore, in keeping with Marshall's theory, if an act of the legislature that is repugnant to the rights that Mr. Justice Scalia admits is squarely in the Ninth Amendment, how could the judiciary not do its duty, as Barnett so violently complains in *Our Republican Constitution*, and strike it down? At least when it comes to the Right to Parent, however, Justice Thomas believed that the Court should use strict scrutiny, its highest level, to strike down a Washington state law.[77]

The opposite view to Originalist is that of University of Chicago law professor David A. Strauss in his book, *The Living Constitution*,[78] one which believes that the Constitution does not require amendments for the Court to create new rights. As the 6th Circuit Court of Appeals explained:

> The theory of the living constitution rests on the premise that every generation has the right to govern itself. If that premise prevents judges from insisting on principles that society has moved past, so too should it prevent judges from anticipating principles that society has yet to embrace. It follows that States must enjoy some latitude

in matters of timing, for reasonable people can disagree about just when public norms have evolved enough to require a democratic response.[79]

In essence, there are no rules, only the ones we can make up as we go. To the Living Constitutionalists, the Constitution is a nullity, the victim of creeping utilitarianism where the ends always justifies the means.

Yet, these two extreme views have one thing in common. They are both consistent with Barnett's theory that decisions of the Supreme Court are political. *Griswold* set up the battle lines that continue until this day, basing decisions, at least in part, on political expedience, taking issues one at a time depending not on the Constitution, but on the will of the populace.[80] Both the far left and the far right wish to impose their views on the nation. As each side of the political equation pushed a constitutional right, the other side would cry foul as a violation of the will of the majority. For example, when the Supreme Court found that political speech included those of an organization in *Citizens United v. Federal Election Commission*,[81] those on the left, including President Barrack Obama, went berserk. On the other hand, conservatives want the will of the people to overrule personal rights when it comes to abortion. Most recently, the June 2016 decision of *Whole Women's Health v. Hellerstadt*[82] is a great barometer for how far the United States Supreme Court will go to hear a particular case in order to force a particular issue to the forefront. In his dissent,

Justice Clarence Thomas echoed the Conservative populace, complaining:

> That decision exemplifies the Court's troubling tendency "to bend the rules when any effort to limit abortion, or even to speak in opposition to abortion, is at issue." *Stenberg v. Carhart*, 530 U. S. 914, 954 (2000) (Scalia, J., dissenting). As JUSTICE ALITO observes, see post (dissenting opinion), today's decision creates an abortion exception to ordinary rules of res judicata, ignores compelling evidence that Texas' law imposes no unconstitutional burden, and disregards basic principles of the severability doctrine. I write separately to emphasize how today's decision perpetuates the Court's habit of applying different rules to different constitutional rights— especially the putative right to abortion.[83]

Ironically, *Roe v. Wade*,[84] itself, was an exercise in measuring political will, and trying to find its center. The three-stage balancing act that Justice Harry Blackmun created in dividing pregnancy into three trimesters was an utter failure. Instead of solving a problem, he simply ignited a firestorm, creating a longstanding political battle that would define politicians by their level of support for or against abortion. The Originalists ignore, not only the Ninth Amendment, but those fundamental rights the Supreme Court has already recognized that are not among those enumerated, such as the right to travel,[85] the right to parent,[86] and, of course, the right to marry. Those on the left have no problem with government intervention if the intervention promotes their agenda. For example, President Barrack Obama decried *Citizens United, supra,* and *District of Columbia v. Heller,* where the Court recognized the right to bear arms.[87] For libertarians, it is all a dizzying affair, with each side crying foul as the other's most favored right comes before the Court, neither side wanting to agree with Mr. Justice Black's dissent in *Adamson,* that the Fourteenth Amendment nullified *Baron,* and that the federal constitutional protections, particularly in the Bill of Rights, applies to the States.

5. *Obergefell*: The Democratic Constitution Marches On

In *Obergefell v. Hodges,* in 2015, the Supreme Court continued the incremental march toward liberty in striking down a state regulation that prohibited same-sex couples the right to obtain a marriage license. Applying strict scrutiny (the highest of three levels of review), the Court found that the statute limiting marriage to one man and one woman violated the Equal Protection Clause in the Fourteenth Amendment. Dissenting, Chief Justice John Roberts, like the majority, based his arguments from the viewpoint of what Barnett tells us is the Democratic Constitution. Therefore, the dispute was not over an interpretation of a provision of the Constitution, but whether society was ready to extend the protection of the right to marry to same-sex couples. Writing for the majority, Justice Anthony Kennedy writes:

The nature of injustice is that we may not always see it in our own times. The generations that wrote and ratified the Bill of Rights and the Fourteenth Amendment did not presume to know the extent of freedom in all of its dimensions, and so they entrusted to future generations a charter protecting the right of all persons to enjoy liberty as we learn its meaning. When new insight reveals discord between the Constitution's central protections and a received legal stricture, a claim to liberty must be addressed.

In dissent, Chief Justice Roberts writes:

Proper reliance on history and tradition of course requires looking beyond the individual law being challenged, so that every restriction on liberty does not supply its own constitutional justification. **The Court is right about that**. Ante, at 18. But given the few "guideposts for responsible decision making in this unchartered area" [*citation omitted*] "an approach grounded in history imposes limits on the judiciary that are more meaningful than any based on [an] abstract formula," [*quoting Moore v. Cleveland*, 431 U. S., at 504, n. 12 (plurality opinion)]. Expanding a right suddenly and dramatically is likely to require tearing it up from its roots.

*Obergefe*ll opens the door to a challenge of state regulation of marriage. Looking back to 1967, *Loving v. Virginia* was decided at a time when a vast majority of the populace saw their vows of matrimony as a lifetime commitment. Therefore, the Court, even if asked, would have been unwilling to take on a challenge to state regulation of marriage as a whole. Instead, it said:

> While the state court is no doubt correct in asserting that marriage is a social relation subject to the State's police power, [citing *Maynard v. Hill*], the State does not contend in its argument before this Court that its powers to regulate marriage are unlimited notwithstanding the commands of the Fourteenth Amendment.[citing *Meyer* and *Skinner v. Oklahoma*].[88]

Going forward then, the question is whether the Court, especially in light of its reasoning in *Obergefell*, would be willing if asked, to take on the subject of state regulation of marriage. In *Obergefell*, Justice Kennedy, for reasons we will discuss in Part II, foreshadowed the abandonment of state regulation in his majority opinion, stating:

> [M]arriage was once viewed as an arrangement by the couple's parents based on political, religious, and financial concerns; but by the time of the Nation's founding **it was understood to be a voluntary contract between a man and a woman. See N. Cott, Public Vows: A History of Marriage and the Nation 9–17 (2000);** S. Coontz, Marriage, A History 15–16 (2005). As the role and status of women changed, the institution

further evolved. Under the centuries-old doctrine of coverture, a married man and woman were treated by the State as a single, male-dominated legal entity. See 1 W. Blackstone, Commentaries on the Laws of England 430 (1765). As women gained legal, political, and property rights, and as society began to understand that women have their own equal dignity, the law of coverture was abandoned. See Brief for Historians of Marriage et al. as Amici Curiae 16–19. These and other developments in the institution of marriage over the past centuries were not mere superficial changes. [*Emphasis added.*]

In endorsing Nancy Cott's finding that marriage at our nation's founding was a private contract, and has since evolved, the Court appears open to return marriage to its original intent under the United States Constitution. This book will present two forms of attack to state regulation of marriage. First, in Part II, it will argue that licensing of marriage is a violation of Religious Liberty under the First Amendment and the Religious Freedom Restoration Act, and the Right to Contract. Second, in Part III, it will argue that state regulation of the terms of the marital agreement are likewise in violation. Next, however, this book will choose the perfect plaintiffs to bring the case.

C. The Turley Track: Why the Utah Polygamist is the Best Plaintiff to Attack

The Supreme Court in *Obergefell* has left an opening in the argument against state regulation of marriage. It is vital, however, to find the right plaintiff to frame the issue. The Supreme Court does not give advisory opinions, meaning there must be an actual case and controversy for the Court to have jurisdiction to rule on the issue.[89] Therefore, first, the persons must have standing to proceed with a matter that is a federal question that directly affects them.[90] Second, the matter must be ripe for review, meaning that the statute must pose an immediate harm to our proposed plaintiffs.[91] As witnessed in *Obergefell*, challenging a statute that directly restricts a constitutional right, such as the right to marry, would fulfill both those requirements. Third, and just as important, the persons with standing must be able to advance the issue to a conclusion without the matter becoming moot, that is that it resolved itself before the Court decision.[92]

George Washington University law professor Jonathan Turley has taken the lead and has provided us with the direction we must take. While he lost his direct attack on the polygamy ban, Professor Turley almost single handedly ended any thought of the State of Utah prosecuting people for entering into polygamous marriages.[93] At the federal district court level, Turley argued that his clients were in danger of criminal prosecution from the Utah ban. He argued that his polygamous clients had the same right to marry as did same-sex couples. Decided two years before *Obergefell*, the district court judge refused his claim, and upheld the Utah statute limiting marriage licenses to one man and one woman.[94]

One argument that Turley apparently did not address was the issue of whether Utah's ban on polygamy violated his clients' religious liberty, triggering not only the First Amendment, but also the Religious Freedom Restoration Act of 1993 (RFRA).[95] As the Supreme Court explained in 2014 in *Burwell v. Hobby Lobby Stores, Inc.*:[96]

> RFRA prohibits the "Government [from] substantially burden[ing] *a person's* exercise of religion even if the burden results from a rule of general applicability" unless the Government "demonstrates that application of the burden to *the person* — (1) is in furtherance of **a compelling governmental interest**; and (2) is the least restrictive means of **furthering that compelling governmental interest.**" [*Emphasis added.*]

The Court has long found that, under the First Amendment Free Exercise Clause, protections are broad. As stated in *Hobby Lobby*:

> [T]he "exercise of religion" involves "not only belief and profession but the performance of (or abstention from) physical acts" that are "engaged in for religious reasons."

As Nancy Cott explains in *Public Vows*, marriage began in America as a private contract, when a vast majority of marrying parties, as they still do today, enter into their nuptials under the tenets of their respective religious beliefs. After all, what is a vow, but a promise? And a contract is nothing more than a series of promises. And, while modern contract law is more than 500 years old, the enforcement of a marital promises, under the guise of religious tenets, is far older.[97] Historically, when couples entered into the vows of marriage, they entered into them with a religious figure as the arbiter, whether it be the Pope or a more local religious leader. Thus, we will build on the foundation that Turley started, selecting plaintiffs in a hypothetical case that have created a written pre-marital agreement stating their intentions to follow the traditional tenets of the Church of the Latter Day Saints (*circa* 1861).

Thus, for the remainder of this essay, we will assume the following facts:

Elizabeth Smith, James Young, and Harmony Jones are devout Mormons and are citizens of the State of Utah. They are part of a sect that practices polygamy. Under the laws of Utah, polygamy is illegal. Elizabeth and James Young were lawfully married three years ago and she has already given birth to their first child. Harmony joined the family as a nanny, and wants to marry into the family. Under the original tenets of the Church of the Latter Day Saints, polygamy was not only acceptable, but the norm. When Utah applied for statehood, Congress made its acceptance

48

into the Union contingent on banning polygamy, forcing true believers to live underground as they have done ever since. Harmony is 21 years of age and converted into the Mormon faith at the age of 18. This is her first marriage.

In 2014, in *Kitchen v. Hebert*, the 10th Circuit Court of Appeals struck down a Utah law that defined marriage as between one man and one woman as an unconstitutional violation of the Fourteenth Amendment as it applied to same-sex couples.[98] Elizabeth, James and Harmony believe that, using the same rationale, the Utah law is unconstitutional when it applies to a polygamous marriage. Further, they want to challenge the Utah ban on polygamy as a violation of their First Amendment right to worship in their faith, and as a violation of the Religious Freedom Restoration Act (RFRA) in that it places an undue burden on their ability to carry out their faith, and, as with same-sex marriage, there is no compelling state interest to interfere in their private marriage. Before applying for a marriage license for the threesome, they entered into a written pre-marital agreement, as follows:

PRE-MARITAL AGREEMENT

COME NOW Elizabeth Smith, James Young and Harmony Jones, all legal adults, and hereby consent to be married under the laws of the Church of Latter Day Saints. As part of this agreement, we state as follows:

1. We are citizens of the State of Utah.

2. We desire to raise a family together under the tenets of our church.

3. We desire to raise our children together under the tenants of our church.

4. We enter into this agreement with full knowledge that polygamy is presently illegal in the United States, and in the State of Utah.

5. We enter into this agreement knowing fully that we might be prosecuted in criminal court.

6. It is our intention to apply for a marriage license for the three of us to be lawfully wed in the State of Utah.

7. We attach hereto as Exhibit A a list of all assets presently owned by us as individuals.

8. We hereby freely agree that all assets set forth in Exhibit A shall, upon our lawful marriage, be the property of the Young Family Trust, and shall only be divided by the terms therein.

9. If any of us wish to dissolve this marriage in the future, we agree that we abandon all of our rights to said property to the family unit.

10. Elizabeth and Harmony acknowledge that if any of us have children during the course of our

marriage, that the children shall be considered of the family unit, and we waive any and all personal rights in the event of our dissolution thereof.

11. We agree that Elizabeth shall hold the title of First Wife, and shall be in charge of all the family finances and husband sharing arrangements.

12. The parties agree that it is their intention to add additional wives to their marriage, and that a unanimous agreement of all parties is required as to any particular choice, and that a substitute agreement adding the new wife would be a prerequisite thereto.

13. The parties hereby waive any right to litigate the terms or conditions of their marriage in the court system.

14. The parties do hereby consent that they submit any dispute to binding arbitration before Bishop Brigham Foster, or his successors.

Signed and Notarized.

After executing the written agreement, the three appear before the County, and request a marriage license. As they expect, the County refuses to issue the license. They then file suit in federal court, using the identical language, of the 10th Circuit decision seeking the court to enjoin the State of Utah, and specifically the license issuer, from relying on the unconstitutional law of Utah, and compel it to issue them a marriage license. Professor Turley did a great service in ending state regulation of marriage by pointing out to the district court of Utah the absurdity of its ban on polygamy, and reminding us all that, despite the will of a Christian nation, people will do as they please when it comes to following the tenets of their chosen faith.

As mentioned above, one year before *Obergefell*, the 10th Circuit Court of Appeals, in *Kitchen v. Herbert,* found that a Utah statute that defined marriage as between one man and one woman unconstitutional as applied to a same-sex couple.[99] In *Kitchen,* plaintiffs brought suit in federal court to enjoin the State of Utah from relying on the statute to deny them the right to marry. The 10th Circuit summarized their claims as follows:

> Plaintiffs allege that Amendment 3 violates their right to due process under the Fourteenth Amendment by depriving them of the fundamental liberty to marry the person of their choice and to have such a marriage recognized. They also claim that Amendment 3 violates the Equal Protection Clause of the Fourteenth Amendment. Plaintiffs asserted their claims under 42 U.S.C. § 1983, seeking both a declaratory judgment that Amendment 3 is unconstitutional and an injunction prohibiting its enforcement.

Our Plaintiffs will piggyback that claim. Moreover, they argue that, unlike same-sex marriage, polygamy was well established in the faith prior to its banning prior to Utah becoming a state, when as the Supreme Court in *Obergefell* (citing Nancy Cott's *Public Vows*) found that during the first fifty years as a nation, marriage was a private affair. They will argue that the banning of a tenet of their faith is a violation of their First Amendment right to religious liberty, as well as being a violation of the Religious Freedom Restoration Act. All of these claims require, as the 10th Circuit reiterated in *Herbert v. Kitchen*:

> The Due Process Clause "forbids the government to infringe certain fundamental liberty interests at all, no matter what process is provided, unless the infringement is narrowly tailored to serve a compelling state interest." *Reno v. Flores*, 507 U.S. 292, 302 (1993) (quotation and emphasis omitted). By the same token, if a classification "impinge[s] upon the exercise of a fundamental right," **the Equal Protection Clause requires "the State to demonstrate that its classification has been precisely tailored to serve a compelling governmental interest."** *Plyler v. Doe*, 457 U.S. 202, 216-17 (quotation omitted). Having persuaded us that the right to marry is a fundamental liberty, plaintiffs will prevail on their due process and equal protection claims unless appellants can show that Amendment 3 survives strict

scrutiny. A provision subject to strict scrutiny "cannot rest upon a generalized assertion as to the classification's relevance to its goals." *Richmond v. J.A. Croson Co.*, 488 U.S. 469, 500 (1989**). "The purpose of the narrow tailoring requirement is to ensure that the means chosen fit the compelling goal so closely that there is little or no possibility that the motive for the classification was illegitimate**." *Grutter*, 539 U.S. at 333 (*quotation omitted*). Only "the most exact connection between justification and classification" survives. *Gratz v. Bollinger*, 539 U.S. 244, 270 (2003). (*Emphasis added*).[100]

Our hypothetical plaintiffs will argue that Amendment 3 is unconstitutional as applied, and that the state's regulation of marriage denies them both their righto marry and their right to practice their faith in accordance to their religious liberty as is also provided under RFRA. They will also argue that their Right to Contract under the Contracts' Clause forbids the state from regulating the terms of the marital agreement, and that the state's interference into their written marital agreement would not support the alleged compelling state interest in fostering, and especially preserving, a stable world for their children. They will also argue that the state of Utah has no right to interfere in their contract, and their choice to arbitrate any dispute arising therefrom permits them to waive any right to judicial intervention.

PART II

THE STATE HAS NO RIGHT TO REGULATE PLAINTIFFS' MARRIAGE

ARGUMENT I:

THE STATE PURPOSE OF MAINTAINING THE ERODING CHRISTIAN FAMILY MODEL BASED ON ANGLICAN LAW IS NOT AN IMPORTANT STATE PURPOSE AND IT CANNOT BE USED TO JUSTIFY INTERFERING IN THE PLAINTIFFS' PRIVATE CONTRACT.

In *Public Vows*, Nancy Cott tells us that the 19th Century was very much about the establishment, preservation and spread of what she called the Christian Family Model. In the past 150 years, states, as well as Congress with DOMA, have continued to push that narrative even in the face of an ever changing society, a society that, in increasing numbers, is rejecting what we call traditional marriage. In 2014, in *Kitchen v. Hebert,* the State of Utah presented four state purposes in defense of its limitation of marriage to one man and one woman:

(1) "[F]ostering a child-centric marriage culture that encourages parents to subordinate their own interests to the needs of their children";

(2) "[C]hildren being raised by their biological mothers and fathers—or at least by a married mother and father—in a stable home";

(3) "[E]nsuring adequate reproduction"; and

(4) "Accommodating religious freedom and reducing the potential for civic strife."

The State of Utah also might cite as precedent the 1985 United States Supreme Court opinion of *Potter v. Murray City*.[101] In that case, plaintiffs asked the federal district court to find unconstitutional a provision of Utah's Enabling Clause that required the outlawing of polygamy as a condition precedent to its entry into the Union in 1896. Rejecting the claim, the 10th Circuit Court of Appeals found a compelling state interest in the state's commitment to a system of domestic relations based on monogamy. The *Potter* court, in refusing to overrule its 1879 precedent *Reynolds v. United States*,[102] stated:

> Monogamy is inextricably woven into the fabric of our society. It is the bedrock upon which our culture is built. *Cf. Zablocki v. Redhail*, 434 U.S. 374 (1978)(marriage is foundation of family and society; "a bilateral loyalty"). In light of these fundamental values, the State is justified, by a compelling interest, in upholding and enforcing its ban on plural marriage to protect the monogamous marriage relationship.

The State of Utah would argue that *Reynolds v. United States* is still good law. It involved the conviction of a devout Mormon who had engaged in a polygamous marriage. In exploring the history of marriage, the Court said:

> Polygamy has always been odious among the northern and western nations of Europe, and, until the

establishment of the Mormon Church, was almost exclusively a feature of the life of Asiatic and of African people. At common law, the second marriage was always void (2 Kent, Com. 79), and from the earliest history of England polygamy has been treated as an offence against society.[103]

In *Reynold*s, the Defendant presented two defenses. First, he argued that he had engaged in polygamy prior to the enactment of the ban. Second, he argued that polygamy is a tenant of his church, and that the statute violated his First Amendment rights. Rejecting his argument, the *Reynolds* court justified the law of the Territory of Utah outlawing the tenant of the Mormon faith:

… it is a significant fact that on the 8th of December, 1788, after the passage of the act establishing religious freedom, and after the convention of Virginia had recommended as an amendment to the Constitution of the United States the declaration in a bill of rights that "all men have an equal, natural, and unalienable right to the free exercise of religion, according to the dictates of conscience," the legislature of that State substantially enacted the statute of James I., death penalty included, because, as recited in the preamble, "it hath been doubted whether bigamy or pol[y]gamy be punishable by the laws of this Commonwealth." 12 Hening's Stat. 691. From that day to this we think it may safely be said there never has been a time in any State of the Union when polygamy has not been an offence against society, cognizable by the civil courts and punishable with more or less severity. In the face of all this evidence, it is impossible to believe that the constitutional guaranty of religious freedom was intended to prohibit legislation in respect to this most important feature of social life. **Marriage, while from its very nature a sacred obligation, is nevertheless, in most civilized nations, a civil contract, and usually regulated by law. Upon it society may be said to be built, and out of its fruits spring social relations and social obligations and duties, with which government is necessarily required to deal.** In fact, according as monogamous or polygamous marriages are allowed, do we find the principles on which the government of the people, to a greater or less extent, rests. … [P]olygamy leads to the patriarchal principle, and which, when applied to large communities, fetters the people in stationary despotism, while that principle cannot long exist in connection with monogamy. [*Emphasis added.*)

In addition to *Potter*, the State of Utah might also cite the writings of noted Originalist scholar and Notre Dame Law School professor Donald L. Drakeman. Drakeman explains that, in *Reynolds*, the defense counsel barely raised the constitutional issue in his brief, choosing to rely instead on English Common Law.[104] Rather, the counsel for the government raised the constitutional issue as a means of seizing upon the slippery slope of harrowing acts and gruesome murders in the name of religion. Drakeman further explains that Chief Justice Waite was able to achieve a near unanimous vote for conviction in raising, but not discussing or answering, how to define "religion." Drakeman argues that what the Court should have done in *Reynold*s, and what Utah would ask here, is to define "religion" as one that was existing at the time of our founding, a definition that, in *Reynolds*, would have excluded the 50-year-old Mormon faith. Instead, Mr. Justice Waite relied heavily on "the greatest historian of his day," George Bancroft, who a contemporary described as "redolent of the ideas of the new Jacksonian democracy ..."

Waite's decision to use the "history of our times' argument is consistent with the Barnett's definition of the Democratic Constitution. According to Drakeman, Waite made the poor decision to attempt to exclude from Constitutional interpretation the ideology of Declaration author and religious liberty advocate Thomas Jefferson, who was in France in 1789 and played no part in its drafting. Drakeman saw the folly in Waite's historical based analysis. After all, as we see now with *Obergefell*, times do change. The Court then was filled with Jacksonians who believed in the Democratic Constitution, as is evident in Waite's conclusion in *Reynolds* that: "we think it may safely be said there never has been a time in any State of the Union when polygamy has not been an offence against society ..." [105]

Just like it would do in *Maynard v. Hill* nine years later, the *Reynolds* court based its judgment not on the Constitution, but on its version of morality. In *Maynard*, the Court proclaimed:

> Marriage, as creating the most important relation in life, as having more to do with the morals and civilization of a people than any other institution, has always been subject to the control of the legislature. That body prescribes the age at which parties may contract to marry, the procedure or form essential to constitute marriage, the duties and obligations it creates, its effects upon the property rights of both, present and prospective, and the acts which may constitute grounds for its dissolution.[106]

After *Reynolds*, the federal attack on polygamy as immoral continued with the 1890 Supreme Court declaration that polygamy constituted "a return to barbarism" and were "contrary to the spirit of Christianity."[107] In the 20th Century, child centered courts also determined that anti-polygamy statutes protect children[108] and "avoid the stigma of illegitimacy." [109]

Further, the State of Utah would adopt the reasoning of Chief Justice Roberts in his dissent in *Obergefell* that the Court should defer the issue to the political process.[110] In essence, Roberts was calling for *Judicial Restraint,* one where:

> The Constitution presumes that, absent some reason to infer antipathy, even improvident decisions will eventually be rectified by the democratic process and

that judicial intervention is generally unwarranted no matter how unwisely we may think a political branch has acted.[111]

In Roberts' view, the Court acted prematurely in overruling the majority of the states that refused to include same-sex couples in their definition of marriage:

Just who do we think we are? It can be tempting for judges to confuse our own preferences with the requirements of the law. But as this Court has been reminded throughout our history, the Constitution "is made for people of fundamentally differing views." *Lochner v. New York*, 198 U. S. 45, 76 (1905) (Holmes, J., dissenting). Accordingly, "courts are not concerned with the wisdom or policy of legislation." Id., at 69 (Harlan, J., dissenting). The majority today neglects that restrained conception of the judicial role. It seizes for itself a question the Constitution leaves to the people, at a time when the people are engaged in a vibrant debate on that question. And it answers that question based not on neutral principles of constitutional law, but on its own "understanding of what freedom is and must become." Ante, at 19. I have no choice but to dissent.[112]

Finally, in *Potter*, the Plaintiff argued that the lack of prosecutions for polygamy rendered the statute as defunct. Ironically, the State of Utah might argue that the lack of prosecutions render unnecessary the need to recognize a fundamental right to enter into a polygamous marriage.[113] After all, in 2013, in Turley's case, a federal district court found that the Utah statute that prohibited conjugal cohabitation was unconstitutional as a violation of the Free Exercise Clause.[114] Nevertheless, in that case, the State of Utah abandoned the moral justifications for banning polygamy that was so prevalent in *Reynolds* and *Potter*. Rather, the Attorney General, perhaps fearful that the ban would be overturned, used legal maneuvering to avoid litigating the issue by filing an affidavit of non-prosecution:

> Defendant swore under penalty of perjury that "[a]s Utah County Attorney, I have now adopted a formal office policy not to prosecute the practice of bigamy unless the bigamy occurs in the conjunction with another crime or a person under the age of 18 was a party to the bigamous marriage or relationship." (Second Buhman Aff. ¶ 8 [Dkt. No. 47-1].)[115]

So, as of 2014, Mormons were free to practice their faith without fear of prosecution, and may cohabit in a conjugal relationship, even holding onto their religious vows so long as they have only one marriage license (between one man and one woman). As of 2015, after *Obergefell*, Utah citizens outside the faith could do the same, including same-sex couples. Therefore, the State of Utah would argue that giving polygamous couples the same rights as monogamous couples is premature and unnecessary.

Yet, the State's own actions in permitting polygamy in practice without fear of criminal prosecution is tantamount to an endorsement. It cannot then use tradition as an argument when, by its own admission, polygamy has remained a practice for more than 150 years. The prohibition against licensing polygamous marriages is nothing more than a paper tiger, and cannot purport to be an important state purpose. Neither can the State cite procreation as an important purpose. The 10th Circuit destroyed that argument in *Kitchen v. Herbert, supra,* as statistically, if not factually, false.[116] The *Kitchen* court found that marriage in America is no longer a social prerequisite for having, raising or adopting children, something we will discuss in detail in Part II when dealing with the terms of the marital agreement.

ARGUMENT II:
THE ACTUAL STATE PURPOSE OF REGULATING MARRIAGE IS TO EFFECTUATE THE CONTINUATION OF A THEOCRACY, AND IT CANNOT BE USED TO JUSTIFY INTERFERING IN PLAINTIFF'S PRIVATE CONTRACT.

Citing *Public Vows*, the Supreme Court in *Obergefell* found that, for the first fifty years of our history, marriage was a purely private affair. Yet, beginning fifty years after our founding, it became a completely public one, where the state was the sole arbiter of who could marry, the terms of the marriage, and its dissolution. This sudden turn away from its original purpose of religious freedom was based on two factors. First, as Barnett explains in *Our Republican Constitution*, the election of Andrew Jackson in 1824 began an era when *We the People* as a collection of individuals became *We the People* as the majority. Second, beginning approximately 1820, a Christian resurgence swept through America causing a popular purge against those that lived outside the faith, especially Mormons.

After the murder of founder Joseph Smith in a Carthage, Illinois, jail in 1844, Brigham Young led the flock to Mexican Territory in what is now Utah in 1847. After the Mexican War, Utah became part of the United States, subjecting the Church to the whims of a hostile Congress that would pass anti-polygamy laws in the territory, and later make the permanent ban a condition precedent to statehood.

The road from the Declaration to the federal and state theocracy that led to the ban on polygamy and state regulation of marriage is paved in revisionist history. This is especially true with the theory that the state is a party to the marital agreement. As was explained in the 1946 California appellate decision *Langdon v. Sayre*:

> [T]he marriage contract is not an ordinary contract; the state is a 'third interested party' in such a contract and in the consequent marriage status; the constitutional protection of contracts against legislative interference does not apply to marriage contracts.[117]

In essence, the marriage of two consenting adults was valid only if the state consented and approved of the marriage.[118] Thus, the state enjoyed the veto power of a theocracy.

True understanding of this phenomenon requires a review of Christian history. The Catholic Church does not permit, nor has it ever permitted, divorce for valid sacramental marriages In Catholicism, in marriage, the two become one flesh in a union joined by God, (Mark 10:8). Jesus speaks about divorce: "Therefore what God has joined together, no human being must separate," (Mark 10:9). So for a marriage that meets the requirements of being a sacrament, divorce in the Catholic Church is **not possible**. Further, the church would only grant an annulment if a marriage is found to be invalid, i.e., that it did not meet the requirements of a sacramental marriage.[119]

Conflicts between the England Church and Roman Authority was common from the time of its founding in 1054. The Magna Carta in 1215 declared that the English Church was an independent of its government.[120] In 1517, Martin Luther began the Reformation when he posted his famous 95 Theses to the door of a church in Wittenberg (Germany), and the news of this certainly reached England. By 1533, when King Henry VIII requested the Pope a special dispensation to end his marriage to Catherine of Aragon so he could marry Anne Boleyn, he had already spent most of his reign challenging the authority of Rome. As a Catholic, he was under the moral authority of the Pope. Of course, the Pope had no say in the marriages of other religions. For example, in Judaism, in order to obtain a divorce, a husband was required to obtain a written document, known in the Talmud as a *sefer k'ritut* (a scroll of cutting off), but more commonly known today as a *get*.[121] Thus, both Jews and Catholics created Ecclesiastic Courts that exercised temporal jurisdiction to determine sacramental matters, including the rights and duties of the marriage.[122]

As a Catholic, Henry VIII feared the power of the Pope to excommunicate him from the church, a horrible punishment at the time. When the Pope refused Henry's request, the King came up with a unique solution. He would order the Archbishop of Canterbury, the head of the Catholic Church in England, to grant him the divorce. Then, in 1534, Parliament made Henry VIII the Head of the newly formed Anglican Church. The country was still Catholic in religious matters, but the Pope had no power over its inhabitants. Shortly, after, in what was called the Dissolution, King Henry VIII, with Thomas Cromwell as his chief minister, began to acquire the vast land holdings of the Catholic monasteries, and used the proceeds to provide for the defense of England. In what is now called the English Reformation, Henry VIII, as Head of the Church, scrubbed the Latin bible in favor of the English bible and ordered that the Lord's Prayer be spoken in English, not in Latin as it had been before. The first translation of the Latin bible into English appeared in 1526. (In 1611, the Authorized Version under King James I, became the standard for English speaking Protestants.) Then in 1562, during the reign of Elizabeth I, the Church of England gained formal structure, using what was a radically simplified version of the Book of Common Prayer, and its use was strictly enforced throughout England. The 1662 English Book of Common Prayer forms the historical basis for most Anglican liturgy around the world. Queen Elizabeth I, as the arbiter of the Church, as the Catholic Church had done, granted to Ecclesiastic Courts temporal jurisdiction to determine disputes on sacramental matters, including the sacrament of marriage.[123]

State control of marriage in England began in 1753 under Lord Hardwicke's Act.[124] Under canon law, the Church only had the power to censure or excommunicate. The Act gave the Anglican Church means of enforcing its canons in civil courts.[125] The

68

Anglican Church, just like the Catholic Church, was the sole arbiter of the rules of marriage.[126] Any marriage outside of the Anglican Church did not have state recognition, and thus did not fall under its jurisdiction. It wasn't until The Marriage Act of 1823 that Parliament recognized non-religious civil marriages, permitting nonconformists and Catholic couples to marry in their own places of worship (as long as they were at least 21 years old or had the permission of their parents). The Act specifically excluded Jews and Quakers, coining the word *nonconformists* to describe them and anyone else who did not abide by the rules of the Anglican Church.[127] It did, however, recognize marriages outside of England as long as they conformed to Anglican law, that is, they were solemnized by a Christian clergyman. Therefore, the state of England expressed no authority over marriages outside the Church, or the dissolution thereof.

Parliament passed the initial divorce law in 1670, and all 300 divorces granted thereafter came through an Act of Parliament. [128] It was not until the Marriage Act of 1836 that divorces in England became the province of the courts, limited to, of course, only marriages that were valid under English law (particularly between Jews and Quakers).[129] In England, there were three types of courts, each having sole jurisdiction over its subject matter. Besides the Ecclesiastic Courts, the Chancery arbitrated matters of equity (such as property rights), and there was separate court to arbitrate damages suits and criminal cases, where the right to trial by jury had its origins.[130]

In the more than two hundred years that would follow Parliament's first divorce law, many sought religious refuge in America. Beginning in 1740, in what historians call The Great Awakening, a new charismatic sect took strength in the Colonies, one that became a major rival to the Anglican Church. The Awakening called for a critical examination of the scripture, and sought non-materialistic ways of looking at God. Renowned Oxford scholar R.G. Collingwood explains in his book *The Idea of History* that advocates of the Enlightenment believed that those that claimed moral authority through religious teachings were "unscrupulous and calculating" … "a class of beings called priests, who, they to seem to have thought, invented it to serve as an instrument of domination over the mass of men." [131]

As Campbell University law professor E. Gregory Wallace explains:

> Underlying the early commitment to religious freedom was the perception that this higher call of God makes the exercise of religious faith a uniquely transcendent and intimate human activity, distinct from other human interests or pursuits. For religious devotion to be authentic, it must be a voluntary matter between the individual and God. The state neither is competent to define the "correct" relation between that person and God, nor may it legitimately use its power to direct or force individual devotion to God. Thus, religion must be treated differently – it should be let alone, regardless of

whether other human activities and institutions are let alone, except when religious exercise obviously endangers either the state's existence or the basic rights of another person.[132]

This awakened thinking would inspire the sense of independence that would foster the American Revolution, especially Thomas Jefferson when he wrote in the Virginia Bill of Freedom:

"That no man shall be compelled to frequent or support any religious worship, place, or ministry whatsoever, nor shall be enforced, restrained, molested, or burthened in his body or goods, nor shall otherwise suffer on account of his religious opinions or belief. . . ."

Jefferson incorporated that idea into the Declaration of Independence, and James Madison did so as well in the First Amendment's Establishment Clause.

At the time of the Revolution, there had emerged two competing religious strongholds, those that followed the Anglican Church, and those that didn't (Presbyterians, Lutherans, Baptists, etc.). Alexander Hamilton, found himself in the midst of the struggle when he attended The City College of New York, an Anglican institution, a college that would become Columbia University.[133] Drakeman tells us that it was the Crown's discrimination against the growing Baptist faith that was at the heart of the Virginians' insistence on religious liberty in the Bill of Rights. Yet, despite the expulsion of the Anglican Church after the Revolution, states would shortly create their own their own theocracies, and find solace in the Supreme Court in 1845's *Permoli v. New Orleans, infra*. As the Supreme Court explained in *Everson v. Board of Education* in 1947:

> A large proportion of the early settlers of this country came here from Europe to escape the bondage of laws which compelled them to support and attend government-favored churches. The centuries immediately before and contemporaneous with the colonization of America had been filled with turmoil, civil strife, and persecutions, generated in large part by established sects determined to maintain their absolute political and religious supremacy. With the power of government supporting them, at various times and places, Catholics had persecuted Protestants, Protestants had persecuted Catholics, Protestant sects had persecuted other Protestant sects, Catholics of one shade of belief had persecuted Catholics of another shade of belief, and all of these had from time to time persecuted Jews. In efforts to force loyalty to whatever religious group happened to be on top and in league with the government of a particular time and place, men and women had been fined, cast in jail, cruelly tortured, and killed. Among the offenses for which these punishments had been inflicted were such things as speaking disrespectfully of the views of ministers of government-established churches, non-attendance at those churches,

expressions of non-belief in their doctrines, and failure
to pay taxes and tithes to support them.[134]

The *Everson* court explained that many of these discriminatory practices continued after the passage of the Constitution and the Bill of Rights to the abhorrence of freedom loving Americans. Yet, there was no judicial remedy. The First Amendment did not apply to the states, and many states, especially in the Northeast, did not give equal rights to Jews, Catholics or anyone that did not conform. Non-Christians were not permitted to vote or take public office if they did not swear to the Christian beliefs.[135] In essence, the states had taken on the role of the Pope in the same way that King Henry VIII had done. In fact, the state had gone much farther.

Alexis de Tocqueville, who visited the United States in the 1820s, wrote that Americans believed that the maintenance of Christianity was necessary to public institutions. Another foreign visitor of that era, James Bryce, noted that federal and state governments had made Christianity a near-official religion. Alexis de Tocqueville's and James Bryce's writings roughly coincided with what Randy Barnett would call the birth of the Democratic Constitution. It also roughly coincided with what was known as the Second Great Awakening, the religious revival that fundamentally altered the character of American religion. This new religious movement rejected the Calvinist idea that emphasized the depravity of human beings in favor of a more optimistic idea that individuals could use their free will in choosing to be saved.[136] As Andrew Sachar reports in his book. *A History of the Jews in America,* Christians were fascinated by the "neglected children of Israel," and made it their solemn duty to convert them to what they believed was a vastly superior religion in Christianity, but used their majoritarian power mostly to exclude Catholics from any form of public office.[137] This populist transformation ended the secular nature of government, in favor of a collection of Christian states. As explained in an 1824 opinion from the Pennsylvania Supreme Court upholding a conviction for blasphemy:

> Christianity is part of the Common Law of this state. It is not proclaimed by the commanding voice of any human superior, but expressed in the calm and mild accents of customary law.[138]

Religious refugee William Penn, the Quaker who founded the colony, would politely disagree, as would its most famous citizen, Benjamin Franklin, who openly opposed his Loyalist son William, the Royal Governor. Christian populism had won the day. And that day lasted for more than a century.

According to Barnett, it was this populism that molded the Democratic Constitution, when the populism of Andrew Jackson doused the flame of the Revolution in the person of his predecessor, John Quincy Adams. Together with majoritarian rule, the assumptions of Christianity's "near enshrined status" that the "respectable" citizenry endorsed Bible readings in public schools and other public rituals, something that our Supreme

Court would not outlaw until the 1950s. Nevertheless, less than fifty years after the Bill of Rights, America had become everything the Founders, especially the Jefferson and Madison, had sought to prevent, a nation, like England, where one religion would impose its morals and beliefs on all of its citizenry.

In 1845, in the case of *Permoli v. New Orleans*, the United States Supreme Court proclaimed that the several states had the authority to set up their own religions, stating:

> The ordinances complained of, must violate the Constitution or laws of the United States, or some authority exercised under them; if they do not, we have no power by the 25th section of the Judiciary Act to interfere. The Constitution makes no provision for protecting the citizens of the respective states in their religious liberties; this is left to the state constitutions and laws: nor is there any inhibition imposed by the Constitution of the United States in this respect on the states. We must therefore look beyond the Constitution for the laws that are supposed to be violated, and on which our jurisdiction can be founded; these are the following acts of Congress.[139]

In Barnett's view, the *Permoli* Court ignored the liberties of *We the People* as individuals, permitting the state religion to come to a vote and impose the result of the election on the minority. In 1859, in *Barber v. Barber*, the Supreme Court mentioned, but refused to rule on, the development of Ecclesiastic Courts in the

Colonies to determine sacramental matters.[140] In 1888, that the Supreme Court in *Maynard v. Hill* relied on English law to justify the development of state theocratic authority over marriage:

> When this country was settled, the power to grant a divorce from **the bonds of matrimony was exercised by the Parliament of England.** The ecclesiastical courts of that country were limited to the granting of divorces from bed and board. Naturally, the legislative assemblies of the colonies followed the example of Parliament and treated the subject as one within their province. [*Emphasis added.*] ...
>
> Says Kent, in his Commentaries: "During the period of our colonial government, for more than one hundred years preceding the Revolution, no divorce took place in the colony of New York, and for many years after New York became an independent state there was not any lawful mode of dissolving a marriage in the lifetime of the parties but by a special act of the legislature." 2 Kent Com. 97.

Parliament took no part in marriages of nonconformists, especially Catholics. Yet, our Supreme Court had no problem citing Parliament as authority to justify the states taking control over the institution for all citizens, stripping the power from religious leaders over their respective flocks, especially the Pope. After assuming state regulation of marriage as an (revisionist) historical given, the *Maynard* Court placed the State in the role of the King:

When the contracting parties have entered into the married state, they have not so much entered into a contract as into a new relation, the rights, duties, and obligations of which rest not upon their agreement, but upon the general law of the State, statutory or common, which defines and prescribes those rights, duties, and obligations. They are of law, not of contract. It was of contract that the relation should be established, but, being established, the power of the parties as to its extent or duration is at an end. **Their rights under it are determined by the will of the sovereign, as evidenced by law.** They can neither be modified nor changed by any agreement of parties. It is a relation for life, and the parties cannot terminate it at any shorter period by virtue of any contract they may make. The reciprocal rights arising from this relation, so long as it continues, are such as the law determines from time to time, and none other." [141]

The populist movement less than fifty years after the Declaration of Independence led to an end to the secular reasoning of *Our Republican Constitution* in favor of a populist, Christian majority. In 1888, America was a Christian nation giving the *Maynard* Court an excuse to usurp the most private freedoms, faith and family. In so doing, it displaced the liberties of *We the People* as individuals with absolute state control similar to what would develop in the Soviet Union 30 years later. State theocracy would continue in the United States until the Supreme Court once again recognized religious liberty in 1940 in *Cantwell v. Connecticut*:

> The essential characteristic of these liberties is, that under their shield many types of life, character, opinion and belief can develop unmolested and unobstructed. Nowhere is this shield more necessary than in our own country for a people composed of many races and of many creeds. There are limits to the exercise of these liberties. The danger in these times from the coercive activities of those who in the delusion of racial or religious conceit would incite violence and breaches of the peace in order to deprive others of their equal right to the exercise of their liberties, is emphasized by events familiar to all. These and other transgressions of those limits the States appropriately may punish.[142]

In the 19th Century, the people's representatives in Congress were no less immune to the religious purge, especially when it came to Mormons. In 1862, President Abraham Lincoln signed into law the Morrill anti-bigamy law that was targeted to eliminate the Mormon Church in the territories.[143] After the Civil War, the Christian majority won the Judiciary Branch with the Supreme Court's decision in *Reynolds v. United States*.[144] The root of the discrimination against polygamy was a "crusade" against "inferior" African and Eastern beliefs:

The court notes that 133 years after *Reynolds,* non-Mormon counsel for Plaintiffs have vigorously advanced arguments in favor of the right of religious polygamists to practice polygamy (through private "spiritual" marriages not licensed or otherwise sanctioned by the state, a relationship to which the court will refer as "religious cohabitation") that would have perhaps delighted Mormon Apostles and polygamy apologists throughout the period from 1852 to approximately 1904. To state the obvious, the intervening years have witnessed a significant strengthening of numerous provisions of the Bill of Rights, and a practical and morally defensible identification of "penumbral" rights "of privacy and repose" emanating from those key provisions of the Bill of Rights, as the Supreme Court has over decades assumed a general posture that is less inclined to allow majoritarian coercion of unpopular or disliked minority groups, especially when blatant racism (as expressed through Orientalism, [imperialism), religious prejudice, or some other constitutionally suspect motivation, can be discovered behind such legislation.(*Footnotes omitted*). [145]

It was with this "crusading" attitude that the Supreme Court, in *Maynard v. Hill,* nine years after *Reynolds,* endorsed what was an unconstitutional state regulation of marriage. By taking control of the family, the state theocracy could control its population, and weed out inferiors, such as the Mormons, all in violation of their First and Fourteenth Amendment rights to religious liberty. For these reasons alone, the Plaintiffs should prevail. This is not to say that the State could not act on behalf of minors, but consenting adults have the right to determine who they will marry and how they will raise their children.

ARGUMENT III:

THE STATE PURPOSE OF MAINTAINING VICTORIAN MORALITY, WHILE IMPORTANT IN THEORY, CANNOT BE USED TO JUSTIFY INTERFERING IN THE PLAINTIFFS' PRIVATE CONTRACT TO ENGAGE IN A POLYGAMOUS MARRIAGE.

In 2013, George Washington University law professor Jonathan Turley challenged Utah's prohibition of polygamy. He did not, however, challenge the validity of state regulation of marriage. Rather, he chose to formulate standing based on a threat to criminal prosecution. While he was unable to convince the district court judge to invalidate the prohibition against polygamy, the district court did strike down a law that criminalized religious conjugal co-habitation. As stated above, the State of Utah avoided litigation of the polygamy ban. At his printing in January 2017, however, Professor Turley has filed a Petition for Writ of Certiorari asking the Supreme Court to permit his to challenge the constitutionality of Utah's ban on polygamy even though Utah has eliminated the possibility of criminal prosecution.

At the district court level, Turley did not have the benefit of the 10th Circuit opinion in *Kitchen v. Herbert,* and most important, the Supreme Court decision in *Obergefell v. Hodges*. If he had, the district court might have agreed with Turley that the 1879 Supreme Court decision in *Reynolds v. United States* was no longer good law.

In our case, as in *Kitchen v. Herbert*, the state of Utah might present the moral argument that permitting polygamy would lead to a destruction in the nuclear family, just as it did in arguing against same-sex marriage:

> Another slippery-slope argument brought forward by appellants is that federal constitutional protection for same-sex marriage might lead to the "wholesale `privatization'" of marriage through the "enactment of a civil-union regime for all couples, with religious and other organizations being free to offer the title of 'marriage' as they see fit."[146]

As the state of Utah argued in *Kitchen v. Herbert*, traditional marriage was geared toward reproduction and rearing children in the faith and homosexual activity obviously would not result in procreation.

Homosexuality is not a tenet of a religion as polygamy is in our case, but the history of intolerance in America is similar. While Mormons suffered the longstanding history of discrimination, it is nothing compared to homosexuals as the Christian state did not tolerate any persons who acted outside its norms. In his concurring opinion in 1986's *Bowers v. Hardwick*, Chief Justice Burger looked to history to underscore the ability of the state to prohibit homosexual activity:

> [T]he proscriptions against sodomy have very "ancient roots." Decisions of individuals relating to homosexual conduct have been subject to state intervention

throughout the history of Western civilization. Condemnation of those practices is firmly rooted in Judeao-Christian moral and ethical standards. Homosexual sodomy was a capital crime under Roman law. See Code Theod. 9.7.6; Code Just. 9.9.31. See also D. Bailey, Homosexuality and the Western Christian Tradition 70-81 (1975). During the English Reformation when powers of the ecclesiastical courts were transferred to the King's Courts, the first English statute criminalizing sodomy was passed. 25 Hen. VIII, ch. 6. Blackstone described "the infamous *crime against nature*" as an offense of "deeper malignity" than rape, a heinous act "the very mention of which is a disgrace to human nature," and "a crime not fit to be named." 4 W. Blackstone, Commentaries *215. The common law of England, including its prohibition of sodomy, became the received law of Georgia and the other Colonies. In 1816 the Georgia Legislature passed the statute at issue here, and that statute has been continuously in force in one form or another since that time. To hold that the act of homosexual sodomy is somehow protected as a fundamental right would be to cast aside millennia of moral teaching.[147]

The moral teaching that sourced the Christian state's prohibition was hardly confined to America. As one libertarian essay in 1975 explained:

Thus for centuries, gays—and even those merely caught in the midst of some momentary gay experience—were the victims of Church-sanctioned State oppression. No secret was made of the "Final Solution" prepared for them, nor were verbal ambiguities considered necessary: the end-goal of their total extermination was written into the law books of the nations of the West. Through long ages, no public humiliation, degradation, torture or painful death was looked on as too cruel to be inflicted on such as them.[148]

The desire for eradication reached extremes as the case of famed English mathematician Alan Turing, the father of the modern computer, known to many Americans today through the recent Academy Award Best Picture nominee, *The Imitation Game*.[149] After his service in breaking the Nazi code, Turing, who was gay, was sentenced to chemical sterilization and eventually committed suicide as a result. While Turing was a resident of Great Britain, American restrictions mostly mimic the harsh punishments of its Mother Country.[150] Sodomy was considered a crime of "moral turpitude" in most states.[151] Many states, with questionable scientific evidence, permitted forced sterilization of individuals who committed acts of moral turpitude until our Supreme Court struck down the penalty in 1942 in *Skinner v. Oklahoma*.[152] The actual number of persons so harmed, however, remains in doubt.

The Anti-Sodomy laws targeted homosexual behavior until 2003, in *Lawrence v. Texas,* when the Supreme Court finally recognized that homosexual activity as a fundamental right. This sudden reversal would be stunning except that, as Barnett would tell us, gay rights became politically fashionable. Just 17 years before, in *Bowers v. Hardwick*, the Court had different ideas:

> Accepting the decisions in these cases and the above description of them, we think it evident that none of the rights announced in those cases bears any resemblance to the claimed constitutional right of homosexuals to engage in acts of sodomy that is asserted in this case. No connection between family, marriage, or procreation on the one hand and homosexual activity on the other has been demonstrated, either by the Court of Appeals or by respondent. Moreover, any claim that these cases nevertheless stand for the proposition that any kind of private sexual conduct between consenting adults is constitutionally insulated from state proscription is unsupportable.[153]

Or, as Chief Justice Burger said in his concurring opinion:

> This is essentially not a question of personal "preferences" but rather of the legislative authority of the State. I find nothing in the Constitution depriving a State of the power to enact the statute challenged here.[154]

Yet, the Supreme Court did more than simply reverse a 17-year-old decision. The *Lawrence Court* eviscerated the entire reasoning of Bowers, finding anti-sodomy laws as a recent development, not one based on "ancient roots."[155] Further, the *Lawrence* court destroyed the ability of any state to use tradition or morality as a basis for a state prohibition of private behavior. If we learn anything from *Maynard v. Hill*, it is that the Supreme Court has historically used revisionist history as an excuse for paltry constitutional analysis, as in the Jacksonian Era's still standing cases of *Maynard v. Hill* and *Reynolds v. United States*. After all, as Nancy Cott tells us in *Public Vows*, before the descent of Christian morality, private behavior was profoundly liberated from state control, including Free Love societies.[156]

The Democratic Constitution, however, still reigns. Only thirteen years after *Lawrence v. Texas*, same-sex couples developed enough political acceptances that they achieved the fundamental right to marry in *Obergefell v. Hodges*. Yet, the Court seemed open to polygamy when it found:

> The ancient origins of marriage confirm its centrality, but it has not stood in isolation from developments in law and society. The history of marriage is one of both continuity and change. That institution—even as confined to opposite-sex relations—has evolved over time. For example, marriage was once viewed as an arrangement by the couple's parents based on political, religious, and financial concerns; but by the time of the Nation's founding it was understood to be a voluntary contract between a man and a woman.[157]

When the majority of the United States Supreme Court reaches back to our founding, discarding the vestiges of our English origins, it is not expanding rights, but rather rediscovering them. As Barnett explains in *Our Republic Constitution*, the State has no authority to disregard the liberties of *We the People* (as a group of individuals, not as the collective). Thus, the State lacks the power to violate our fundamental liberties precisely because the people never afforded the State that right in its Constitution.

Regardless, if the Supreme Court adopts Barnett's model, the current court will look on polygamy, as it did with homosexuality, and find that consenting adults have the ability to reach any type of agreement, including a marital one. And when a state grants a license to marry to adult different-sex or same-sex couples, it is required, under the Fourteenth Amendment Equal Protection Clause, to grant a license to polygamous threesomes, especially those that are doing so under their traditional faith. Considering the four alternatives that the district court in *Brown v. Buhman* laid out in its Equal Protection analysis, polygamous marriage is far superior to out-of-wedlock births:

Class I: Couples who reside together in lawful marriage.

Class II: Couples of traditional Mormon beliefs that reside together in lawful marriage, who also engage in polygamy in conjugal cohabitation with additional women.

Class III: Couples of traditional Mormon beliefs that reside together in lawful marriage, who also engage in polygamy as solemnized in their faith in conjugal cohabitation with additional women acting as Sister Wives.

Class IV: Three or more persons consisting of a man and at least two women, one acting as First Wife, and the remainder acting as Sister Wives, under the doctrines of the Mormon faith prior to Utah's entry into the Union in 1896, and all licensed to marry.

As explained in Argument IV below, more than 40 percent of all children born in America today have unmarried parents. If social mores prefer parents raising children in a lawful marriage, it certainly would be better to raise children in a polygamous marriage, especially so when that marriage is a legal one. As further explained below, the primary purpose of legal marriage was to ascertain the legal rights of their offspring, and today, genetic testing overrules any legal presumptions from marriage. The secondary purpose of marriage was to raise children in the faith and thus spread the word of God. That is exactly what the Plaintiffs here are attempting to do, and why they should prevail.

ARGUMENT IV:

PLAINTIFFS' POLYGAMOUS MARRIAGE WOULD SERVE THE INTENDED STATE PURPOSE OF PROVIDING THEIR CHILDREN WITH FAITH, STABILITY AND GOOD PARENTING IN AN ERA OF DECLINING MARRIAGE AND FIDELITY.

In 2014 in *Kitchen v. Herbert*, the State of Utah, presented four justifications as a shield in defending its statute that limited the definition of marriage to one man and one woman:

(1) "[F]ostering a child-centric marriage culture that encourages parents to subordinate their own interests to the needs of their children";

(2) "[C]hildren being raised by their biological mothers and fathers—or at least by a married mother and father—in a stable home";

(3) "[E]nsuring adequate reproduction"; and

(4) "Accommodating religious freedom and reducing the potential for civic strife."[158]

Ironically, the Plaintiffs in our case can use these same four justifications as a sword in defeating the prohibition against polygamy. Which is better?

1. A man with six children by different mothers, never married.

2. A woman with six children by six different fathers, never married.

3. A man cohabiting with three women, never married.

4. A man, under the doctrine of the Mormon Church, in the years prior to Utah's entry into the Union, married to three women.

The answer is obvious. A family acting in their faith, not only produces children, but also educates them in their faith and provides them with a stable home. In Professor Turley's case, the State of Utah abandoned the field of enforcing anti-polygamy laws, while the district court struck down Utah's criminalization of conjugal cohabitation as unconstitutional. Thus, Mormon families that practiced polygamy in secret for more than a century were free to practice their faith in the open. Yet, under Utah law, the children born to the sister wives would be classified as born out of wedlock. If, on the other hand, Utah granted marriage licenses to sister wives and their husbands, all of the children would be born inside a lawful marriage. While, *illegitimacy*, as it was known just fifty years ago, is no longer a social stigma, it would be, as Utah argued in *Kitchen v Herbert,* preferable for a child to be raised in a lawful marriage. Moreover, since the early 1960s, the percentage of children born outside of marriage has risen from less than two percent to more than 40 percent today. In *America Solved*, I explain how in the 1960s, unwed girls who became pregnant were social pariahs. In middle class America, up through the 1970s, a high school girl who became pregnant would disappear from her classmates as if she were kidnapped by aliens. As the Welfare State gained traction, economic necessity of marriage begat social change, and gradually having a child out of wedlock became socially acceptable.

All four of the compelling interests Utah argued in *Kitchen* are at the root of what Nancy Cott calls *The Christian Family Model*, a lifelong partnership to raise their children in the faith. Former Louisiana State law professor Katherine Spaht explains:

> Marriage served the purpose of channeling sexual expression between a man and a woman into a desirable institution that could provide a stable environment for any resulting children. The female was the guardian of societal moral standards, no doubt for the very practical reason that she would bear the consequence of any failure of self-control. The "double standard" which distinguished between the acceptability of sexual experience for a man and such experience for a woman was simply recognition of her unique position as the bearer of offspring and her risk of graver consequences should she fail to exercise sexual self-control.[159]

And, so it was in late 19th Century America. After *Maynard v. Hill,* states began to advance their regulatory power primarily focusing on banning interracial marriage. Eventually states created a complex, contract based action for divorce. This Fault System permitted divorces only to those couples where there was a breach of the marital contract. The State was a theocracy, and its jurists would be the arbiter, permitting the trial judge to delve deep into the intimacies of a marriage to determine if either party was worthy of a divorce.[160] Just as in any other breach of contract action, the act must be material to the agreement (adultery, for example), and directly cause the breakup of the marriage. In no case could the person at fault obtain a divorce.

Well into the 1970s, it had become apparent to legal scholars and state legislatures that couples who wanted to divorce would fabricate a fault where none existed, conspiring to commit perjury in order to circumvent the system. Beginning with California, states completely abandoned the fault model for a no-fault system, where either party could obtain a divorce by simply stating that the marriage was broken. Forty years later, as I describe in detail in *America Solved*, state courts have become virtual divorce factories,, with states creating fill-in-the-blank forms that lay persons could complete to simplify the process. In essence, the state, rather than acting as an impediment to divorce, began to facilitate it. This begs the question. If people can simply get a divorce by applying for it, why couldn't they just make a public announcement that they are divorced? It is, in reality, a return to the post-Revolutionary War period, as Nancy Cott describes in *Public Vows*, when many spouses were doing just that.

Since the birth of the Welfare State, divorce rates have skyrocketed. Marriages that fifty years ago were lifetime cruises are becoming ten-, five- or even two-year excursions. In fact, three generations of divorce and out-of-wedlock children in America have all but ended the knowledge of how to remain married, especially with the growth of feminism and the diminishing need of women to be, and remain, married. Barbara Dafoe Whitehead in her book, *The Divorce Culture*, performed a study of no-fault divorce in the 1970s and 1980s showing that false expectations is the key reason why women are the decision makers in termination, and the key reason why the modern divorce is far more difficult on men than on women.[161] According to Dr. Whitehead, for most men, a marriage is an agreement. If he adheres to his part, he expects the wife to do the same, leaving him clueless when she wants to move on without him. Dr. Whitehead found that the wife was the one deciding to terminate the marriage 85 percent of the time, not because of something the husband did wrong, but mostly because she was not happy in the relationship.[162]

When marriage becomes a choice, rather than a necessity, or even an obligation, women can choose divorce, or single parenthood, rather than having to endure life with a man, or at least a particular man. Dr. Whitehead's studies in the 1970s are consistent with anthropologist Margaret Mead's theory that women choose their mate, and not vice versa. Under Mead's theory, the male had to prove his worth, that he had the ability to support her, and the female would award him her virginity in exchange.[163] If the male failed to live up to his promise to make her happy and secure, why wouldn't women choose to terminate the agreement if it was socially acceptable to do so?

The answer is plainly yes. The 1970s began what sociologist Lenore Weitzman called *The Divorce Revolution*.[164] According to the Center for Disease Control (CDC) and the U.S. Census

Bureau, heterosexual couples marrying in 2010 had a 66 percent chance of divorce in their lifetime. The odds of African Americans divorcing was even higher.[165] Moreover, fewer and fewer couples are choosing to marry, but rather to cohabit, or to just "hook up" as mutual pleasure seekers, producing children by accident rather than by mutual agreement. In 1972, the Supreme Court determined, in *Gomez v. Perez* that children born outside of marriage enjoyed an equal right to support from their fathers as children born of a marriage. Thereafter, the federal government set up an immense bureaucracy to establish parentage and to establish and collect child support.[166] In this system, marriage became almost irrelevant as DNA testing became the key to establishing paternity, even overruling the husband's presumption of fatherhood for a child born during a lawful marriage.[167] By 1996, the testing was so widespread, that it became affordable and readily available to all state agencies. The 1996 welfare reform act required states to alter their paternity laws to make paternity affidavits available at birth hospitals for new parents to sign, regardless if the mother was married to the natural father.[168] This system has greatly contributed to the steady decrease in marriage and the steady increase in children born outside of marriage.

In this environment, the idea of religious polygamy is by far preferable, and more stable for children, especially in a nation that is increasingly secular, and increasingly selfish where its children is concerned. The traditional Mormon family would reverse the trend toward the destruction of marriage, and would, in fact, grace

Utah with a generation of children raised to respect their faith, as well as their community. Polygamy, then, would be a great boon to the State, certainly not the scourge that the State of Utah would certainly argue.

PART III

STATE REGULATION OF THE TERMS OF THE PLAINTIFFS' MARITAL CONTRACT VIOLATES FEDERAL LAW AND THE CONSTITUTION

ARGUMENT V:

UTAH'S DOMESTIC RELATIONS STATUTORY SCHEME UNCONSTITUTIONALITY INTERFERES IN PLAINTIFFS' MARITAL CONTRACT.

A. PLAINTIFFS HAVE STANDING TO CHALLENGE STATE CONTROL OVER THE TERMS OF THEIR MARITAL AGREEMENT.

The State of Utah, as with all states in the union, has created a regulatory scheme giving statutory authority to the judiciary to decide, not only whether to grant a divorce, but also the terms of that divorce, including division of property, custody of children, and spousal and child support. In this system, the judiciary is given broad discretion to place burdens on the parties not envisioned in their private agreement. In anticipation of their challenge, Plaintiffs have entered into the following:

PRE–MARITAL AGREEMENT

COME NOW Elizabeth Smith, James Young and Harmony Jones, all legal adults, and hereby consent to be married under the laws of the Church of Latter Day Saints. As part of this agreement, we state as follows:

1. We are citizens of the State of Utah.

2. We desire to raise a family together under the tenets of our church.

3. We desire to raise our children together under the tenants of our church.

4. We enter into this agreement with full knowledge that polygamy is presently illegal in the United States, and in the State of Utah.

5. We enter into this agreement knowing fully that we might be prosecuted in criminal court.

6. It is our intention to apply for a marriage license for the three of us to be lawfully wed in the State of Utah.

7. We attach hereto as Exhibit A a list of all assets presently owned by us as individuals.

8. We hereby freely agree that all assets set forth in Exhibit A shall, upon our lawful marriage, be the property of the Young Family Trust, and shall only be divided by the terms therein.

9. If any of us wish to dissolve this marriage in the future, we agree that we abandon all of our rights to said property to the family unit.

10. Elizabeth and Harmony acknowledge that if any of us have children during the course of our

marriage, that the children shall be considered of the family unit, and we waive any and all personal rights in the event of our dissolution thereof.

11. We agree that Elizabeth shall hold the title of First Wife, and shall be in charge of all the family finances and husband sharing arrangements.

12. The parties agree that it is their intention to add additional wives to their marriage, and that a unanimous agreement of all parties is required as to any particular choice, and that a substitute agreement adding the new wife would be a prerequisite thereto.

13. The parties hereby waive any right to litigate the terms or conditions of their marriage in the court system.

14. The parties do hereby consent that they submit any dispute to binding arbitration before Bishop Brigham Foster, or his successors.

Signed and Notarized.

Plaintiffs seek to avoid state control of their marital contract as it interferes with their right to religious liberty under the Constitution and under the Religious Freedom Restoration Act

(RFRA). They ask the federal district court to enjoin the State of Utah from taking future action to terminate or otherwise grant relief to any party that is not specified in their contract. Further, they seek to enjoin the judiciary from taking any action because the parties have agreed to binding arbitration to resolve any dispute that might arise out of their contract.

In support of their claim, Plaintiffs argue that the Supreme Court in *Maynard v. Hill* was incorrect it asserting:

> [T]he constitutional protection of contracts against legislative interference does not apply to marriage contracts; the legislature in dealing with the subject of marriage has plenary power; and the rights of the husband in the wife's affections and society are not 'property' within the due process clause.

As the Supreme Court found in *Obergefell v. Hodges*, marriage in the United States began as a private contract.[169] In Western Civilization, the concept began in Roman law, usually in arranged marriages, as an agreement between the father of the bride and the groom. In 1950, the Supreme Court of Wyoming explained:

> It was the custom for a woman who was to be married to bring to her husband a dowry, provided by herself, or her father or some other party, which should serve as part of a common fund to provide for the support of the family. During the time of the empire a custom arose, under the influence of the customary practice of the Orient, for the husband to give to the wife a prenuptial

gift, equal in amount to the dowry brought by the wife. This gift was later allowed to be made even after marriage. Both the dowry and the prenuptial or postnuptial gift were under the control of the husband during the marriage, but became the absolute property of the wife upon the death of her husband.[170]

The track from Roman law to the American Constitution is no accident. Rome developed an advanced theory of the rights of citizenry that reemerged in the Enlightenment. According to Barnett, our Founding Fathers, especially Jefferson and Madison, relied heavily on writings of John Locke, who, in reality, simply reached into Rome's history to rediscover the concept of individual liberty that is the basis for our Constitution. That fact is most obvious in the creation of the U.S. Senate as a copy of the ancient Roman senate as an elected legislative body.

Marriage contracts under Roman law, as the Wyoming Supreme Court explains, was a purely private affair, with fathers arranging for marriages for their daughters to ensure their continued care.[171] In medieval times, these agreements set specific damages for breach, including, that the husband, upon divorce, was to refund the dowry to his bride's father. As Nancy Cott describes in *Public Vows,* at our nation's founding, men and women would enter into their own private marital agreement without the assistance of their parents, and might later also agree to divorce. As a private agreement, those couples were relying on the basic rule of contract, one that English law also adopted from Roman law.

In *Maynard v. Hill*, the Supreme Court refused to treat the marital agreement as an ordinary contract, mistakenly applying Anglican Church doctrine in violation of the parties' rights to religious liberty. As an ordinary contract, upon a dispute, the court would look to the intent of the parties rather than any preexisting rule of the State. As the Supreme Court of California explains:

> "Every contract imposes upon each party a duty of good faith and fair dealing in its performance and its enforcement." (Rest.2d Contracts, § 205.) This duty has been recognized in the majority of American jurisdictions, the Restatement, and the Uniform Commercial Code. (Burton, *Breach of Contract and the Common Law Duty to Perform in Good Faith* (1980) 94 Harv. L. Rev. 369.) Because the covenant is a contract term, however, compensation for its breach has almost always been limited to contract rather than tort remedies. As to the scope of the covenant, "` [t]he precise nature and extent of the duty imposed by such an implied promise will depend on the contractual purposes." [*Citation omitted*]. Initially, the concept of a duty of good faith developed in contract law as "a kind of `safety valve' to which judges may turn to fill gaps and qualify or limit rights and duties otherwise arising under rules of law and specific contract language."

(Summers, *The General Duty of Good Faith — Its Recognition and Conceptualization* (1982) 67 Cornell L. Rev. 810, 812, fn. omitted; see also Burton, *supra,* 94 Harv. L. Rev. 369, 371 ["the courts employ the good faith doctrine to effectuate the intentions of parties, or to protect their reasonable expectations" (fn. omitted)].) As a contract concept, breach of the duty led to imposition of contract damages determined by the nature of the breach and standard contract principles.[172]

Adjudicating a marriage agreement as an ordinary contract is far superior to the vagaries of modern marriage laws that are based on the outdated canons of the Anglican Church. An arbiter of an ordinary contract dispute looks to the four corners of the writing (if there is one) to determine the intent of the parties as to the meaning of any particular term of their agreement. In fact, most private (especially commercial) contracts contain provisions as to Choice of Law, that is, what state's law would apply in the event of a dispute.[173] Divorce laws are different. If a couple married in California, lived there for 50 years, and became "bona fide" residents of Utah for three months, Utah, not California would have jurisdiction to adjudicate their divorce.[174] Jurisdiction for divorce is based on the residence of the parties on the date of filing, not the state that they resided when entering their marital agreement.[175]

This is the historical flaw in the theory that the state is a party to the marital agreement, one that the Supreme Court ignored in 1888 in *Maynard v. Hill.* [176] In that case, the marriage took place in Ohio, but that the husband left his family behind and traveled to Oregon Territory, where he petitioned successfully to the legislature for a divorce. His wife, still an Ohio resident, complained that the divorce should have taken place in Ohio. After all, if, as the Supreme Court found, the state was a party to the marital agreement, wouldn't the State of Ohio have a stake in its dissolution? In England, except for nonconformists, there was but one court of jurisdiction. In America, interstate travel to seek out one's fortune has always been a fact of life. Thus, applying Anglican law, as the Supreme Court did in *Maynard*, would inevitably lead to a conundrum that continues through today. When a couple marries, what are they actually agreeing to do? They cannot predict the future to see when or where they might divorce. Further, even if they enter into the standard pre-nuptial agreement, the court that might interpret it would apply its own law, not the law of the state of its inception, as with ordinary contracts.[177] For example, a couple could marry in California, a community property state, and move to Utah, an equitable division state, creating an outcome far different from what the parties had originally agreed.[178]

Maynard v. Hill stands as the sole precedent to state regulation of marriage. In *Loving v. Virginia,* the Supreme Court expressed it as a given. In *United States v. Windsor*, the Court looked to tradition in determining that states had the sole authority to define marriage. Yet, as the Court also said in *Lawrence v. Texas*, tradition is not a rationale for constitutionality. The parties entering into a marital agreement have the right to contract, just as they have the right to marry. As Barnett tells us, our constitutional rights are inalienable. Since *We the People* could not grant to the state the power to regulate marriage, it is a solely private affair, and thus state interference in that private agreement is unconstitutional.

B. COMMON LAW MARRIAGE UNDERCUTS THE THEORY IN *MAYNARD V. HILL* THAT THE STATE IS A PARTY TO THE MARRIAGE CONTRACT.

For almost 60 years after *Maynard*, interstate disputes over jurisdiction rose to such a fervor that Congress passed a law requiring that state courts give judgments of sister states full, faith and credit, as long as the judgment itself was otherwise valid under the Constitution.[179] Beginning in the 1970s, the federal government invaded the family law arena, instituting laws intended to provide unity and interstate cooperation in custody and support disputes.[180] Yet, as the Supreme Court said in *Windsor*, each state had retained the respective authority to define marriage, and thus to decide whether a couple was legally married. For example, while most states require an actual license to marry for the marriage to be valid, some states hold onto the 19th Century phenomenon of common law marriage.

Common law marriage permitted a couple to declare themselves as married just as Nancy Cott described in *Public Vows,* without requiring a license or a state sanctioned ceremony. The current New Hampshire law is a good example:

> Persons cohabitating and acknowledging each other as husband and wife, and generally reputed to be such, for 3 years shall thereafter be deemed to have been legally married, until one of them dies.[181]

States that recognize common law marriage permit one of the parties to present evidence to prove its existence. Yet, interstate travel creates a problem for the couple who might have proved up their marriage in a common law state, but move to a jurisdiction that does not recognize it,[182] This was especially true of state rivals, such as Kansas (traditionally a common law marriage state) and Missouri (that despised it). And, of course, the very idea of common law marriage begs the question not considered in *Maynard*: If a couple enters into a common law marriage, how could the state be a party to that contract when the state did not grant a license?

The very concept of common law marriage highlights, not only the absurdity of the Supreme Court argument in *Maynard v. Hill* that the state was a party to that contract, but to the very purpose of contracts: To set the standards of behavior of the contracting parties, especially in case of dispute or dissolution. In the current system, state courts nationwide have broad discretion in carrying out the terms set, not between the parties, but by the state legislature of the jurisdiction of its dissolution. Therefore, even within the same state, the results of a certain dissolution proceeding might vary widely not just county to county, but judge to judge. And while Utah might argue that it is this very uncertainty that might cause couples to think twice about divorce, statistics do not bear that out.

ARGUMENT VI:

THE STATE'S STATUTORY SCHEME IN DICTATING AND/OR INJECTING TERMS INTO THE PLAINTIFFS' MARITAL AGREEMENT IS UNCONSTITUTIONAL.

A. STATE INTERFERENCE AS TO THE TERMS OF THE MARITAL AGREEMENT VIOLATE THE CONTRACTS CLAUSE OF THE UNITED STATES CONSTITUTION.

Plaintiffs want to avoid the uncertainty of the Utah regulatory scheme. Rather, they want to make certain that their agreed upon terms trump any existing state laws that might seek to void or modify the intent of the parties. They move that the District Court to enjoin the State of Utah from applying its statutory scheme in that: (1) it places an undue burden on their right to marry under the Fourteenth Amendment; and (2) it interferes with their right to contract under the Contracts' Clause of the United State Constitution.[183]

The Contracts Clause is specific in its prohibition, as Chief Justice Burger once explained:

> One of the fundamental premises of our popular democracy is that each generation of representatives can and will remain responsive to the needs and desires of those whom they represent. Crucial to this end is the assurance that new legislators will not automatically be

bound by the policies and undertakings of earlier days. In accordance with this philosophy, the Framers of our Constitution conceived of the Contract Clause primarily as protection for economic transactions entered into by **purely private parties** …. (*Emphasis added.*) [184]

That was the very definition of a marital agreement, as Nancy Cott tells us, at our founding. Now that the Supreme Court acknowledged that fact in *Obergefell v. Hodges,* the door has swung open to a new constitutional attack on state regulation of marriage. Application of the Contracts Clause to a marital agreement is a case of first impression, as courts nationwide have assumed that ordinary contract rules do not apply based on *Maynard v. Hill, supra.* [185] Since, as argued above, the State is not a party to the marital agreement, there is no other reason to interfere with the parties' purely private contract. In Contracts Clause cases, the Supreme Court has long stated that "an impairment may be constitutional if it is reasonable and necessary to serve an important public purpose."[186] The Court, in 1993, in *Buffalo Teachers Association v. Tobe,* said:

> To determine if a law trenches impermissibly on contract rights, we pose three questions to be answered in succession: (1) is the contractual impairment substantial and, if so, (2) does the law serve a legitimate public purpose such as remedying a general social or economic problem and, if such purpose is demonstrated,

(3) are the means chosen to accomplish this purpose reasonable and necessary.[187]

Assuming then that *Maynard v. Hill* is no longer good law, there is no doubt that Utah's statutory scheme substantially interferes in the parties' written agreement in that it imposes on them the rules of the Anglican Church. Plaintiffs also argue that the state's hold on this last vestige of duties based on Anglican Law violates their fundament Right to Parent, as the Supreme Court found in 1924's *Meyer v. Nebraska.*[188] Plaintiffs further argue that the statutory scheme does not further an important state purpose because application and enforcement has actually served to dissuade marriage and personal responsibility. Further, Utah's statutory scheme is not reasonable and necessary because it only applies to marrying couples who adjudicate their dispute before a state court judge. It does not apply to parents who marry and never divorce, nor does it apply to parents that never marry or adjudicate their dispute.

Further, since the Fault System has long since ended, the state no longer has a role in whether a couple can divorce, leaving it up to the parties to either work out the matter between themselves or to litigate and leave their fate in the hands of a legal stranger. Even when it comes before a trial judge, that judge has tremendous discretion in interpreting the rules of the statutory scheme. Even then, the parties are free to ignore the findings of the court, and do whatever they please, as long as they are in agreement. Therefore, the present no fault scheme is so arbitrary in its interpretation and in its enforcement that it is useless as a tool of morality or promoting social responsibility. And, thus, the Utah statutory scheme is unconstitutional as applied.

In defending the authority of the state, Utah would argue, as Randy Barnett tells us in *Our Republican Constitution*, that the Court has adopted a deferential approach to state regulatory schemes, something that Barnett considers an abandonment of its constitutional duty.[189] Utah would also argue that, with regard to spousal support, it has an important interest in preventing the spouse from being a public charge. It would argue, with regard to the custody and support of children, that: 1) The child cannot be bound to an agreement of his parents; 2) The state is charged with the best interest of the child; and 3) The state has an interest in the child not being a public charge.

B. NATIONAL TREND IS TO TREAT PRE-MARITAL AGREEMENTS AS ORDINARY CONTRACTS.

Utah, as with a vast majority of the states, "permits" parties to enter into a binding prenuptial agreement, and will enforce them unless the court deems them to be invalid under ordinary contract principals. Yet, Utah gives the trial court the discretion to invalidate the parties' written agreement, frequently second guessing the outcome rather than enforcing the intent of the parties.[190] As the Utah Supreme Court found in 1999 in *Reese v. Reese*:

> We also have been unwilling to deprive trial courts of their equitable powers to modify agreements made by

spouses in contemplation of divorce. "[A]greements between spouses to fix their property rights... are generally not held to be so absolute as to prevent a court under its equity powers in divorce actions from doing that which justice and equity require for the interest and welfare of the parties involved." [191]

Further, while most states have adopted the provisions the Uniform Premarital and Marital Agreements Act (set out in Appendix A below), Utah places a unique exception to the waiver of spousal support:

If a provision of a premarital agreement modifies or eliminates spousal support and that modification or elimination causes one party to the agreement to be eligible for support under a program of public assistance at the time of separation or marital dissolution, a court, notwithstanding the terms of the agreement, may require the other party to provide support to the extent necessary to avoid that eligibility.

Beginning in the mid to late 20th Century, marriage law in America has been in the process of evolving from complete state control toward a private agreement. In the 1930s, state courts rejected the ability of a party to a marital agreement to waive her right to inherit from her husband.[192] Prior to the 1970s, state courts routinely rejected premarital agreements that would limit the power of the state to intervene, as an Illinois appellate court explained in 1972:

The most frequent argument made for holding agreements limiting alimony invalid is that such agreements encourage or incite divorce or separation. There is little empirical evidence to show that this assertion is well founded. It is true that a person may be reluctant to obtain a divorce if he knows that a great financial sacrifice may be entailed, but it does not follow from this that a person who finds his marriage otherwise satisfactory will terminate the marital relationship simply because it will not involve a financial sacrifice. It may be equally cogently argued that a contract which defines the expectations and responsibilities of the parties promotes rather than reduces marital stability.[193]

The emergence of judicial and legislative acceptance of the prenuptial agreement roughly coincided with the uniform rejection of the fault system. As the Illinois court explained:

The assumptions on which these reasons are based should be examined. It is often declared that the state has a vital interest in the maintenance of the family, but this interest does not require that persons, once married, must live together forever without regard to the breakdown of their relationship. The necessity of granting divorces is recognized, and the grounds upon which one can be granted are expanding. Where no minor children are involved, as here, and where the husband and wife can function in society separately and independently, the interest of the state in the continuance of the marriage is small.[194]

By 1980, states had almost uniformly accepted the prenuptial agreement, and the rights of marrying couples to predetermine property division, spousal support, and waiver of estates, as long as it met certain notice and fairness requirements, and, of course, consideration. [195] As the Florida Supreme Court explained in 1987:

[T]he fact that one party to the agreement apparently made a bad bargain is not a sufficient ground, by itself, to vacate or modify a settlement agreement. The critical test in determining the validity of marital agreements is whether there was fraud or overreaching on one side, or, assuming unreasonableness, whether the challenging spouse did not have adequate knowledge of the marital property and income of the parties at the time the agreement was reached. A bad fiscal bargain that appears unreasonable can be knowledgeably entered into for reasons other than insufficient knowledge of assets and income. There may be a desire to leave the marriage for reasons unrelated to the parties' fiscal position. If an agreement that is unreasonable is freely entered into, it is enforceable. Courts, however, must recognize that parties to a marriage are not dealing at arm's length, and, consequently, trial judges must carefully examine the circumstances to determine the validity of these agreements.[196]

By the late 1980s, state judiciaries began to reverse the public policy argument, and expanded the contract principals approach to postnuptial agreements.[197] As with any ordinary contract, the parties to the agreement could specify what state's law would apply to its validity and enforcement. Further, states have permitted, as the Plaintiffs have here, to contractually bind themselves to a resolution of disputes through binding arbitration.[198] Others have permitted to the parties to bind themselves to religious duties just as the Plaintiffs have here.[199]

The Utah legislature promulgated its Premarital Agreement Act in 1994. Reported cases, as limited as they are, however, show a continuing judicial distaste and overall reluctance to obey the law as written, courts choosing instead to follow case law that predates the Act.[200] Prior to the enactment of the statute, public policy concerns remained in the minds of the state courts, as a Utah Appellate decision explained:

Notwithstanding the relative ease with which parties to a deteriorated marriage can obtain a dissolution on grounds enumerated in Utah Code Ann. § 30-3-1(3) (1989), we believe the statutes regulating marriage and divorce still reflect that it is the public policy of this state to preserve marriage and disfavor dissolution. "**When [the marriage] status is created the rights involved are not merely private, but they are also of public**

concern. The social system and welfare of the state having their foundation in the family, the state is an interested party...." [*Emphasis added.*][*Citation omitted.*]. The public interest in stable, harmonious marriages was more recently expressed by our supreme court while examining a "reconciliation agreement" by which the parties settled and dismissed a prior divorce action: "The marriage itself and the obligations inherent in it are matters which it has always been recognized cannot be left entirely to private contract." [*Citation omitted.*]. We therefore adopt the Restatement view and hold that a promise in a prenuptial agreement regarding the disposition, upon divorce, of property brought to the marriage by the parties is unenforceable if it tends unreasonably to encourage divorce or separation.[201]

The view of the Utah courts had its roots in the Christian Family Model, made a part of the state constitution in its Enabling Act passed at the height of the Jacksonian Democracy and the Democratic Constitution.[202] When the United States Supreme Court in *Maynard* adorned us as a Christian Nation, it also adopted all of the Anglican court decisions, including the terms of the marital contract, even though, as above stated, those terms did not apply to nonconformists, but only to those that married in the Anglican Church. The *Maynard* court distinguished the marital contract from the ordinary one, claiming it was between the marrying parties and their King, as being the head of the Anglican

Church. And while Colonial governors might have applied Anglican Law for hundreds of years prior to the Revolution, Colonial law predates the Declaration and the Constitution, and its posterity should have ended in 1789. The Right to Contract is one of those inalienable rights mentioned in the Declaration, and entering into a private marital agreement, as was the case at our founding, is outside the business of the state, just as is the privacy of our bedrooms, our use of contraceptives as stated in *Griswold v. Connecticut, supra*, or are sexual preferences, as found in *Lawrence v. Texas, supra.*

C. STATE INTERFERENCE INTO THE TERMS OF PLAINTIFFS' MARITAL CONTRACT AS TO THEIR INTERSPOUSAL DUTIES IS UNCONSTITUTIONAL BECAUSE IT IMPOSES THE RELIGIOUS DUTIES OF THE ANGLICAN CHURCH, THUS VIOLATING PLAINTIFFS RIGHT TO RELIGIOUS LIBERTY.

In order for a couple to obtain the recognition of the Catholic Church, they must agree to its terms, including, but not limited to, raising their children in the faith. Since the Anglican Church was Catholic in all but name, it followed similar procedures, except, due to the merging of the church and the state, the Anglican Church had the force of law behind its canons, while the Pope only had the power of excommunication. In the Anglican Church, state recognition was a prerequisite to enforcing marital duties in the English court, and that recognition only came if a couple married in the Anglican Church and entered into an agreement with the King to abide by its rules. Nonconformists need not apply, especially Jews and Quakers.[203]

Those rules became what American jurisprudence calls the Common Law. But since Anglican marital duties were conditional, they were not rights at all, but contractual obligations to their spouse and to the King. Our Supreme Court in *Maynard v. Hill,* however, made a broad overreach in forcing the Common Law on all citizens. While equating the state with the King, the Court made no exception for nonconformists. Just as the English monarch, in conflating the church and the state, had more power than the Pope, our Supreme Court in *Maynard v. Hill* gave to the states more power than the English monarch. In America, the state was not only a theocracy, it was a democratic one, one where majority rule trumped the rights of any minority. After *Maynard*, the Christian majority had the power to impose its authority on non-Protestants, whether they be Jews, Catholics or Mormons or of any other faith, including, and especially, the rights of marriage.

Whether or not the *Maynard* court was being duplicitous, or just dishonest, the prejudices of the Jacksonian era fit tightly with the canons of the Anglican Church. Women, under this view, were inferior to men, and any other culture was inferior to Christianity (including polygamy). Under Anglican law, the rule of coverture meant that, when a woman married, all of her worldly possessions proceeding the marriage became the property of her husband. As the Supreme Court explained in 1859 in *Barber v. Barber*:

By Coke and Blackstone it is said: "That by marriage, the husband and wife become one person in law; that is, the very being or legal existence of the woman is suspended during the marriage, or at least is incorporated or consolidated into that of the husband, under whose wing and protection she performs everything. Upon this principle of union in husband and wife, depend almost all the rights, duties, and disabilities that either of them acquire by the marriage. For this reason, a man cannot grant anything to his wife, nor enter into a covenant with her, for the grant would be to suppose her separate existence, and to covenant with her would be only to covenant with himself; and therefore it is generally true, that all compacts made between husband and wife, when single, are voided by the intermarriage." (Co. Lit., 112; Bla. Com., vol. 1, p. 442.) So, too, Chancellor Kent, (vol. 2, p. 128:) "The legal effects of marriage are generally deducible from the principle of the common law, by which the husband and wife are regarded as one person, and her legal existence and authority in a degree lost and suspended during the existence of the matrimonial union."[204]

Under this view, it was permissible for a state to deny women the ability to work in a man's profession. In 1879, in *Bradwell v. State*, the United States Supreme Court adopted that theory in rejecting the claim of a woman seeking membership to the state

120

bar of Illinois that had excluded her based on her gender.[205] In a concurring opinion (denying her claim), Justice Joseph P. Bradley set out what was the proper place for a married woman:

It certainly cannot be affirmed, as an historical fact, that this has ever been established as one of the fundamental privileges and immunities of the sex. On the contrary, the civil law, as well as nature herself, has always recognized a wide difference in the respective spheres and destinies of man and woman. Man is, or should be, women's protector and defender. The natural and proper timidity and delicacy which belongs to the female sex evidently unfits it for many of the occupations of civil life. The constitution of the family organization, which is founded in the divine ordinance, as well as in the nature of things, indicates the domestic sphere as that which properly belongs to the domain and functions of womanhood.

As for unmarried women, Justice Bradley commented:

It is true that many women are unmarried and not affected by any of the duties, complications, and incapacities arising out of the married state, but these are exceptions to the general rule. **The paramount destiny and mission of woman are to fulfil the noble and benign offices of wife and mother.** This is the law of the Creator. And the rules of civil society must be

121

adapted to the general constitution of things, and cannot be based upon exceptional cases. (*Emphasis added.*)[206]

Further, in the Anglican view, when the husband and wife exchanged vows of matrimony, the wife's duty was to make herself available to the husband's sexual pleasures, and her failure to do so would result in a public punishment. For example, when residing in the English colony of Jamaica, Alexander Hamilton's mother was charged with refusing her husband and placed in the pubic jail for her offense.[207] The sacrament of marriage under English Law, for women meant, as the Supreme Court explained about English Law in 1859 in *Barber v. Barber*:

> {W}hilst yet she is wife, still bound by her conjugal obligations, the faithful observance of which, on her part, is the foundation of her claim to maintenance as wife, and which claim she would forfeit at any time by a violation of these obligations. Indeed, the form of her application is an acknowledgment that she is not sui juris, and not released from her conjugal disabilities and obligations, for she sues by prochein ami.[208]

Under English law, the state's perceived interest in inter-spousal obligations, including and especially spousal support, was based on the theory that women were incapable of supporting themselves. As our Supreme Court stated in 1948:

> [State of marital domicile] evinced a concern with this broken marriage when both parties were domiciled [there]. … [It] was rightly concerned lest the abandoned

spouse be left impoverished and perhaps become a public charge. The problem of her livelihood and support is plainly a matter in which her community had a legitimate interest.[209]

Since the wife was deemed incapable of supporting herself, the common law placed solely on the husband the role of provider. Since the husband was responsible for the wife, he was also responsible to third parties who provided care for his wife, as well as being subject to spousal support upon divorce.[210] If the wife violated the terms of their marital agreement, or otherwise took on the responsibility of supporting herself, she would forfeit any right to receive an allowance from her husband.[211] These common law duties of support continued through the fault system, and remain with us today in the form of spousal support.

In America, under the fault system, the judges could only award a divorce to the innocent party. Thus, if a wife ran off with another man, only the *innocent* husband could obtain the divorce. And, even if that husband did file for divorce, the trial judge might not award her any alimony, perhaps believing the wife's new lover took on that responsibility. If, however, it was the husband who ran away with another woman, the judge would be more likely to award alimony to the wife as being the injured party. If they were both at fault, neither could obtain a divorce and they would be stuck together. In fact, where both spouses sought a divorce claiming the other one was at fault, a judge could determine neither was worthy of a divorce.[212]

Even today, the role of women in America is still in great dispute among feminist scholars, some seeking gender equality while others embracing their historical role.[213] In 1949, in her book, *Male and Female*, anthropologist Margaret Mead theorized that married women embodied society, and that it was the women's role to educate her daughters in the proper role of women in society, as it was the father's role to provide:

In every known human society, everywhere in the world, the young male learns that when he grows up one of the things which he must do in order to be a full member of society is to provide food for some female and her young. ... Within the family, each new generation of young males learn the appropriate nurturing behavior and superimpose upon their biologically given maleness this learned parental role. When the family breaks down — as it does under slavery, under certain forms of indentured labor and serfdom, in periods of extreme social unrest during wars, revolutions, famines, and epidemics, or in periods of abrupt transition from one type of economy to another — this delicate line of transmission is broken. Men may founder badly in these periods, during which the primary unit may again become mother and child, the biologically given, and the special conditions under which man has held his social traditions in trust are violated and distorted. [214]

Anglican law morphed into what Nancy Cott calls the Christian Family Model, with clear and separate gender roles. Husbands were to produce for his family while his wife was in charge of the home. Yet, in modern day America, changing gender roles have proven a difficult adjustment for both men and women. Beginning in the 1980s, men gradually increased their role in childrearing, and assumed that women would take a greater role in income producing.[215] While women have achieved equal rights as income producers, many continue to expect men to adhere to their role under the outdated Christian Family model.[216]

In the Fault Era, the family reaped the benefits of the husband's successes, and endured his failures. It was the American Dream. It was all about risk and reward. Yet, husbands and wives would endure together because, under the Christian Family model, there was little choice. It was first and foremost about survival, and it was far easier to survive as a family unit. President Harry S Truman and his wife, Bess, for example, struggled with three failed businesses and three bankruptcies before joining the political world.[217] In and after the Fault Era, spouses could live apart, being married in name only, both responsible for their own support regardless of the economic disparity. And, while spousal support is directly tied to the marriage, a husband could not, under the fault system, establish residency in another state as a means of escaping his responsibility.[218]

The No-Fault Era roughly coincides with the Supreme Court's taking action to strike down laws that discriminated based on gender. This was especially true in the family law arena. Equal Protection now requires that either spouse could be responsible to the other for their support.[219] This is true even in same-sex marriage cases.[220] In the elimination of fault as a prerequisite to obtaining a divorce, and of obtaining spousal support, a cheating spouse could breach the marital contract and still benefit from it in the same way as if that spouse was the innocent party.

Self-sufficiency became the national mantra. In *Noble v. Noble*, in 1988, the Supreme Court of Utah outlined the authority of a trial judge in an original divorce proceeding to award spousal support:

> We require that a trial court, in setting alimony, attempt to provide support for the receiving spouse sufficient to maintain that spouse as nearly as possible at the standard of living enjoyed during the marriage. In determining the amount of the award necessary to accomplish this aim, the trial court must make adequate findings and conclusions demonstrating that it has considered three factors: (i) the financial condition and needs of the party seeking alimony, (ii) that party's ability to produce a sufficient income, and (iii) the ability of the other party to provide support. [Citations omitted.] In weighing those three factors, it is entirely appropriate for the trial court to take into account whether physical or mental

disabilities arising during the marriage, regardless of their cause, have made the receiving party's needs greater or reduced that party's ability to produce an income. The fact that such disabilities may have resulted from the tortious acts of another, including the divorcing spouse, certainly does not preclude the trial court from considering those disabilities.[221]

When a couple signs a pre-nuptial agreement, they are setting their own terms, and their own expectations, opting out of the obligations in the licensing state. They rely on the standard rules of contract law. Conflicts of Laws calls for the postnuptial contract to be interpreted under the laws of the state in which it was created, or under the laws as dictated in the agreement.[222] In our mobile society, forcing a couple to adhere to the rules of the divorcing state defeats the purpose of creating an agreement in the first place. And, any state placing limitations on enforcement of a pre-marital agreement, as with Utah in limiting the waiver of spousal support, is likewise irrelevant to a married couple that relocated to or from Utah after executing the pre-nuptial agreement. And, as long as pre-nuptial agreements are the subject of family, rather than equity courts, they will viewed through the prism of a legal stranger, who will apply his or her own biases to the terms of the agreement. Utah, especially its courts, seemingly want to hold on to their prejudices that originated in the Christian Family model, a model that had its origins in the Anglican Church.

Agreements are made up of a series of promises, and the familiar wedding vows are no different. Under the canons of the Anglican Church, the wedding vows were not just words. They were real promises made for a lifetime partnership.[223] In taking these vows, they were bonding to each other for life, and agreed to their prescribed duties. The Anglican theory was that, if a couple married, each did so with an inherent knowledge of their respective responsibilities. Thus, the Chancery Court would enforce those duties post-marital, including the duty of the husband to support the wife. When Equal Protection forced states to rethink the theory of spousal support, courts and state legislatures instinctively expanded, rather than retracted, spousal duties. In the 1970s, breadwinner wives suddenly realized that they had the same duty as their husband, even though that might not have been the case when they married. Further, as states expanded their rules of marriage to same-sex couples, they were telling both spouses that they had the inherent duty to support each other.

Obviously, applying common law duties that were based on a contract with the Anglican Church made little sense in 1888 when the Supreme Court imposed them on the entire populace in violation of religious liberty. Applying those rules to 2017 America is completely nonsensical. The two worlds could not be more different. Marriage began as an economic necessity, and morphed into a religious commitment. Judaism and Catholicism entered into agreements with their respective flocks to commit to carrying out God's will, and spreading the word. The Anglican Church did the same, entering into contracts with parishioners that, if you wanted the force of law behind your religious commitment, you had to adhere to its rules. The commitment was completely voluntary, as you could always leave the church. Many left for America in search of religious liberty. Ironically, our Supreme Court, in *Maynard v. Hill*, believed that the majority could impose its will, and any marriage, regardless of faith, became the will of the state to enforce at its discretion in accordance with its rules.

D. FEUDALISTIC ANGLICAN LAWS OF MARRIAGE WERE GEARED TO PRESERVE TITLE AND TO FACILITATE INHERITANCE, NOT TO INSTITUTE MORALITY.

Anglican rules of marriage were more than religious promises. They were based on feudal laws of title and property, laws that were based on the scarcity of real estate and its inheritance. Under Anglican law, the wife was the property of her husband.[224] In fact, the crime of adultery was an offense against property, subject to an action for civil damages, as the Pennsylvania Supreme Court explained in 1959:

> Criminal conversation, at early common law, was an action brought by the husband against the other man with whom his wife committed adultery. The action was one of trespass *vi et armis* … (*Citation omitted.*)

[Criminal conversation was in] many states of America was the civil counterpart of the criminal charge of adultery, the only difference being that in the former the private right was vindicated and in the latter the public proscription.[225]

Yet, given the scarcity of land in England, economics, not morality, was at the heart of adultery laws, as the Utah Supreme Court explained in 1991:

The tort of criminal conversation came into existence primarily because of the great importance that feudal society placed on insuring that the right of inheritance to property, title, and office descended to legitimate children only. Conflicting claims to titles, property, and estates could lead to discord and even violence. The law afforded a remedy designed to prevent illegitimate children by allowing a husband to sue another man who had intercourse with his wife. Stone, *The Family, Sex and Marriage* 316 (abridged ed. 1979).[226]

If a man induced another man's wife to leave the marriage, he had committed the tort of alienation of affection.[227] The same was not true in reverse. At common law, only the husband had the ability to sue because the wife surrendered that right when she got married.[228] It was only when, beginning in America in the late 19th Century, that married women obtained the right to sue or be sued in their own name, and thus given the right to pursue actions against other women for tortuously interfering in her marriage.[229]

As with spousal support, however, the original purpose for criminal conversation and alienation of affection were lost to time, as was its meaning. Instead, with the creation of the Christian state, these torts became actions of morality rather than economics. As the Supreme Court in Utah explained in 1991:

> The argument that the tort of alienation of affections is an historical anomaly is incorrect. Certainly, **many of the common-law concepts concerning the nature of the marriage relationship and the jural rights of spouses with respect to each other and to family property are no longer accepted by any court.** Few today would challenge the proposition that a sound marriage relationship is intrinsically deserving of protection from outside assaults made by those who use improper means to interfere with it. The obsolete procedural **and property theories that once attended the tort, and are relied on by the dissenters as reasons for abolishing the tort, have long been abandoned**; if applied today, they would be unconstitutional.[230] [*Emphasis added.*]

Most states, however, believe that these torts does nothing to preserve marriage, and that any claim that it does is pure fiction.[231] Still other states, as with Utah, hold onto alienation of affection as the only civil means to protect "the love, society, companionship, and comfort that form the foundation of a marriage." [232] Since the beginning of the 20th Century, however, these actions dissipated, and a majority of states have abandoned criminal conversation and alienation of affection as archaic.[233]

Anglican law was not about morality, nor the preservation of marriage, but about social stability. When the husband married in the Anglican Church, it was his contract with his sovereign to support his wife and any children born of the marriage. Anglican courts created this duty to prevent women from becoming public charges. Yet, the fundamental basis for these common law rules was to create offspring that would inherit both title and property, something that was vital to the preservation of a feudal society. That is why the common law rejected any claim that a father of a child born outside of marriage was responsible to support that child, absent a specific agreement to do so.[234] Further, the right of a wife to support was geared to encourage women to marry, while encouraging them to remain chaste prior to marriage with the punishment of having to support any child born to them outside of marriage (along with the corresponding public shame to themselves and their bastard child) [235] As well, courts created the common law tort of seduction, punishing any man who coerced a girl to give up her virginity, and provided damages for the loss.[236] In America, where land is abundant, and we have no knights, barons or other nobles, application of these archaic Anglican laws is absurd, especially in times, as discussed below, where right to inheritance has found itself dwarfed in importance to the duty of support.

D. STATE REGULATION OF MARRIAGE AND DIVORCE, PARTICULARLY ITS INTERFERENCE IN TERMS OF SPOUSAL SUPPORT, FAILS IN ITS STATED PURPOSE TO PROVIDE SOCIAL STABILITY.

The purpose of common law marital rights and duties in feudal England was to maintain the stability of the nation. Marriage developed in Western Civilization on its own out of economic necessity. Religion set forth the rules of conduct in society, especially when it came to family. The Anglican Church developed specific rules, and within that society, men and women knew what they were supposed to do, and behaved accordingly. As University of Chicago professor Eric Posner points out, in *Law and Social Norms*, shame is the most effective means of social compliance.[237] Shaming creates voluntary action, with people choosing to either comply with social mores, or risk exclusion from the community. The Anglican Church, much like the Catholic Church before it, seemingly understood that concept when it came to marriage. If people wanted the blessing of the church, they had to comply with its rules, or otherwise suffer the wrath of exclusion. Thus, if a couple wanted to marry within the Anglican Church, they had to voluntarily enter into an agreement with the King, and only those that married within the rules of the Anglican Church were entitled to enforce them in English courts.

When the Supreme Court in *Maynard v. Hill* implemented state regulation of marriage, it removed the voluntary nature of the Anglican contract. The mistake of the Democratic

Constitutionalists was that forcing the will of the majority is by its nature involuntary. And, with all types of purely private conduct, the Christian majority failed to eliminate the vices that it deemed unseemly, Prohibition being its most infamous example. Crimes of vice are the most illustrative examples in American history of this phenomenon. From the turn of the 20th century, gambling was a vice and illegal in all communities until Nevada broke the mold. Now gambling boats, usually placed on ponds, exist from sea to sea. Lotteries, known in the gambling world as the Numbers Game, was illegal until it became a state sponsored activity. Prostitution, as with gambling, long the target of the morality police, is now legal in Nevada. In all such cases, these vices never ended; rather, they became the subject of yet another crime, the bribery of public officials. Most interesting in this vein is the history of New Orleans, where before Prohibition, the city actually created a self-monitoring vice district with the nickname of Storyville to wall of its immorality from respectable communities.[238] The wealthiest of those practitioners within the District would contribute massively to campaigns of state officials in order to maintain their quarter.

Libertarians recognize that, as long as there are prohibitions of purely private conduct, there will be rebellion, and that rebellion will continue until their cause, like marijuana legalization, the recognition of same-sex marriage and, as in this case, the recognition of plural marriage, wins the day. In short, neither federal and state, nor local communities have the power to eliminate the purely private conduct known as vice, just as the federal government, with all of its power, did not have ability to even hinder devout Mormon families that wished to practice polygamy.

As the Supreme Court finally admitted in *Obergefell v. Hodges* in 2015, marriage in America originated as a purely private affair. When the Supreme Court, in *Barron ex rel. Tierman v. Mayor of Baltimore*, all but extinguished the Bill of Rights by limiting it to the actions of the federal government, it gave states, as the Court would find in 1845 in P*ermoli v. New Orleans,* the authority to become Christian theocracies. When, after the Civil War, Congress drove through the Fourteenth Amendment to nullify *Baron,* the Court refused to abide.[239] When the Court in *Maynard v. Hill* in 1888 thrust the will of the Christian majority on all, states quickly adopted the teachings of the Anglican Church, permitting its trial judges to look into the most private intimacies of a marriage to determine whether a couple was worthy of a divorce. When, after World War II, couples would conspire to commit perjury, or to travel to Reno, Nevada, to obtain a divorce, states finally gave in and quickly adopted the no-fault system triggering an explosion in the 1970s of what sociologist Lenore Weitzman called *The Divorce Revolution*.[240]

Despite a push for privatization of marriage in the 1960s and 1970s, state governments held onto their grasp.[241] But, to what end? The statistics are overwhelming. Marriage as we once knew it has been dying out. Certainly, states have no moral pedestal on which to stand. Greek philosopher Aristotle tells us that, for a community to enforce social mores, it must be small enough to be within shouting distance for the rules to be known to all. Thus, it was much easier for a small nation like England to create harmony of decisions than the United States, with its more than three thousand counties spread across more than three thousand miles, with tens of thousands of family court judges inserting their personal biases into the outcomes. In the Anglican Church, and even in America before the 1960s, divorce was so rare, and communities were so tight nit, that all were aware of a single judicial decision, and that decision might have an impact on behavior of those within shouting distance. In today's America, family courts have no interest in what impact their decision might have on the community at large. Even if they did, the sheer number of cases with all of their variations would have no impact other than on those immediately affected.

State regulation of marriage is now irrelevant to the financial support of children since both the United States Supreme Court and the United States Congress have rejected any discrimination as to children born out of wedlock, and require parents to provide for their support.[242] Thus, if a woman chose not to marry, as many have done, her intent to birth children is irrelevant to her marital status. In feudal times, marriage was important to determine lineage. Today, with the advent of genetic testing, marriage is all but irrelevant to lineage.[243]

State regulation of marriage does not save welfare costs. Women do not have to be married to become public charges, as nearly half the population of the United States is today on some form of public assistance.[244] In fact, Utah, in refusing to permit persons entering into a prenuptial agreement to waive their statutory right to maintenance, might actually increase reliance on the public dole.[245] Why should a spouse, who has waived her right to spousal support in a prenuptial agreement make any effort to advance her employment when she knows she can rely on the Utah statute to invalidate her waiver?

Further, since the beginnings of the no-fault era, lifetime spousal support has morphed into rehabilitative maintenance, like welfare, a temporary help up until the receiving spouse can become self-sufficient.[246] Today, women enjoy equal rights to support themselves, being one of the main reasons why most states have permitted them to waive rights to spousal support in a prenuptial agreement.[247] As the Illinois Appellate Court explained in 1972:

> When the rules regarding the husband's duty of support were first enunciated, the roles of a husband and wife were more rigid and defined. The husband worked and brought income into the family while the wife maintained and managed the household. The woman generally did not seek outside employment partly, because "her place was in the home", and partly because few opportunities for meaningful employment were available. Married women nowadays are increasingly

developing career skills and successfully entering the employment market. Where a woman is trained, healthy, and employable, and where a woman's efforts have not contributed to her husband's wealth or earning potential, the necessity for an alimony award upon breakup of the marriage is not great.[248]

In fact, the 1980s brought a surge of women into the workforce dramatically increasing the numbers of female breadwinners and stay-at-home dads.[249]

Moreover, state regulation of marriage, especially in setting the terms of the marital agreement, is actually discouraging people from marrying. In the 1960s and 1970s, the anointed Christian state of the 19th Century morphed into an anointed class of high minded ideals that led to social degradation that has been documented beyond issue.[250] As I explain in my 2015 book, *America Solved*, the drastic change in social norms that came with the Welfare State and the Divorce Revolution has displaced the positive reward system for hard work with a system that rewards, rather than, punish bad behaviors, discouraging, rather than encouraging, personal responsibility. The result of these oppressive policies have left our youngest generations gun shy, preferring to live together, rather than tie themselves down in marital paperwork, with all of its unknown obligations.[251] Further, those that do marry are waiting as long as possible to bind themselves to each other, and those that do marry are hardly making a lifetime commitment, as the average length of marriage has been dropping steadily for the past 40 years.[252] Further still, the current system has scared an entire segment of the male population to drop out of the workforce, remaining sexless bachelors, rather than being productive members of society who would, as was the goal of the Anglican Church, to bind themselves to a woman for life and populate the society with children raised in its teachings. [253]

Last, state regulation of marriage is so arbitrary in its outcomes that it has no reason to exist. Utah, as with every other state, has retained inside its statutory law, a single term of the marital contract in the Anglican Church, the duty of support. Thus, when brought before a state trial court judge, a legal stranger with a law degree is given the ability to insert their historical biases and prejudices, and enforce it under the edifices of judicial discretion.[254] Perhaps, nothing is more variant in the family courts across America as the issue of spousal support, where the trial judge is free to project an income to either spouse to achieve a desired result.[255]

And even so, Utah courts, like any other family court in America, encourage parties to settle their differences and in most cases would gladly rubber stamp any settlement agreement that may also contain a projected income of either spouse. No person entering into the bounds of matrimony in the United States knows their future, and they certainly do not know in what state or county that their marriage might come to an end. Even if they did, they would not be able to predict its outcome regardless of their actions during the marriage. Thus, nothing within these rules or realities supports Utah's argument that its regulatory scheme provides social stability; in fact, it does the opposite. It promotes fear, not of violating the state's perceived social norms, but of divorce, and the state's power to ruin.

Enter the premarital agreement. Like a white knight, once universally enforced, it will again encourage couples to overcome their fear of a bad judicial outcome. It will promote marriage, thus meeting head on the main reason as to why the courts of Utah have rejected its enforcement.[256] It will take out of the hands of meddling family court judges the power to inject their beliefs, and rather confine judges to the four corners of the written agreement, as stated in a landmark law review article cited in Eric Posner's *The Law and Social Norms*:

> The choice of marriage also signals their shared belief that, through mutual investments, their relationship can produce an expected "value" greater than the sum of their individual investments. Thus, we might expect the parties to assign each other specific and precise responsibilities according to relative advantages and preferences in order to maximize the expected relational value. In agreeing to such an assignment of responsibilities, of course, each party must be at least as well off under the relational bargain as she would have been otherwise.[257]

And, while most states have taken baby steps toward approving premarital agreements, Utah lags behind, permitting judges to modify its terms, placing on it conditions that any judge could easily thwart, rendering it, at least as to the terms of spousal support, nearly worthless. The very nature of a contract is predictability. Predictability creates trust. Without trust, commerce would die. And without trust in a judicial system to enforce the terms of a contract, there is no predictability, and thus no commerce. That defines the nature of marriage in America. Until the federal courts establish once and for all that the State cannot interfere in a private contract between two citizens who are relying on its terms, marriage will continue its steep decline into oblivion.

ARGUMENT VII:

OTHER THAN IN CASE OF IMMINENT HARM TO CHILDREN, THE STATE STATUTORY SCHEME THAT DICTATES, AND OR INJECTS, TERMS INTO PLAINTIFFS' MARITAL AGREEMENT REGARDING CUSTODY AND SUPPORT OF CHILDREN VIOLATES THER FUNDAMENTAL RIGHT TO PARENT UNDER THE NINTH AND FOURTEENTII AMENDMENTS TO THE CONSTITUTION.

A. PLAINTIFFS ARE PRESUMED TO BE FIT AND PROPER PARENTS FOR THEIR CHILDREN, AND THUS STATE'S INTERFERENCE IN PARENTAL AUTHORITY OVER THEIR CHILDREN IS EXTREMELY LIMITED.

The Founders never envisioned state interference in the family. As former colonies, the newly formed states only saw parenting in terms of property rights and contractual obligations. Yet, state interference in parental rights has stirred a century of litigation, prompting the Supreme Court to declare in 1981, it is "plain beyond the need for multiple citation" that a natural parent's "desire for and right to `the companionship, care, custody, and management of his or her children' " is an interest far more precious than any property right.[258]

In fact, state interference in parental rights is a 20th Century phenomenon. At common law, the parents were entitled to the labors of their children. During the Gilded Age, children were sent to factories to earn for their families in conditions so harsh that state and federal governments decided to step in and overrule parental decisions.[259] Reformers argued that there was an overriding importance of ensuring that children will grow up to be good citizens, including requiring compulsory education. As a University of Alabama law professor explains in 1971:

> Our society, because of culture ethnocentrism and an unwillingness to admit that poor people were entitled to full citizenship, continued to derogate the children's right to liberty and the parent's right to custody. By calling the statutes "protective" and of borrowing the idea of *parens patriae* the reformers were able to state their task elegantly and to dazzle their observers, in their time and ours.[260]

Parents began to push back, as the Supreme Court decisions of *Meyer v. Nebraska, supra,* and *Pierce v. Society of Sisters*, vividly displays. As the Court stated in *Pierce*:

> The fundamental theory of liberty upon which all governments in this Union repose excludes any general power of the State to standardize its children by forcing them to accept instruction from public teachers only. The child is not the mere creature of the State; those who nurture him and direct his destiny have the right, coupled with the high duty, to recognize and prepare him for additional obligations.[261]

But the struggle between the state and the parent had just begun. In 1944, in *Prince v. Massachusetts*, the Supreme Court addressed whether a parent, who was a Jehovah's Witness, could use her children to hand out literature preaching her faith.[262] The Court sought to find equilibrium in the competing interests:

> To make accommodation between these freedoms and an exercise of state authority always is delicate. It hardly could be more so than in such a clash as this case presents. On one side is the obviously earnest claim for freedom of conscience and religious practice. With it is allied the parent's claim to authority in her own household and in the rearing of her children. The parent's conflict with the state over control of the child and his training is serious enough when only secular matters are concerned. It becomes the more so when an element of religious conviction enters. Against these sacred private interests, basic in a democracy, stand the interests of society to protect the welfare of children, and the state's assertion of authority to that end, made here in a manner conceded valid if only secular things were involved. The last is no mere corporate concern of official authority. **It is the interest of youth itself, and of the whole community, that children be both safeguarded from abuses and given opportunities for growth into free and independent well-developed men and citizens**. Between contrary pulls of such weight, the safest and most objective recourse is to the lines already marked out, not precisely but for guides, in

narrowing the no man's land where this battle has gone on. (*Emphasis added*.).[263]

The battle came to a head in 1982, in *Santosky v. Kramer*, when the Court entered a decree that states, in parental termination hearings, must prove with clearing and convincing evidence (the highest civil standard), saying:

> The fundamental liberty interest of natural parents in the care, custody, and management of their child does not evaporate simply because they have not been model parents or have lost temporary custody of their child to the State. Even when blood relationships are strained, parents retain a vital interest in preventing the irretrievable destruction of their family life.[264]

Absent any finding of their future unfitness, however, Plaintiffs enjoy the fundamental right to make decisions that are in the best interests of the children. As the Court found in 1979 in *Parham v. J.R.*:

> "[O]ur constitutional system long ago rejected any notion that a child is the mere creature of the State and, on the contrary, asserted that parents generally have the right, coupled with the high duty, to recognize and prepare [their children] for additional obligations. . . . The law's concept of the family rests on a presumption that parents possess what a child lacks in maturity, experience, and capacity for judgment required for making life's difficult decisions. More important,

145

historically it has recognized that natural bonds of affection lead parents to act in the best interests of their children."[265]

Yet, in the 1980s and 1990s, state legislatures began an incursion into parental rights with the newest fad, grandparent rights. Under this view, the best interest of the child trumped parental authority, as defined by a legal stranger. The worst offender was the State of Washington, where its law extended visitation rights to any one, regardless of family relationship, until the Supreme Court in *Troxel v. Granville, supra,* voting 8-1 with only Justice Scalia dissenting, restated its position in Parham and found the statute unconstitutional as applied.[266] As a result, states greatly trimmed back grandparent rights, or the claims of any person not a legal parent to a child.[267]

B. NATIONWIDE TREND TOWARD PUSHING PARTIES TO SETTLE THEIR OWN CUSTODY DISPUTES UNDERMINES ANY CLAIM THAT STATE REGULATION IS NECESSARY AND FAILS IN ITS PURPOSE OF PROVIDING STABILITY FOR CHILDREN.

Beginning with the fault system at the turn of the 20th Century, state court judges had the authority to determine not only whether to grant a divorce, but to determine the custody of any children born of the marriage. When the fault system ended, with a sheer avalanche of cases, state court judges struggled with weight of that responsibility. State court judges, unlike their federal counterparts, are not the cream of the crop, but rather political lackeys that find their way to the bench more because who they know, rather than what they know. Far from being extraordinary, state court judges are extraordinarily ordinary, containing little wisdom in the making of far reaching decisions that could place a lifetime scar on those involved. As demonstrated below, state court judges have recognized their inherent limitations, deferring to the parental authority whenever possible.

As of 2017, however, no state permits parties to pre-determine their rights and obligations to children born of their marriage in a premarital agreement, and states have retained their police power to determine custody and support of children. In fact, the Uniform Marital and Premarital Agreements Act, published in 2012, forbids the parties from binding their children to parental decisions as to support or custody, reserving for the state court the authority to determine what is in the best interest of their children.[268] Therefore, in defending the rights of the state, Utah would argue that 1) The child cannot be bound to an agreement of his parents; 2) The state is charged with the best interest of the child; and 3) The state has an interest in the child not being a public charge.

Just like the fault system before it, Utah's no fault falsely assumes that state knows best, and that its elected or appointed trial judge has wisdom the of Solomon. In the fault system, parties would conspire to avoid judicial scrutiny of their marriage, carrying out a plot where one spouse would commit perjury and admit a nonexistent fault just so that the court would grant it.[269] The no-fault system that followed has overwhelmed our court system by its sheer volume, rendering fair and impartial judicial review impossible, and any attempt from the state legislatures to provide direction ignored in the haste of clearing a docket. Settlement techniques are, and have been, for decades, part and parcel of judicial training throughout the nation to empower the parties to come to an agreement and avoid the nastiness of trial. Interfering in a proposed settlement of divorcing parties would be detrimental to that end. When a case does go to trial, requiring the judge to decide, litigants in family court are frequently shocked to find that the outcome is more based on the likeability of the litigants, and the quality of representation, rather than any rule of law. And, as their attorneys will tell them, "the best interest of the child" means whatever the judge thinks it means at the given moment of decision, and that the judge will make its factual and legal findings in accordance with the outcome. Given the discretion given to trial court judges in divorce or paternity proceedings, any result would hold up on appeal, no matter how ludicrous it might appear to the litigants and their respective attorneys.[270]

Even when the judge is not involved in settlement negotiations, and lawyers present the court with a completed settlement agreement, the court is almost always happy to clear a case from its docket rather than disturb it. Further, even when there might be a problem pushing the settlement past a judge's inquiring eyes, lawyers understand that the court's inquiry might be cursory at best, and will parse facts to avoid judicial interference, just as a judge would want to avoid appellate interference if the matter did not settle. For example, a stay-at-home wife in a long-term marriage may feel empowered and decide she doesn't want any support from her ex-husband, or she may feel guilty for leaving him for another man. Or, a mother of a child born outside of marriage might enter into an agreement to waive support for a child on the condition that she be the sole parent. Or, parties might agree on a custody arrangement that permits a parent to relocate to another state on condition they receive no child support. The possibilities are endless, and they may have nothing to do with the best interest of the child as the state would define it.

In litigation or not, parents are free to bind their children to settlement agreements just as they would bind them in a prenuptial one, perhaps not in writing but through their actions. After all, in actuality, even a judicial settlement involving support and custody is little more than a contract in itself, leaving the parties with the choice of settling any dispute through binding arbitration, and away from the prying eyes of the state.[271] Moreover, for couples, married or just co-parents, who work out their differences without litigation, outside the bounds of judicial interference, enjoy the right to parent their children away from the prying eyes of the state, absent, of course, an action for abuse or neglect in juvenile court. Those parents get to decide what is in the best interest of their child.

Therefore, the only time that the state actually uses its police power to determine the best interest of the child is when the cased is litigated and proceeds to trial, or when it, in the body of the trial judge, is vocal in its settlement. Still, these few times are far afield from the days of the fault system when parties could not divorce without state approval. Rather, family law in America in 2017 is more like the first fifty years of our nation's history when, as Nancy Cott finds in *Public Vows*, married couples would self-marry and self-divorce, the time before the emergence of what Randy Barnett calls the Democratic Constitution, when the majority began to make the rules for all. This majority asserted control over individual liberties, especially the right to parent, and imposing duties and obligations into what was a private contract, not founded on our Constitution, but on the same Anglican Church our Founders had evicted in asserting our freedom from English rule.

C. THE "BEST INTEREST" STANDARD IS A 20TH CENTURY INVENTION THAT IS SO VAGUE THAT IT HAS NO VALUE IN SETTING STANDARDS OF BEHAVIOR.

Anglican Law at the time of our founding treated children as property. Upon divorce, the father always received custody of his children.[272] As Nancy Cott explains in *Public Vows*, the Christian Family model placed the husband at the head, giving him ownership, not just of the wife's property, but of their offspring.[273] A 1981 opinion of the Alabama Supreme Court criticized the notion as outdated:

> At common law, it was the father rather than the mother who held a virtual absolute right to the custody of their minor children. [*Footnote omitted.*] This rule of law was fostered, in part, by feudalistic notions concerning the "natural" responsibilities of the husband at common law. The husband was considered the head or master of his family, and, as such, responsible for the care, maintenance, education and religious training of his children. By virtue of these responsibilities, the husband was given a corresponding entitlement to the benefits of his children, i. e., their services and association.[274]

Up until the 20th Century, children of a marriage were free labor, often subject, as Abraham Lincoln was as a boy, to being loaned out to supplement the family income. In consideration, the offspring born into the lawful marriage were entitled to inherit property from their father, something that was especially important in England were land is scarce.[275] Yet, the one can see the beginnings of state intervention in an opinion of the Supreme Court of Mississippi in 1900:

> [I] t is presumed to be for the real interest of the child that it should be in the custody of its father, as against collateral relatives, and he, therefore, who seeks to withhold the custody against the natural and legal

presumption, **has the burden of showing clearly that the father is an unsuitable person to have the custody of his child**. (*Emphasis added.*) [276]

By contrast, at common law, the mother had no rights to custody of her children born to a lawful marriage:

> [T]the wife was without any rights to the care and custody of her minor children. By marriage, husband and wife became one person with the legal identity of the woman being totally merged with that of her husband. As a result, her rights were often subordinated to those of her husband and she was laden with numerous marital disabilities. As far as any custodial rights were concerned, Blackstone stated the law to be that the mother was "entitled to no power [over her children], but only to reverence and respect." 1 W. Blackstone, *Commentaries on the Law of England* 453 (Tucker ed. 1803).[277]

As society changed its attitudes toward parenthood, however, so did the state courts. Between the late 19th and mid-20th Centuries, the paternal preference in England became a maternal preference. It began with an 1839 law that permitted the Chancery Court to award custody of children born of a lawful marriage to a mother in a divorce proceeding if the children were less than seven years old.[278] Maryland became the first state court in the United States to grant to mothers a rights of custody based on what it believed was in the child's best interests (according to its own prejudices):

Yet even a court of common law will not go so far as to hold nature in contempt, and snatch helpless, puling infancy from the bosom of an affectionate mother, and place it in the coarse hands of the father. The mother is the softest and safest nurse of infancy, and with her it will be left in opposition to this general right of the father.[279]

By the late 19th Century, state legislators and state courts, again being the arbiter of social norms, began to swing the pendulum in the opposite direction, awarding custody of children to their mother until they reached the age of seven, where they would be returned to their father.[280] Again, social norms and prejudices were at the forefront of the ideology that a father was incapable of raising a young child:

This provision is a recognition of the fact that during the very tender years of the child the husband has not an unqualified right to its custody, even when the wife is at fault in the separation. Mothering of a young child is one of its rights. None but the real mother can meet this high duty in full measure.[281]

After World War II, the Baby Boom era reversed the ideology of father custody in favor of the stay-at-home mother. Called the *tender years' presumption*, the mother was presumed to be best fitted to guide and care for children seven years old or younger, and, in order to obtain custody, the father would have to prove that the mother was unsuitable to care and nurture their children.[282]

Beginning in the 1970s, with the advent of Equal Protection, states and courts called into question "the constitutionality of statutes which distinguish between males and females on the basis of 'old notions,' notions based upon stereotyped distinctions between the sexes," striking down most laws that were not gender neutral as being in violation of the Fourteenth Amendment.[283] By 1980, the *tender years' presumption*, at least in the eyes of the courts and the state legislatures, was both antiquated and unconstitutional.

By the 1980s, fathers grew more into caretakers, and mothers grew more into income providers. In fact, a recent census reveals more than 18 percent of single parents receiving child support were fathers.[284] Yet, the evolving door of social correctness continued to sway. At first, courts were loath to divided custody on the belief that sole custody promoted stability as described in a 2007 Iowa Supreme Court decision, finding that "divided custody is destructive of discipline, induces a feeling of not belonging to either parent, and in some instances can permit one parent to sow seeds of discontent concerning the other."[285] The Iowa court cited precedent, finding:

> Although a child's best interests will be served by associating with both parents, "an attempt to provide equal physical care may be harmfully disruptive in depriving a child of a necessary sense of stability.[286]

Clearly, keeping up with the latest psychological fad is beyond the purview of the average family court judge, and many recognize their limitations as both a fact finder and an evaluator of what is in the child's best interest in a custody dispute. Rather, courts frequently appoint psychologists, or family court attorneys, or both to make recommendations on how the trial court should divvy up custody of the children.[287] The Iowa Supreme Court set its own standard based on its favored psychological theory, attachment theory:

> [S]ocial science research related to child custody issues is now richer and more varied than it was in the past. In the past, many scholars and courts rejected joint physical care based on the influential writings of Joseph Goldstein, Anna Freud, and Albert J. Solnit. These scholars utilized attachment theory to emphasize the need to place children with a single "psychological parent" with whom the children had bonded. Joseph Goldstein, Anna Freud, & Albert J. Solnit, *Beyond the Best Interests of the Child* 98 (1979). Although the research upon which the "psychological parent" attachment theory was based rested upon studies of infants, it was also thought to apply throughout the life cycle of a child. Shelley A. Riggs, *Is the Approximation Rule in the Child's Best Interests?*, 43 Fam. Ct. Rev. 481, 484 (2005). The psychological parent approach stressed the important role of a strong, caring parent-child dyad and embraced what is sometimes termed a monotropic view of infant-child bonding. Robert F. Kelley and Shawn L. Ward, *Social Science Research*

and the American Law Institute's Approximation Rule, 40 Fam. Ct. Rev. 350, 355-59 (2002); Peggy Cooper Davis, *The Good Mother: A New Look at Psychological Parent Theory,* 22 N.Y.U. Rev. L. & Soc. Change 347, 360 (1996).[288]

The various child custody theories, as well as the prejudices of trial court judges, psychologists and family court attorneys who all claim to be acting in the child's best interest, demonstrates how varied a result might be depending, not necessarily on the facts of the case, but the jurisdiction of the eventual decider, with states sometimes fighting over which state has the true authority to make that decision.[289] They also vary on the individuals who are making the decisions in a certain case, and the outcome could vary widely from state to state or judge to judge, evaluator to evaluator. It is essentially a lottery of decision makers, the result not based on some higher power of understanding, but on sheer luck, or sheer timing as to the favored theory in place at the time of the date of decision.

The debate over what type of custody plan was in the best interest of the child has had so many variations it is too voluminous to mention here. It is sufficient to note that, despite the reasoning of the Iowa Supreme Court, the trend is now toward joint parenting. How long that trend continues, however, is anybody's guess. Yet, the truth is that nobody really knows, especially the State, and especially the trial judges. That is why parents should have the final say, and should do so within the confines of their written marital agreement rather than the random swings in the whims of state legislatures and trial judges.

D. SINCE STATE'S FAMILY COURT HAS VAST DISCRETION TO DETERMINE CUSTODY AND SUPPORT, THE INCONSISTENT RESULTS FAIL TO PROMOTE ANY MORAL FRAMEWORK, AND THUS ITS INTERFERENCE IN THE MARITAL CONTRACT HAS NO STATE PURPOSE.

State control over marriage in England began in 1753 under Lord Hardwicke's Act. As explained in the last section, the purpose of state regulation of marriage was to ensure stability, and facilitate the transfer to the children born of the marriage their parents' title and property after their deaths. Thereafter, as the Chancery Courts set forth duties and rights in order to effectuate the transfer, society developed social rules in support. It was the purpose of the courts to punish those that violated it rules, and in so doing, reinforcing the strict moral codes. As Eric Posner explains in his book, *Law and Social Norms*, consistency is vital to the enforcement of moral codes. According to Posner, punishment is the worst method of enforcing moral codes, necessitating judges to act in concert with the will of the majority. For example, in the 1970s, Congress passed Sentencing Guidelines in order to create consistency in punishment for its federal courts.[290] While initially successful, eventually judges and lawyers found holes in the guidelines to justify any reasonable result leading to its utter failure in its purpose, and ending with the

Supreme Court deeming the legislative guidelines not as strict rules, but only as advisory in nature, effectually rendering them useless to their original purpose.[291]

As the Iowa Supreme Court has shown, the same is true in family law. State legislators have issued specific directives to its judges to effectuate its policies as to custody, and, under a federal mandate, have issued child support guidelines. And, since "illegitimate" children gained Equal Protection in 1968 with *Levy v. Louisiana*,[292] these guidelines also apply to children born outside of marriage. Congress and state legislatures have desperately tried to create some sort of consistency in results, mandating in 1996, that each state develop a formula to determine the amount of support, resulting in as I describe in *America Solved*, fifty different formulas each with so many discretionary variations as to render them useless as a tool of consistency. Further, just as with the federal sentencing guidelines, judicial discretion reigns, permitting trial court judges to avoid legislative directives.

Iowa is demonstrative of the ongoing battle between the legislatures and the courts, each believing that it is the best arbiter. The legislature passed a statute requiring that the trial courts presume that joint custody is best, but the Iowa Supreme Court, in interpreting that statute, saw it differently:

> With respect to joint custody, the legislature has declared that if the court does not grant joint custody, it shall "cite clear and convincing evidence" that joint

custody is unreasonable and not in the best interests of a child. Iowa Code § 598.41(2)(*b*). ,,, We disagree, however, with the court of appeals as to whether the 1997 and 2004 amendments have affected any change in substantive law. While the amendments clearly require that courts consider joint physical care at the request of any party and that it make specific findings when joint physical care is rejected, the legislation reiterates the traditional standard — the best interest of the child — which appellate courts in the past have found rarely served by joint physical care. The amendments only require the courts to consider and explain the basis of decisions to deny physical care.[293]

The ongoing battle between Iowa's legislature and judiciary is just one example of the massive inconsistencies that exist in our nation's family courts, inconsistences that completely undercut the intended purpose of setting standards for behavior. After all, unlike England, where historically the House of Lords had been the final court of appeal, trial courts don't answer to the legislature, only to appellate courts. And appellate courts are made up of former trial court judges, who are empathetic to the trial judge, and not the complaining litigant creating strong deference for the trial judge's decision.[294] The logical result of this broad discretion is that trial judges feel more and more empowered to do whatever they decide is best regardless of statutes, court rules, or even appellate precedent. Finally, this concoction of legislative directive and trial court discretion leads to a cacophony of results so varied in their very nature that no reasonable person would have any idea how their actions or inactions in real life would be viewed in any future family court.

E. FEDERAL LAWS UNDERCUT THE STATE'S ARGUMENT THAT STATE REGULATION OF MARRIAGE IS ESSENTIAL TO PROVIDE FOR CHILDREN'S BEST INTERESTS.

As the Supreme Court explained in *United States v. Windsor*, *supra*, the federal courts have traditionally stayed away from cases involving Domestic Relations. In 1890, the Supreme Court declared:

> The whole subject of the domestic relations of husband and wife, parent and child, belongs to the laws of the States and not to the laws of the United States.[295]

In fact, federal courts have actually refused to take jurisdiction over a matter for no other reason that it might interfere in a state domestic relations case.[296] And, even though Congress has had the ability to preempt state law under the Supremacy Clause, it wasn't until the 1970s that Congress did so in force.[297]

Using the benefits of the Great Society as bait, Congress used its Spending Power to force state legislatures to adopt laws as a precondition for receiving those federal benefits for its citizens.[298] The system removed from the states the ability to refuse benefits to any individual on moral grounds, setting into motion an explosion in the number of persons receiving those benefits.[299] In 1968, in *King v. Smith*, the Supreme Court found unconstitutional an Alabama law that refused benefits to a mother of a child who was co-habiting with a man not her husband. Alabama was on strong moral ground as it was permissible under federal law for the state to refuse her benefits if she were co-habiting with her own husband and father of the child. But, as the State of Alabama learned in that ruling, Congress and morality are not a good match. It makes more sense for women economically to have a child by one man and live with another, thereby gaining economic assistance from their current lover without losing their federal benefits. Eventually, economic necessity begat social change. As a result, Congress legislated many fathers out of their homes, and funded an epidemic of single-parent households.[300]

Congress would not relent. In 1974, it required each state to enact laws that would continue payment of child support for all children until age 18.[301] (Of course, the states could not require intact families to support their children.[302]) The massive bureaucracy had as its stated goal to seek reimbursement of welfare payments from the fathers.[303] Under this system, the mother receiving benefits assigned her right to collect child support to the government. [304] As I explain in more detail in *America Solved*, Congress passed this law with full knowledge of the 1965 Moynihan Report's finding that poor children generally had poor fathers who were unable to support them.[305] As the Moynihan Report would have predicted, as of 2003, 90 percent of the $96 million owed in back child support in the United States was owed by men earning $10,000 per year or less, and 70 percent was owed not to the mothers, but to the government.[306] Poverty programs not only kept people in poverty, they destroyed the African American family, ignoring the dire warning of the Moynihan Report, which said:

> In a word, a national effort towards the problems of
> Negro Americans must be directed towards the question
> of family structure. The object should be to strengthen
> the Negro family so as to enable it to raise and support
> its members as do other families.[307]

Congress cannot claim originality in its stupidity, but if its intention was to injure the fledgling American-American family, it could do no worse. Just after the Civil War, Christian missionaries in the Freedman's Bureau tried to force the former slaves into the Christian Family Model, with all of its duties and responsibilities, including teaching the newly freed females that they were the property of their husbands.[308] One hundred years later, the Moynihan Report found that African Americans had rejected the patriarchal family, stating:

> There is, presumably, no special reason why a society in
> which males are dominant in family relationships is to
> be preferred to a matriarchal arrangement. However, it

162

is clearly a disadvantage for a minority group to be operating on one principle, while the great majority of the population, and the one with the most advantages to begin with, is operating on another. This is the present situation of the Negro. Ours is a society which presumes male leadership in private and public affairs. The arrangements of society facilitate such leadership and reward it. A subculture, such as that of the Negro American, in which this is not the pattern, is placed at a distinct disadvantage

In *The Idea of History*, Collingwood tells us that man is the only animal that has the capacity to learn from the experiences of others.[309] Congress, however, seems immune from that truth, and states theocracies have done no better. As demonstrated with the continuation of the Mormon faith and plural marriage, both state and federal government have failed to learn the lesson of the Anglican Church. Participation, while encouraged, must be voluntary for a policy to succeed. The virtues of the Christian Family model did not come from government. As Locke wrote, elected officials are the servants of the people, not their rulers. Virtues begin at home, and develop with the religious and moral teachings of church and community, and grow over time, building generation after generation, just as they did in the Anglican Church for three centuries prior to our Founding.

In the Anglican Church, like the Catholic Church before it, failure to adhere to the agreed upon rules meant excommunication. As Eric Posner explains in *The Law and Social Norms*, shame is the best form of social modification and punishment the worst.[310] Lots of carrots. Very few sticks. Yet, as I explain in *America Solved*, believing it was saving the family rather than destroying it, Congress consistently pushed the punishment pedal harder and harder as its policies continued to fail. The result of this all stick and no carrot policy has been the total devastation of the African American family, with a steady increase of children born outside of marriage reaching 72 percent according to the CDC compared to a still astounding 30 percent for white families.[311] But it's far worse than that. An epidemic of hopelessness has spread across poor and especially the African American community, and has metastasized into the general population. As Nicholas Eberstadt tells us in his 2016 book, *Men Without Work: America's Invisible Crisis*, there is a smaller percentage of men in the workforce today than any time since the end of World War II.[312] According to Eberstadt, the number of prime-age men outside the workforce exploded in the time period between 1965 and 2015 to more than 7 million, 6.5 times higher than a half a century before, growing at a rate of three times those inside the workforce or those looking for work. At the same time, as discussed above, a higher percentage of our citizenry is on some form of public assistance than in our nation's history.

What is absolutely clear after fifty years of these idiotic policies is that Congress has no mirror, and has refused to accept that its policies are the reason for these calamities. When it comes to the family, Congress should heed the words of Walt Kelly in his comic strip Pogo: "We have met the enemy, and he is us." Instead, Congress, in an effort to prove itself right, passed the ill-conceived Personal Responsibility and Work Opportunity Reconciliation Act of 1996 to decrease the rising percentage of those receiving public assistance, and in so doing, stuck a dagger in what was left of the nuclear family. Congress, still refusing to adhere to the recommendations of the Moynihan Report, was bound and determined to squeeze out of the poorest of Americans reimbursement for whatever it was paying in welfare. It even adopted what was called the Bradley Amendment, a rule that states were prohibited from renegotiating any child support debt owed to the federal government.[313] Therefore, while the rich who failed to pay taxes could make a deal with the government to discount the debt, the poor got the stick yet again. As well, Congress created a huge bureaucracy headed by the Office of Child Support Enforcement to oversee and execute its task. Congress also altered its bankruptcy laws so that no one could escape from government imposed obligations regarding support, forced states to pass laws making the failure to pay child support a felony, and paid for jail space for violators.[314] Never mind that these costs of administration and punishment exceeded by a thousand fold the actual debt it was trying to collect. It was fiscal idiocy, and remains so today.

Yet, the biggest victim of the single minded purpose of the Child Support System was the   state court's duty to protect the best interest of the child. By 1996, the science of genetic testing had advanced dramatically, and the cost of each test was so cheap, that paternity establishment became the primary focus. The state court system, however, was seen as slow and methodical, requiring actual service of process on those accused. The poor often didn't have regular employment, and more often didn't have fixed addresses making it difficult for sheriff's deputies to do their jobs right, leading to a high rate of false returns, which in turn led a national default rate in state filed paternity cases of nearly 70 percent nationwide, meaning support orders were entered without the input of the accused, and much less a genetic test.[315]

The Office of Child Support Enforcement has long claimed that children are entitled to know their biological parents. Yet, in the court process, federal law demands that the state be able to enter support orders without a custody decree, something required for all private litigants. The government could have funded a process using court social workers to help develop the father-child relationship. Further, as I explain in *America Solved*, if the biological relationship was so vital to the government, Congress could have insisted, using its Spending Power, on genetic testing at birth (as only a swab is necessary) for all children regardless of whether the parents are married to each other as a precondition for the issuance of a birth certificate. Yet, Congress has been only willing to pay for genetic testing in contested paternity proceedings and only when the state is a party because Congress, and especially the vast bureaucracy that is the Child Support

System, has no interest in helping children know their biological parents.[316] Rather, it is, and has been, federal policy to get someone, anyone, to sign off on the responsibility for supporting a child, and it has been federal policy to use any means necessary to obtain that goal.

At common law, and prior to 1996, state laws uniformly found that there was a legal presumption that a child born during a lawful marriage was the husband's child, and a court would not disturb that finding without clear and convincing evidence.[317] In fact, if, during a court proceeding, either the husband or the wife claimed that the husband was not the natural father of the child, the court generally appointed an attorney to act on behalf of the child to represent his or her interests.[318] When genetic testing became available, trial court judges, anxious to protect the child, used their discretion to deny requests for testing rather than ruin the life of a child that had been raised by his or her father regardless of biology.[319] By way of illustration, in the early 1990s, I represented a father of five in a custody dispute, with children ranging in ages from eight to sixteen. When he filed for custody, his wife of nearly 20 years asked the court to declare that the middle child was not his, claiming he was sired from an affair. Under the 1973 version of the Uniform Parentage Act, the trial court used her discretion in denying the wife's motion for genetic testing that might prove her claim.[320] If that case came before the same judge after 2002, however, she would have been required to order genetic testing as the new version of the UPA removed that discretion.[321] State court judges and even some legislatures were forced to invent new ways to protect children from this trauma, even inventing a doctrine of "equitable parent" in order to find parental rights for a man who has acted as the child's father for a lengthy period, many times believing he was, in fact, the biological father.[322]

For Congress, however, the judiciary (and the Constitution) was long seen as an impediment to its single minded goal. At common law, a child born outside of marriage was the child of no one, as explained above, with its mother having the primary duty of support.[323] In 1974, federal law required states to enact statutes permitting prospective fathers of these children to sign a paternity affidavit to place their name on the child's birth certificate, creating a legal presumption of paternity equivalent to that of a child born during a lawful marriage.[324] As stated above, under the Uniform Parentage Act, a genetic test would provide the necessary clear and convincing evidence to rebut the presumption.[325]

In the 1996 Act, Congress, again using its Spending Power, forced states to adopt laws to establish paternity legally without judicial intervention.[326] Hospitals would be required to present prospective fathers with paternity affidavits, binding them to the child for life without further legal proceedings.[327] As I explain in *America Solved*, it is actually federal policy to trick men, regardless of the facts, into taking financial responsibility for a child at the "magic moment" of birth. In order to appear fair, the federal law requires states to provide to the prospective parents the legal ramifications of signing.[328] Federal regulations based on the 1996 law require that the state must provide to birthing hospitals "[c]opies of a written description of the alternatives to, the legal consequences of, and the rights (including any rights, if a parent is a minor, due to minority status) and responsibilities of acknowledging paternity." The federal agency permits states to hire private attorneys to explain the legal rights to prospective parents, but it is a suggestion rarely, if ever, taken when the federal government failed to fund the program.[329] Of course, that was all part of Congress' fraudulent scheme. If your object is to trick someone, you would want them to believe you are looking out for their interests when they sign a statement that they received legal advice as to the ramifications for signing the affidavit without even knowing what that advice might look like. A master criminal could do no better. After all, studies show that as much as 30 percent of men who signed the paternity affidavit would be excluded by genetic testing.[330]

But Congress' shame has no bounds, as federal law even seeks to entrap minors into signing paternity affidavits. In judicial proceedings, when litigants are minors, courts have historically bent over backwards to protect the interests of those considered legally incompetent.[331] In a paternity proceeding, when the parents are themselves minors, judicial intervention would have required that legal adults be appointed to represent their interests.[332] Therefore, while most states that would not permit a minor to unilaterally enter into matrimony,[333] federal law would permit them to bind themselves into being legally responsible for a child, a responsibility that could lead to loss of custody (for the mother) and possible incarceration for failing to support the child.[334]

Finally, the 1996 Act circumvented judicial protection of minors who were born to a lawful marriage. As stated above, if either parent sought to rebut the presumption of paternity, courts appointed attorneys to represent their interests. Under the affidavit process, however, a married couple and another man could erase the presumption without judicial approval.[335] All it takes is the consent of the married couple, and an affidavit of a willing party.

In conclusion, Congress, in an effort to justify its burgeoning welfare policies, has dramatically undercut what was a state interest in protecting the best interest of children, removing old fashioned barriers like Due Process and actual proof. As we examine Utah's authority for regulating marriage, therefore, we see it through the prism of a federal government that has stripped it of its very purpose, especially for children born outside of marriage.

ARGUMENT VIII:

OTHER THAN IN INSTANCES OF CHILD ABUSE, UTAH'S STATUTORY SCHEME VIOLATES PLAINTIFFS' RIGHT TO RELIGIOUS LIBERTY UNDER THE RELIGIOUS FREEDOM AND RESTORATION ACT BY INJECTING TERMS INTO THEIR MARITAL AGREEMENT AND VIOLATING THEIR CHOICE TO LIMIT RESOLUTION OF ANY DISPUTES TO BINDING ARBITRATRATION WITH THEIR CHOSEN ARBITER.

A. UTAH'S STATUTORY SCHEME VIOLATES PLAINTIFF'S RELIGIOUS FREEDOM UNDER THE ACT AS IT PERTAINS TO THEIR FUNDAMENTAL RIGHT TO PARENT.

America's laws are based in part on Western Tradition developed from Greco-Roman humanism, and the theory that man is essentially a rational animal, capable of reason. Thus, the measure of his wisdom is the degree that he reaches his potential. But as R.G. Collingwood explains in his book, *The Idea of History*, "the idea that every agent is a wholly and directly responsible for everything that he does is a naïve idea that takes no account of certain important regions in moral experience." Rather, "people don't know what they are doing until this are actually doing it" and with that knowledge they learn what becomes of their actions.[336]

In the Hebrew (and Eastern) tradition, the religious leader (and king) was considered divine, giving him the inner wisdom to judge men and women for their behaviors. We know now that these kings were just as human as their subjects, and that their mortality did not cloak them in the Wisdom of Solomon. Thus, it is a rational absurdity to grant the power of Solomon to a single random family court judge cloaked only in a robe and a law degree. Rather, it creates only one filter of irrational human fallibility over another, especially when it comes to parenting of children. Permitting parents to choose their arbiter in advance permits them to focus their behavior on the rule of that arbiter, and to have some knowledge that of how their actions might be judged. After all, as our Supreme Court said in *Meyer v. Nebraska* and *Stanley v. Illinois*, [337] parents have a fundamental right to raise their children. Parents who choose never to litigate their dispute have the right to make the decision outside of state control (absent actions that put the children in mortal or severe physical harm that would merit juvenile court involvement).

The state of Utah, as any state in the Union, bases its authority to interfere in those rights, not on the Constitution, but on the rules of the Anglican Church, the same one that our Founders rejected in establishing religious liberty in the First Amendment to the United States Constitution. As explained above, the Supreme Court found in *Obergefell v. Hodges* that marriage in America began as a private contract, and evolved to the federally and state controlled contraption that it is today. Our Founders rejected the religious obligations associated with the Anglican Church, choosing instead the Enlightenment theory of religious liberty. As explained above, the growth of the Democratic Constitution in the early 19th Century coincided with a religious resurgence that historians call "The Second Great Awakening."

In 1888, in *Maynard v. Hill,* our Supreme Court accepted as historical fact that the rules of the same Anglican Church were imbued in the states to arbitrate what had been a private marital agreement. It didn't matter to the *Maynard* court that, even in England, the state didn't have control over any marriage outside the faith until the 19th Century. It didn't matter that, in England, the state's control over marriage did not apply to *nonconformists,*[338] Quakers, Jews, and then only to those other Christians that succumbed to the will of the Anglican theocracy. It did not matter that the original thirteen colonies gained control over marriage and divorce through an act of Parliament, and not the Constitution. Rather, with extraordinary audacity, the *Maynard* court adopted rules of religious intolerance that our nation was founded to escape. It did not matter to the *Maynard* court that the sovereign discussed in the Anglican marital contract was in fact the King, and the marrying couple were agreeing to comply with the rules of the Church as a condition for enforcement of those rules in English courts.

In essence, in declaring the United States a union of theocracies in the image of their Mother Country, the Court was telling our citizenry that the Revolution never occurred, and that thing we called religious liberty is just a suggestion. The *Maynard* court issued a proclamation that Americans were still subjects of the

King, or at least were subject to his rules, including his interpretation of the meaning of the marital vows, specifically the duties of husband and wife, the scourges of illegitimacy, and, of course, polygamy.[339] And it was the mission of American theocracy, and of every good Christian, including and especially government officials, to civilize nonconformists in the ways of the superior faith.

Georgetown professor Randy Barnett explains in *Our Republican Constitution* that the views of the Court in the mid-19th to early 20th Centuries were based on prejudices based on flawed scientific beliefs, especially the view that women and non-Whites, and non-Christians were inferior to white Anglo-Saxon men. According to Nancy Cott in *Public Vows*, this Christian superiority complex charged the Freedman's Bureau with the job of civilizing the former slaves in ways of the Christian Family model.[340] As well, The Indian Bureau was charged with the job of civilizing the savage Native Americans in the teachings of Christianity so they would be able to assimilate into our culture, and, of course, lose their former identity. Most Americans today see the flaw in this superiority complex, as Albert Einstein explains in a 1946 published letter:

> The ancient Greeks also had slaves. They were not Negroes but white men who had been taken captive in war. There could be no talk of racial differences. And yet Aristotle, one of the great Greek philosophers, declared slaves inferior beings who were justly subdued

and deprived of their liberty. It is clear that he was enmeshed in a traditional prejudice from which, despite his extraordinary intellect, he could not free himself.

A large part of our attitude toward things is conditioned by opinions and emotions which we unconsciously absorb as children from our environment. In other words, it is tradition—besides inherited aptitudes and qualities—which makes us what we are. We but rarely reflect how relatively small as compared with the powerful influence of tradition is the influence of our conscious thought upon our conduct and convictions.

It would be foolish to despise tradition. But with our growing self-consciousness and increasing intelligence we must begin to control tradition and assume a critical attitude toward it, if human relations are ever to change for the better. We must try to recognize what in our accepted tradition is damaging to our fate and dignity— and shape our lives accordingly.[341]

So it was with the Mormons. As stated above, in 1879, in *Reynolds v. United States*, the Supreme Court declared the superiority of the Anglo-Saxon Christian over Asian or African traditions that it considered uncivilized, particularly the Mormon doctrine of polygamous marriage. In 1890, in *Mattox v. United States*, the Court showed the difficulty in prosecuting anyone for violating the federal and state law banning polygamy, explaining why it continues to thrive through today.[342] And, as explained above, the State of Utah has made absolutely no effort to extinguish the religious practice, even going as far as to file an affidavit in 2013's *Brown* v. *Buhman*, stating it had no intention of prosecuting any person that married under the sacrament as long as only man and his First Wife were licensed under the state.[343] Polygamy in the Church made national headlines in various sects when child abuse was an issue, but the faith found a positive message in television, first with the HBO show, *Big Love*, and then with the reality show, *Sister Wives*. Moreover, the state of Utah has made no effort to interfere with the parenting of children in polygamous families, and the teaching of their children of its virtues in order to continue with the tradition.

Nearly a century after *Reynolds*, the Supreme Court in *Wisconsin* v. *Yoder* made inroads into the strict restrictions of Christian state control over the religious beliefs of others.[344] The 1972 decision involved an Amish family that challenged the right of the state to force their children to attend secondary school. The parents argued that the state compulsory education statute violated their First and Fourteenth Amendment rights to parent their children:

> The trial testimony showed that respondents believed, in accordance with the tenets of Old Order Amish communities generally, that their children's attendance at high school, public or private, was contrary to the Amish religion and way of life. They believed that by sending their children to high school,

they would not only expose themselves to the danger of the censure of the church community, but, as found by the county court, also endanger their own salvation and that of their children. The State stipulated that respondents' religious beliefs were sincere.[345]

After finding the state requirement a compelling interest, the Court nonetheless rejected Wisconsin's argument, finding the statute violated the Amish families' First Amendment right to Free Exercise of their religious beliefs, as well as their fundamental right to parent under the (Ninth and) Fourteenth Amendments:

> The conclusion is inescapable that secondary schooling, by exposing Amish children to worldly influences in terms of attitudes, goals, and values contrary to beliefs, and by substantially interfering with the religious development of the Amish child and his integration into the way of life of the Amish faith community at the crucial adolescent stage of development, contravenes the basic religious tenets and practice of the Amish faith, both as to the parent and the child.
>
> The impact of the compulsory-attendance law on respondents' practice of the Amish religion is not only severe, but inescapable, for the Wisconsin law affirmatively compels them, under threat of criminal sanction, to perform acts undeniably at odds with fundamental tenets of their religious beliefs. *See*

Braunfeld v. Brown, 361 U.S. 599, 605 (1961). Nor is the impact of the compulsory-attendance law confined to grave interference with important Amish religious tenets from a subjective point of view. It carries with it precisely the kind of objective danger to the free exercise of religion that the First Amendment was designed to prevent. As the record shows, compulsory school attendance to age 16 for Amish children carries with it a very real threat of undermining the Amish community and religious practice as they exist today; they must either abandon belief and be assimilated into society at large, or be forced to migrate to some other and more tolerant region.[346]

This inroads into religious freedom was short lived, however. In 1990, the Supreme Court rejected the strict scrutiny in religious freedom arguments in *Employment Div., Dept of Human Resources of Ore. v. Smith*.[347] In that case, a person claimed that the use of peyote in a religious ceremony gave him First Amendment rights that the state could not impinge. The majority disagreed. As Justice Blackmun explained in his dissent:

This Court over the years painstakingly has developed a consistent and exacting standard to test the constitutionality of a state statute that burdens the free exercise of religion. Such a statute may stand only if the law in general, and the State's refusal to allow a religious exemption in particular, are justified by a compelling interest that cannot be served by less restrictive mean. *[Footnote omitted.]*

Until today, I thought this was a settled and inviolate principle of this Court's First Amendment jurisprudence. The majority, however, perfunctorily dismisses it as a "constitutional anomaly." *[Citation omitted.]* As carefully detailed in JUSTICE O'CONNOR's concurring opinion *[Citation omitted.]*, the majority is able to arrive at this view only by mischaracterizing this Court's precedents. **The Court discards leading free exercise cases such as [*Wisconsin v. Yoder*] as "hybrid."** *[Citation omitted.]* The Court views traditional free exercise analysis as somehow inapplicable to criminal prohibitions (as opposed to conditions on the receipt of benefits), and to state laws of general applicability (as opposed, presumably, to laws that expressly single out religious practices). *[Citation omitted.]* The Court cites cases in which, due to various exceptional circumstances, we found strict scrutiny inapposite, to hint that the Court has repudiated that standard altogether. *[Citation omitted.]* In short, it effectuates a wholesale overturning of settled law concerning the Religion Clauses of our Constitution. One hopes that the Court is aware of the consequences, and that its result is not a product of overreaction to the serious problems the country's drug crisis has generated. [***Emphasis added***.]

Congress agreed with Justice Blackmun, and three years later, passed the Religious Freedom Restoration Act of 1993 (RFRA)[348] to protect its citizenry them from governmental intrusion into their religious beliefs.[349] As the Supreme Court explained in 1997 in *City of Boerne v. Flores*:

These points of constitutional interpretation were debated by Members of Congress in hearings and floor debates. Many criticized the Court's reasoning, and this disagreement resulted in the passage of RFRA. Congress announced:

"(1) [T]he framers of the Constitution, recognizing free exercise of religion as an unalienable right, secured its protection in the First Amendment to the Constitution;

"(2) laws `neutral' toward religion may burden religious exercise as surely as laws intended to interfere with religious exercise;

"(3) governments should not substantially burden religious exercise without compelling justification;

"(4) in Employment Division v. Smith, 494 U.S. 872 (1990, the Supreme Court virtually eliminated the requirement that the government justify burdens on religious exercise imposed by laws neutral toward religion; and

"(5) the compelling interest test as set forth in prior Federal court rulings is a workable test for striking sensible balances between religious liberty and competing prior governmental interests." 42 U. S. C. § 2000bb(a).

The Act's stated purposes are:

"(1) to restore the compelling interest test as set forth in [*Wisconsin v. Yoder*] and to guarantee its application in all cases where free exercise of religion is substantially burdened; and

"(2) to provide a claim or defense to persons whose religious exercise is substantially burdened by government." § 2000bb(b).

As the Supreme Court decision in 2014's *Burwell v. Hobby Lobby Stores, Inc.,*[350] states:

RFRA prohibits the "Government [from] substantially burden[ing] *a person's* exercise of religion even if the burden results from a rule of general applicability" unless the Government "demonstrates that application of the burden to *the person* — (1) is in furtherance of **a compelling governmental interest**; and (2) is **the least restrictive means** of **furthering that compelling governmental interest.**" [*Emphasis added.*]

The Court further explained:

[T]he "exercise of religion" involves "not only belief and profession but the performance of (or abstention from) physical acts" that are "engaged in for religious reasons."

Plaintiffs here are seeking to prevent the state from interfering in their fundamental religious beliefs as to how they raise their children under their faith. They have entered into a written marital agreement to determine the method as to how they wish to adhere to the tenets of their religion, and applying *Wisconsin v. Yoder*, Utah's child custody and support statutory scheme is a "grave interference" with those "important" tenets. As with *Yoder*, the Utah statutory scheme is "precisely the kind of objective danger to the free exercise of religion that the First Amendment was designed to prevent." [351] Further, as argued above, the statutory scheme authorizes persons outside the faith to interpret the duties set forth in the faith, or worse, to inject duties created by the state based, not on the Constitution, but on the duties of the Anglican Church. And, finally, and most important, the state cannot argue, based on all of the horrific statistics as to the state of marriage in America, that its statutory scheme promotes marriage, family, and especially economic stability. In fact, given the wide array of possible interpretations of the statutory scheme depending on the arbiter, the state's system actually discourages marriage for fear of an unwanted result in the event of divorce. Therefore, even if the state purpose was compelling, it is not narrowly tailored to meet its intended purpose, where, as argued above, the ability of parties to a marital contract to understand in full the terms of their agreement gives them a full understanding of their contractual duties, and the consequences of their failure to perform them. As I explained in *America Solved*, for a marriage to work, the parties have to be *all in* from the start, and there is no better way of accomplishing that goal than by setting out the expectations in a written contract.

B. THE STATE'S STATUTORY SCHEME IS BOTH ARBITRARY IN ITS APPLICATION AND CAPRICIOUS AS TO ITS EXECUTION, AND THUS PLAINTIFFS' CHOICE OF THEIR LOCAL RELIGIOUS LEADER AS THEIR SOLE ARBITER TO ANY AND ALL DISPUTES THAT ARISE FROM THEIR MARITAL AGREEMENT IS FAR SUPERIOR TO THAT OF A FAMILY COURT JUDGE.

In the Ecclesiastic Courts of England, and in the Catholic and Jewish faiths, all matters of sacrament were presented to the local religious leader. The leader would listen to the arguments of both parties and issue a decree that they, as members of his flock, would follow else they may suffer the wrath of the community. So it was in Colonial America as to marital issues. So it was at our founding. So it was with the Mormon faith. In all such cases, the loser of the decision of the chosen arbiter would have two choices: Follow the decree or leave the community. So it still is with local Amish communities, one in particular that challenged the right of the state to interfere with the right to parent before the United States Supreme Court, as in *Yoder*, above.

As Eric Posner argues throughout his book, *Law and Social Norms*, the strongest method to convince members of a community to adhere to social norms is through the act of shaming. For example, a corporate executive was publicly shamed because he gave money to California campaign to outlaw same-sex marriage. The National Basketball Association was shamed into stripping the ownership of an elderly, and longtime, member of its club based on an illegally taped conversation where he used improper language that was insulting to African Americans.[352] Of course, as citied above, in the Anglican Church, Alexander Hamilton's mother was publicly shamed, put in the local jail, because she refused her husband access to her body in violation of Anglican law. In the Victorian era, young women in England and in the United States were shamed when they violated the religious and moral tenets of having premarital sex, especially when that violation resulted in her pregnancy. As Posner argues, the entire basis of the law is to set standards of behavior and enforce them in a full and fair way, and it is only with a full knowledge of the rules, and their punishments for violation, that society can create adherence to those rules. In *Law and Social Norms*, Posner explains why putting a violator on public display in the stocks worked as a deterrent:

> Although part of the punishment was the physical pain
> that resulted from confinement, and from being pelted
> with refuse, an important purpose of the punishment was

communicating to other people that offender had committed a crime.[353]

Beginning with Hammurabi's Code, Western Civilization has always understood that for punishment to act as a deterrent to bad behavior, the law must be based on predetermined consequences of that bad behavior. The Torah, for example, sets forth for the Jewish people, a detailed list of crimes of punishments in the book of Deuteronomy. When a member of the community violated those tenets, all the remaining members would participate in the punishment. It is not unlike the theory of behavioral psychology, where there is cause and effect. Pavlov's dog would not salivate if it did not know that the bell signaled that it was dinner time. Opponents of capital punishment are not incorrect when they argue it has lost its usefulness when the Supreme Court found that it was not a deterrent to crime, especially when the punishment was not on public display, and the process took so long that its remoteness from the act itself greatly diminished it as a teaching tool.[354]

Modern civil law is no different. In tort law, the Supreme Court permits punitive damages (an additional amount over and above actual damages) to further a state's legitimate interests in punishing unlawful conduct and deterring its repetition.[355] In liable law, the Court is constantly searching for the right balance between promoting freedom and punishing bad behavior. In *Gertz v. Robert Welch, Inc.*, the Supreme Court permitted punitive damages in a liable case based on the balance between free speech

185

and the state's legitimate interest in protecting its citizens, permitting such damages only when there is a showing of knowledge of falsity or reckless disregard for the truth.[356] In contract law, the parties, not the state, define their respective duties and punishments for violation. As Eric Posner, in *The Law and Social Norms*, explains:

> Most people are able to cooperate without resorting to the threat of legal sanction. In ordinary life, people constantly make and keep promises, and legal retaliation for cheating is never an option because the cost of invoking the law exceeds the amount at stake. The common wisdom might be revised, then, to hold that non-legal cooperation occurs among people in communities, where information flows freely and reputation are known, but not among strangers.[357]

When a party to a contact behaves in such a way that constitutes a tort, the Court accepts a judgment for punitive damages when there was a tort involved, i.e., fraud, bad faith, etc.[358] In commercial behavior, however, Posner explains that the parties to contracts are not strangers to each other because they are part of the same economic community, requiring an unspoken trust that they will adhere to their promises. Employment contracts, too, create an expectation that the employer would protect and reimburse its employees and the employees will behave in such a way to seek bonuses and avoid termination.[359] When the agreement is in writing, parties expect that, not only will the other party perform their duties therein, but that, if there is a dispute, the state court would enforce the terms of that agreement.

Plato, in his book, *Republic*, explains that community is a natural human endeavor because the individual man is not self-dependent, that he needs the economic services of others in order to satisfy his own desires. As an economic being, he must have the state to survive.[360] Plato's student and disciple, Aristotle, however, tempered this belief by telling us that for a community to enforce social mores, it must be small enough to be within shouting distance for the rules to be known to all.[361] Thus, religious regulation of marriage worked in the Anglican Church at the time of our founding because the rules were so knowable, and because enforcement, both societal and legal, was strict.

As Margaret Mead explains in her book *Male and Female*, marriage is learned behavior.[362] Information is passed on from generation to generation, each one learning from the last two before it. As explained above, when the Fault Era ended, states eliminated the corresponding social norms, rendering the wedding vows a perfunctory tool. At the time of our founding, England's common law courts carried out the decree of the Ecclesiastical Courts in punishing those that violated the sacrament. Unmarried women, for example, were schooled in the virtue of virginity, and charged with keeping control over their own bodies. If they failed to do so, and their actions resulted in pregnancy, they would be left, absent the father acknowledging the child, to raise their child alone at their own expense.[363] This policy, although seemingly harsh today, had the effect of impressing on young women to remain chaste until marriage. When the Supreme Court, in 1968, in *Levy v. Louisiana*, ended the longstanding sanction against out-of-wedlock children, it was in fact greenlighting a societal change, and was, as was stated in Louisiana Attorney General's brief, the end of marriage as we knew it. [364]

Yet, Congress and the state legislatures have been determined to hold on to power over the private lives of their citizens, enforcing arbitrarily selected norms of what Nancy Cott calls the Christian Family model. The result, as one should logically see, is mass confusion, and an utter contempt for an out-of-control judiciary. As I explain in *America Solved*, the generational escalator has long since stopped. Just as the ancients handed down vital information of life, so did the teachings of ethics and morals, especially the knowledge of how to stay in a lifelong marriage. No wonder our federal and state governments express frustration when their constituents don't behave in conformity with its (inconsistently enforced) draconian rules. In *America Solved*, I explain that the State's primary role in the Fault Era was to prevent divorce, whereas today states have become utter divorce factories whose outcomes are in the hands of random strangers who put their own moral stamp on the outcome, which in turn has deterred our citizenry from marrying, choosing rather to co-habit, destroying the social stability that marriage was intended to create. Again, for marriage to work, as I said in *America Solved*, the parties must be "all in," and have the mutual goal of being life partners. The current system cannot achieve that goal, rather the marrying parties must set their own plan, setting their own rules, in order to succeed. Thus, the only way then to resurrect marriage as an institution in America is to end of state regulation and a return to the private contract that it was at the time of our nation's founding.[365]

C. PARTIES' HAVE THE RIGHT TO ENFORCE THEIR PREMARITAL AGREEMENT IN TOTAL, INCLUDING THE ABILITY TO AVOID STATE INTERFERENCE THROUGH BINDING ARBITRATION OF ANY AND ALL CLAIMS THAT ARISE OUT OF THAT CONTRACT.

When prenuptial agreements entered into the sphere of the family courts, especially in Utah, they were reluctant to enforce them. And, while Utah, along with most states, have accepted and enforced prenuptial agreements, some states linger behind.[366] The history of family law in America since the end of the 19th Century has been geared toward the protection of women, even creating the doctrine of separate maintenance to combat a history of discrimination in the workplace.[367] Thus, trial courts refused to enforce prenuptial agreements on public policy grounds in order to protect innocent women from their evil husbands who were using the written agreement to deprive their wives from receiving their due.[368] These courts reasoned that negotiating a premarital agreement, with or without attorneys, made them ripe for manipulation and fraud, and it was the job of the family court to protect the victim, i.e., the wives, requiring the courts to hold the enforcement of the contract to a much higher standard.

For example, in 1986, when automobile mogul John DeLorean divorced, the prenuptial agreement he had signed with his wife of 13 years would have left her with "relatively little" of his 20 million dollar estate (she herself was worth millions and earned a salary that earned her millions more each year).[369] These were also the days when lawyers created complex contracts using a scribe, and later manual and then electric typewriters, long before the era of the Internet and its fill-in-the-blank, PDF printable, forms and online preprinted contracts. Those were the days before licensed real estate agents were permitted to fill in the blanks on preprinted forms or PDF fill-ins without being accused of the unauthorized practice of law.[370] As technology has expanded the availability of prenuptial agreements to the masses, the state courts and legislatures have been increasingly accepting, applying contract principles, removing the additional burden of "the utmost good faith" that does not exist in ordinary contracts.[371] As former Louisiana State law professor Katherine Shaw Spaht told us in her 2003 law review article, "The Last One Hundred Years: The Incredible Retreat of Law from the Regulation of Marriage":

> Not surprisingly, people in Western countries have concluded that marriage is a private relationship which the law has no right to regulate and whose consequences

affect only the parties to the marriage, not the general public, not even their own children. The singular and most crucial purpose of marriage as the incubator of future civilization has been replaced in Americans' cultural imagination by a very different purpose. No longer does the general public intuit that the married couple is the instrumentality charged with civilization's most burdensome, time-consuming but indispensable task, the acculturation of children. The new purpose of marriage is best described as the public recognition of a private, sexually intimate, and privileged relationship created for the satisfaction, support, nurturance and fulfillment of the two parties.[372]

As is usually the case, it was California that tried to push the envelope by applying marital agreements to unmarried, cohabitating couples. The California Supreme Court case involved actor Lee Marvin and his girlfriend:

In summary, we base our opinion on the principle that adults who voluntarily live together and engage in sexual relations are nonetheless as competent as any other persons to contract respecting their earnings and property rights. Of course, they cannot lawfully contract to pay for the performance of sexual services, for such a contract is, in essence, an agreement for prostitution and unlawful for that reason. But they may agree to pool their earnings and to hold all property acquired during the relationship in accord with the law governing community property; conversely they may agree that each partner's earnings and the property acquired from those earnings remains the separate property of the earning partner. So long as the agreement does not rest upon illicit meretricious consideration, the parties may order their economic affairs as they choose, and no policy precludes the courts from enforcing such agreements.[373]

Despite the uproar of the Marvin decision, it had little impact on family law, and was quickly dismissed as an anomaly.[374] Nevertheless, if the State of Utah were to adopt the California decision as their own, they would then enforce the polygamy co-habitation contracts for those that, under *Brown v. Buhman*,[375] would be able to enter into a similar agreement without the judicial scrutiny. Of course, since these couples are not married in the eyes of the state, they could confine their disputes to binding arbitration under the laws of the State of Utah, as the Plaintiffs do in this matter.[376]

Binding arbitration before a person known to the parties would provide the stability that the State of Utah finds to be an important state purpose.[377] In the *DeLorean* case, the New Jersey family court sustained a provision in the prenuptial agreement that limited any remedy for dispute to binding arbitration before a designated arbitrator:

Arbitration is a consensual, voluntary contract entered into by parties to a dispute for the purpose of securing a "final disposition in a speedy, inexpensive, expeditious, and perhaps less formal manner of [one or more of] the controversial differences between the parties." [*Citation omitted*]. Arbitration offers many benefits: it reduces the length and cost of the court process, it enables the parties to select their own judge who they believe has the ability, fairness and expertise to render a just decision, and the dispute can frequently be resolved in a private forum in which the decision, absent an appeal, will not become a public record.[378]

Plaintiffs here have chosen their religious leader to act as arbiter of their disputes. He is a person known to them, and a person they trust implicitly. And, since he is their bishop, they have the added benefit of seeking his advice on how he might interpret a clause in their agreement and thus resolving the dispute before it came to litigation. Thus, Plaintiffs arbitration provision would create the stability and tend to preserve marriage, the very important state purpose that Utah used to justify its ban on same-sex marriage. In fact, as explained above, the state regulatory scheme creates instability in the face of a statistical upward trajectory in divorce, out-of-wedlock children, and a similar downward trajectory in length of marriage. Therefore, permitting the parties to engage in a known remedy before a known arbitrator would revitalize the original purpose of state enforcement of marital contracts.

CONCLUSION

For the past 150 years, polygamous families held themselves out in their community as being married, just like same sex couples did in their communities, and just like married couples did at our Founding, each devoid of state recognition. Since Utah has abandoned any attempt to prosecute, polygamous families stand in the same ground as same-sex couples after the Supreme Court's decision in *Lawrence v. Texas, supra,* where the Court found that their purely private conduct was outside the purview of the State. In *Obergefell v. Hodges,* as with all Equal Protection cases, the issue was one of discrimination between competing classes, and specifically about state issued marriage licenses. If the state did not issue marriage licenses to anyone, it could not be discriminating against any class of individuals.

The question presented here is not whether polygamous marriages should also receive marriage licenses, but whether the Constitution permits states to act as gatekeepers for what is purely private behavior. State regulation of marriage and divorce had a dubious beginning, based on the worst kind of judicial dishonesty. Historians look back with disdain at decisions of the United States Supreme Court from the mid to late 19th Century, particularly, the Dred Scott case and *Plessy v. Ferguson*. The cases of *Reynolds v. United States* and *Maynard v. Hill* deserve the same level of distaste. They stand for state interference in our most fundamental freedom, religious liberty, and with it the right to raise our children as we see fit. In 1972, the Supreme Court in *Wisconsin v. Yoder*, *supra*, rediscovered this freedom, and it is now codified in the Religious Freedom and Restoration Act. It was with this freedom that marriage developed, not through some government edict, but by choice of individuals in a free market deciding that it was mutually beneficial to mold their resources and to raise their children in their chosen faith.

In the 21st Century, America has accepted alternative lifestyles rather than punish them, with the federal government seeking to protect even the smallest minorities, such as transsexuals. We are far removed from the Christian nation that was the late 19th Century, when as R.C. Collingwood describes in *The Idea of History*, the idea of European superiority flowered under the teachings of Johann Gottfried Herder, the father of anthropology.[379] His egocentric ideas created the imperative duty for Europeans to socialize those less fortunate, at the same time spawning the eugenics movement that would end with Adolph Hitler's vision of Aryan superiority that would justify the slaughter of millions. It was this same sense of superiority that brought us the Christian state's imposition of its ideology on American families, especially in its illegal usurpation of authority over marriage and divorce. It is high time that we throw off the last vestiges of these repressive decisions in favor of the freedom that our Founders sought from government control of our daily lives, whether it be our families or our faith or something else.

John Quincy Adams, the last founding father, saw religion as nothing more than ethics, a means to teach the moral codes of society, and pass them on from generation to generation.[380] Adams, the product of a mostly European education, agreed with Voltaire that reason, not religion should rule. Thus, in Adam's view, marriage was a private contract, a private vow between the couple and their creator to live as life partners under the rules as set forth in their chosen faith. When Harvard professor Nancy Cott came to the conclusion in *Public Vows* that marriage in at our founding was a private contract, she was speaking of the era before Jackson, when Adams' beliefs prevailed, when our leaders believed in religious freedom. As Randy Barnett explains *in Our Republican Constitution*, the Jacksonian era and the birth of the Democrat party emerged to protect the institution of slavery, one that our Founders believed would die out.

It was Andrew Jackson and the Democrat party that laid waste to the Bill of Rights as a means to preserve and spread slavery. The eternal fiction of state's rights emerged to justify the spreading of its evil, and a countervailing religious movement emerged to combat it. As Barnett explains, states have no rights, just limited authority granted to them by their citizens in accordance with the Declaration of Independence, a grant that, by definition, could not include intrusion on the inalienable rights of the citizenry. Reacting to blowback from Great Britain's move to abolish slavery, fearing a dissolution of the Union and Andrew Jackson in general, Mr. Chief Justice John Marshall nullified most of the Bill of Rights in *Baron ex rel. Tierman v. Mayor of Baltimore, supra,* in 1833. By the time Congress passed the Fourteenth Amendment to nullify *Baron,* however, the Jacksonian Democracy was so well entrenched that, as Mr. Justice Hugo Black observed in his dissent in *Adamson v. California,* the Supreme Court nullified not *Baron,* but the Amendment itself. By the time the Supreme Court heard *Reynolds v. United States* and *Maynard v. Hill,* the Christian revival that begat the Abolitionist movement had spread to all corners of government, leading to theocratic control of marriage, and the outlawing of Mormon traditions.

The Jacksonian Democracy sought to impose the views of the majority on every individual, and do so from the highest pinnacles of government, not unlike socialism and communist dictatorships. That can, and will, never work, despite the continuing efforts of Congress, as its feeble attempt to criminalize polygamy in 1862 demonstrates. Eric Posner tells us that social norms begin with We the People as individuals, and any enforcement of those norms must come at the community level, not from the halls of the state or federal legislatures. In his book, *The Tipping Point*, author Malcolm Gladwell explains how a product, or an idea, comes into general use and acceptance, and nowhere in that book will you find a mandate from government. [381] In fact, the opposite is true. Defiance of government edicts develops and grows until their will changes the minds of the legislators who created them. Case in point is Congress' 1974 imposition of the 55-mph speed limit on federal highways. People in the larger, flatter states saw this rule as idiotic and shortly began to defy it. The public defiance grew to a shattering scream until Congress repealed the law in 1995.[382] The same is true in the 150 years of federal interference in the family. The rebellion against these federal edicts is apparent and lives on in the polygamous families in Utah.

A national rebellion against theocratic morality has been brewing since the 1960s. Conservative commentators decry millennials as soft and positively narcissistic, unable to tolerate, much less withstand, any other point of view but their own. Yet, this generation is nothing more than the logical consequence of federal interference in the family beginning with the Kennedy administration's policy to separate the poor fathers from their families and replace them with a check. As I explain in detail in *America Solved*, Congress and the Johnson administration refused to reverse this destructive policy despite the pleadings from the Moynihan Report.

Congress' solution to each failure was to double down on stupid and push for more and more federal control, spending a thousand fold in enforcement what it might actually collect. For example, the alleged welfare reform bill in 1996 requires states to incarcerate men for the crime of being poor at an average annual cost of nearly $60,000 per person, far exceeding their actual debt. As a result, men, beginning at the lowest level of society, began to realize that there was little to gain from success. This was particularly true in an African-American community that began to decry education as a sucker bet, and chastised any member who believed otherwise.[383] That viewpoint has seeped passed the tipping point as psychologist Helen Smith points out in her 2013 book, *Men on Strike: Why Men are Boycotting Marriage, Fatherhood, and the American Dream*.[384] Smith tells us how so many young men would rather get high and play video games than take on any form of responsibility that were part of social norms of the 1960s, while fewer others become what college age girls now call F*** Boys, who use willing girls to meet their base needs in the devolving hookup culture. The Great Society is a well-documented failure, especially for women seeking a respectful and hardworking husband. Young men feel marginalized, and living in every increasing hopelessness, one that leads to an early death in gang membership and/or drug addiction. As Nicholas Eberstadt tells us, this invisible crisis has led to the lowest labor participation rate for men of prime working age since the Great Depression.[385] When it comes to the family, however, government seems fixed in some time warp, believing we still live in the days when marriage was a community game of musical chairs, where young men and women were determined to find a life mate before all the good ones were taken.

In truth, however, the federalization of family law has all but destroyed what had been traditional marriage in America. In *The Idea of History*, Collingwood tells us that man is the only animal that has the capacity to learn from the experiences of others. Up until the 1970s, there existed in America a generational escalator where grandparents would teach parents how to parent and so forth. Or, as Margaret Mead tells us in *Male and Female*, it was the job of a young woman to socialize her future husband, and together, they would prepare their children for the ruggedness of life.[386] Since the 1970s, however, that escalator has slowed to a stop in most of our increasingly secular nation. This begs the question, after three generations, who is training the women how to be wives? With fifty years of easy divorce and single parenthood, especially for those raised without a strong religious and moral core, the answer is no one. Aristotle teaches us that happiness takes a lifetime to attain, and the Declaration of Independence together with our Constitution guarantees liberty in pursuing it. Yet, as I explain in *America Solved*, the current generation believes they are entitled to happiness, that their very wish and desire is theirs to take.

When John Quincy Adams suggested that religion was just ethics, he was telling us that religion provided a framework for our existence, for our very purpose, one based on The Ten Commandments.[387] Civilization is defined as the process by which a society reaches an advanced stage of development. The same is true of individuals. In the 19th Century, Benjamin Disraeli said, "The secret of success is the constancy of purpose." In the 20th Century, social scientists such as Erik Erickson, Abraham Maslow and Lawrence Kohlberg attempted to trace our development and categorize our levels of achievement. Maslow proposed five levels to enlightenment, the first one being the satisfaction of our needs and the second being the realization of the needs of others. Kohlberg presented a similar scale in his stages of moral development. What we are seeing in this current generation is the de-civilizing of America. While religion's primary purpose was to teach ethics, Christianity flourished because it gave people a purpose, especially dealing with loss of loved ones, that it was part of some greater plan, that there was a reward for moral behavior. Our Founders were creatures of the Enlightenment, and envisioned a nation that worshipped the Constitution, a nation of laws. They believed that, if the people truly believed in the freedoms it espoused, and took pride in what Alex De Tocqueville described as our exceptionalism, we would all be worshipping in the same house. The Christian work ethic begat the American Dream, each in accordance with his or her talents, where once chosen, success would come through perseverance.

Yet, the American Dream begins and ends with the family. We see our parents succeed, and we want to be just like them. We listen. We observe. We copy. We follow their roadmap to happiness. When parents failed in this endeavor, many turned to faith for guidance. As our country has become increasing secular, however, faith in God turned to faith in government. The Warren Court restored the faith of many in our Constitution as the barriers to freedom that were set in *Baron* disappeared one by one. In the 1970s, it appeared that freedom and true equality were just beyond the horizon. There was truly a reason to be optimistic. When the fault era ended in the 1970s, however, parents forfeited their primary purpose, seeking instead the illusory goal of happiness, and finding only a regression toward narcissism, producing children that were increasingly egocentric and rudderless in their purpose. As well, people have lost faith in the institutions of government, particularly the courts. They see the creeping utilitarianism for what it is: Power without purpose, rules that exist on paper, but are completely arbitrary in application.

History is meaningless if we don't learn from the mistakes of others. Looking back, it would be easy to say that the Supreme Court was duplicitous in its opinion in *Maynard v. Hill*. As Collingwood tells us, these members of the Court were simply men of their times, armed with a false sense of superiority of Christendom rather than the ideals of the Declaration and the Constitution. Now with its decision in *Obergefell v. Hodges*, our Supreme Court has reopened the discussion of state regulation of marriage and divorce by adopting Nancy Cott's conclusions that marriage in America began as a purely private affair. *Maynard v. Hill* begat the Fault Era where states sought to preserve marriage, albeit under the strict guidelines of the Anglican Church. In 1968, when the Supreme Court determined that children born out of wedlock were entitled to equal rights to those who were born of a marriage, it was clear that the Fault Era was on life support. When it finally ended in the 1970s, so did the very purpose of state regulation of marriage and divorce. Rather, the current system is so arbitrary in its application of law, and so capricious in its enforcement that its borders on despotism. But neither people nor institutions give up power freely, and the resultant grasp has led us to the virulent mess we have today, where marriage as a lifelong partnership is a fading memory, as is the very purpose of the institution itself.

Marriage, however, is the stabilizing force of our society and must be preserved. Ask any economist, and they will tell you that stability is the key to productivity, because stability permits risk taking, and marriage is the ultimate risk in a nation of scattered divorce laws and ever more scattered judges. Businessmen would not enter into a partnership without a fully negotiated agreement, setting forth not only the duties and obligations, but of the conditions for, and determination of, its eventual dissolution. The free market ideals contained in our Constitution is the only solution to this crisis and that is why government must remove itself from the field. After all, common law rights were not rights at all, because they did not apply to nonconformists, those that chose to live outside the rules of the Anglican Church. Rather, when a couple entered into matrimony in conformity with its rules, they were entering into a contract with their sovereign to abide by those rules. Couples marrying in the Anglican Church did so voluntarily, and understood their obligations, knowing that, because they married in the Anglican Church, they had also agreed that the English courts had the authority to enforce their vows

Marriage only works when the partners are all in, and religious beliefs historically provided the rule book for them to live. The State cannot, and should not, be interfering in setting those rules, especially when the source of those rules is not the Constitution, but on the Anglican Church. Rather, those that enter into matrimony should do so with open eyes, and should set their own rules and regulations, doing so within the framework of their religious beliefs, even if they are atheists. The prenuptial and postnuptial agreement has provided us the method to where the partners can set forth their own terms, where they can come together and plan out their future without fear of interference from the state. Technology has provided us with the means with fill-in-the-blank on-line forms. One can easily imagine couples picking and choosing predetermined clauses from a creative website, or entrepreneurial attorneys offering mediation services, or whatever the unlimited talents of America might render.

Achieving this goal will not come easy. It may take a person like Jonathan Turley to push the envelope on religious freedom, to spark the fire that will incinerate the remains of the dying institution of state control, and to restore our liberty that our Founders worked so hard to accomplish. My greatest hope, however, is that young people will so tire of the current system that, perhaps after reading this book, that they will reengage the power of We the People, and use my suggestions to create a new and lasting marriage revolution.

About the Author

Attorney Alan W. Cohen is a graduate of the University of Missouri School of Journalism and Washington University School of Law (in St. Louis). Now retired from practice, Mr. Cohen represented hundreds of men and women in the family courts in the St. Louis area for more than 25 years. Besides his 2015 book, *America Solved*: *A New Family for the 21st Century*, he is the author of the Child Support Trap three-book series on instruction on how to navigate through the calamities of federal involvement in family law, as well as two beginner's books on parentage law, *The Unwed Mom and The Unwed Dad,* all of which are available on Amazon. Besides his books, Mr. Cohen has authored scholarly articles on the subjects of paternity, child custody and child support.

Appendix A

UNIFORM PREMARITAL AND MARITAL AGREEMENTS ACT

Drafted by the

NATIONAL CONFERENCE OF COMMISSIONERS

ON UNIFORM STATE LAWS

and by it

APPROVED AND RECOMMENDED FOR ENACTMENT

IN ALL THE STATES

at its

ANNUAL CONFERENCE

MEETING IN ITS ONE-HUNDRED-AND-TWENTY-FIRST

YEAR

NASHVILLE, TENNESSEE

JULY 13 - JULY 19, 2012

WITH PREFATORY NOTE AND COMMENTS

COPYRIGHT 8 2012

By

NATIONAL CONFERENCE OF COMMISSIONERS

ON UNIFORM STATE LAWS

January 2, 2013

ABOUT ULC

The **Uniform Law Commission** (ULC), also known as National Conference of Commissioners on Uniform State Laws (NCCUSL), now in its 121st year, provides states with nonpartisan, well-conceived and well-drafted legislation that brings clarity and stability to critical areas of state statutory law. ULC members must be lawyers, qualified to practice law. They are practicing lawyers, judges, legislators and legislative staff and law professors, who have been appointed by state governments as well as the District of Columbia, Puerto Rico and the U.S. Virgin Islands to research, draft and promote enactment of uniform state laws in areas of state law where uniformity is desirable and practical.

• ULC strengthens the federal system by providing rules and procedures that are consistent

from state to state but that also reflect the diverse experience of the states.

• ULC statutes are representative of state experience, because the organization is made up

of representatives from each state, appointed by state government.

• ULC keeps state law up-to-date by addressing important and timely legal issues.

• ULC's efforts reduce the need for individuals and businesses to deal with different laws as they move and do business in different states.

• ULC's work facilitates economic development and provides a legal platform for foreign entities to deal with U.S. citizens and businesses.

• Uniform Law Commissioners donate thousands of hours of their time and legal and drafting expertise every year as a public service, and receive no salary or compensation for their work.

• ULC's deliberative and uniquely open drafting process draws on the expertise of commissioners, but also utilizes input from legal experts, and advisors and observers representing the views of other legal organizations or interests that will be subject to the proposed laws. ULC is a state-supported organization that represents true value for the states, providing services that most states could not otherwise afford or duplicate.

DRAFTING COMMITTEE ON UNIFORM PREMARITAL AND MARITAL AGREEMENTS ACT

The Committee appointed by and representing the National Conference of Commissioners on

Uniform State Laws in drafting this Act consists of the following individuals:

BARBARA A. ATWOOD, University of Arizona, James E. Rogers College of Law, 1201 E.

Speedway, P.O. Box 210176, Tucson, AZ 85721-0176, *Chair*

TURNEY P. BERRY, 500 W. Jefferson St., Suite 2800, Louisville, KY 40202

STANLEY C. KENT, 90 S. Cascade Ave., Suite 1210, Colorado Springs, CO 80903

KAY P. KINDRED, University of Nevada, Las Vegas, William S. Boyd School of Law, 4505 S.

Maryland Pkwy., Box 451003, Las Vegas, NV 89154-1003

SHELDON F. KURTZ, University of Iowa College of Law, 446 BLB, Iowa City, IA, 52242

ROBERT H. SITKOFF, Harvard Law School, 1575 Massachusetts Ave., Cambridge, MA 02138

HARRY L. TINDALL, 1300 Post Oak Blvd., Suite 1550, Houston, TX 77056-3081

SUZANNE B. WALSH, P.O. Box 271820, West Hartford, CT 06127

STEPHANIE J. WILLBANKS, Vermont Law School, 164 Chelsea St., P.O. Box 96, South

Royalton, VT 05068

BRIAN H. BIX, University of Minnesota Law School, Walter F. Mondale Hall, 229 19th Ave.

S., Minneapolis, MN 55455-0400, *Reporter*

EX OFFICIO

MICHAEL HOUGHTON, P.O. Box 1347, 1201 N. Market St., 18th Floor, Wilmington, DE

19899, *President*

GAIL HAGERTY, South Central Judicial District, P.O. Box 1013, 514 E. Thayer Ave.,

Bismarck, ND 58502-1013, *Division Chair*

AMERICAN BAR ASSOCIATION ADVISOR

CARLYN S. MCCAFFREY, 340 Madison Ave., New York, NY 10173-1922, *ABA Advisor*

LINDA J. RAVDIN, 7735 Old Georgetown Rd., Suite 1100, Bethesda, MD 20814-6183, *ABA*

Advisor

EXECUTIVE DIRECTOR

JOHN A. SEBERT, 111 N. Wabash Ave., Suite 1010, Chicago, IL 60602, *Executive Director*

Copies of this Act may be obtained from:

NATIONAL CONFERENCE OF COMMISSIONERS

ON UNIFORM STATE LAWS

111 N. Wabash Ave., Suite 1010

Chicago, Illinois 60602

312/450-6600

www.uniformlaws.org

UNIFORM PREMARITAL AND MARITAL

AGREEMENTS ACT

TABLE OF CONTENTS

1

UNIFORM PREMARITAL AND MARITAL AGREEMENTS ACT

Prefatory Note

The purpose of this act is to bring clarity and consistency across a range of agreements between spouses and those who are about to become spouses. The focus is on agreements that purport to modify or waive rights that would otherwise arise at the time of the dissolution of the marriage or the death of one of the spouses. Forty years ago, state courts generally refused to enforce premarital agreements that altered the parties' right at divorce, on the basis that such agreements were attempts to alter the terms of a status (marriage) or because they had the effect of encouraging divorce (at least for the party who would have to pay less in alimony or give up less in the division of property). Over the course of the 1970s and 1980s, nearly every state changed its law, and currently every state allows at least some divorce-focused premarital agreements to be enforced, though the standards for regulating those agreements vary greatly from state to state. The law relating to premarital agreements affecting the parties' rights at the death of a spouse had historically been less hostile than the treatment of such agreements affecting the right of the parties at divorce. The ability of a wife to waive her dower rights goes back to the 16th century English Statute of Uses. 27 Hen. VIII, c. 10, § 6 (1535). Other countries have also moved towards greater legal recognition of premarital agreements and marital agreements, though there remains a great diversity of approaches internationally. *See* Jens M. Scherpe (ed.), *Marital Agreements and Private Autonomy in Comparative Perspective* (Hart Publishing, 2012); *see also* Katharina Boele-Woelki, Jo Miles and Jens M. Scherpe (eds.), *The Future of Family Property in Europe* (Intersentia, 2011).

The Uniform Premarital Agreement Act was promulgated in 1983. Since then it has been adopted by 26 jurisdictions, with roughly half of those jurisdictions making significant amendments, either at the time of enactment or at a later date. *See* Amberlynn Curry, Comment,
"The Uniform Premarital Agreement Act and Its Variations throughout the States," 23 *Journal of the American Academy of Matrimonial Lawyers* 355 (2010). Over the years, commentators have offered a variety of criticisms of that Act, many arguing that it was weighted too strongly in favor of enforcement, and was insufficiently protective of vulnerable parties. *E.g.*, Barbara Ann Atwood, "Ten Years Later: Lingering Concerns About the Uniform Premarital Agreement Act,"

19 *Journal of Legislation* 127 (1993); Gail Frommer Brod, "Premarital Agreements and Gender

Justice," 9 *Yale Journal of Law & Feminism* 229 (1994); J. Thomas Oldham, "With All My

Worldly Goods I Thee Endow, or Maybe Not: A Reevaluation of the Uniform Premarital

Agreement Act After Three Decades," 19 *Duke Journal of Gender and the Law* 83 (2011).

Whatever its faults, the Uniform Premarital Agreement Act has brought some consistency to the

legal treatment of premarital agreements, especially as concerns rights at dissolution of marriage.

The situation regarding marital agreements has been far less settled and consistent. Some states have neither case law nor legislation, while the remaining states have created a wide range of approaches. Additionally, other legal standards relating to the waiver of rights at the death of the other spouse, by either premarital agreements or marital agreements, seem to impose somewhat different requirements. *See, e.g., Uniform Probate Code*, Section 2-213; *Restatement (Third) of Property*, Section 9.4 (2003); *Model Marital Property Act,* Section 10 (1983); and *Internal Revenue Code*, Sections 401 and 417 (stating when a surviving spouse's waiver of rights to a qualified plan would be valid).

The general approach of this act is that parties should be free, within broad limits, to choose the financial terms of their marriage. The limits are those of due process in formation, on the one hand, and certain minimal standards of substantive fairness, on the other. Because a significant minority of states authorizes some form of fairness review based on the parties' circumstances at the time the agreement is to be enforced, a bracketed provision in Section 9(f) offers the option of refusing enforcement based on a finding of substantial hardship at the time of enforcement. And because a few states put the burden of proof on the party seeking enforcement of marital (and, more rarely, premarital) agreements, a Legislative Note after Section 9 suggests alternative language to reflect that burden of proof.

This act chooses to treat premarital agreements and marital agreements under the same set of principles and requirements. A number of states currently treat premarital agreements and marital agreements under different legal standards, with higher burdens on those who wish to enforce marital agreements. *See, e.g.*, Sean Hannon Williams, "Postnuptial Agreements," 2007 *Wisconsin Law Review* 827, 838-845; Brian H. Bix, "The *ALI Principles* and Agreements:

Seeking a Balance Between Status and Contract," in *Reconceiving the Family: Critical*

Reflections on the American Law Institute's Principles of the Law of Family Dissolution (Robin

Fretwell Wilson, ed., Cambridge University Press, 2006), pp. 372-391, at pp. 382-387; Barbara

A. Atwood, "Marital Contracts and the Meaning of Marriage," 54 *Arizona Law Review* 11

(2012). However, this act follows the American Law Institute, in its *Principles of the Law of*

Family Dissolution (2002), in treating the two types of agreements under the same set of

standards. While this act, like the American Law Institute's *Principles* before it, recognizes that

different sorts of risks may predominate in the different transaction types – risks of unfairness

based on bounded rationality and changed circumstances for premarital agreements, and risks of

duress and undue influence for marital agreements (*Principles of the Law of Family Dissolution,*

Section 7.01, comment *e*, at pp. 953-954) – this act shares the American Law Institute's view

that the resources available through this act and common law principles are sufficient to deal

with the likely problems related to either type of transaction.

UNIFORM PREMARITAL AND MARITAL AGREEMENTS ACT

SECTION 1. SHORT TITLE. This [act] may be cited as the Uniform Premarital and

Marital Agreements Act.

SECTION 2. DEFINITIONS. In this [act]:

(1) "Amendment" means a modification or revocation of a premarital agreement or

marital agreement.

(2) "Marital agreement" means an agreement between spouses who intend to remain married which affirms, modifies, or waives a marital right or obligation during the marriage or at separation, marital dissolution, death of one of the spouses, or the occurrence or nonoccurrence of any other event. The term includes an amendment, signed after the spouses marry, of a premarital agreement or marital agreement.

(3) "Marital dissolution" means the ending of a marriage by court decree. The term includes a divorce, dissolution, and annulment.

(4) "Marital right or obligation" means any of the following rights or obligations arising between spouses because of their marital status:

(A) spousal support;

(B) a right to property, including characterization, management, and ownership;

(C) responsibility for a liability;

(D) a right to property and responsibility for liabilities at separation, marital

dissolution, or death of a spouse; or

(E) award and allocation of attorney's fees and costs.

(5) "Premarital agreement" means an agreement between individuals who intend to marry which affirms, modifies, or waives a marital right or obligation during the marriage or at

separation, marital dissolution, death of one of the spouses, or the occurrence or nonoccurrence of any other event. The term includes an amendment, signed before the individuals marry, of a premarital agreement.

(6) "Property" means anything that may be the subject of ownership, whether real or personal, tangible or intangible, legal or equitable, or any interest therein.

(7) "Record" means information that is inscribed on a tangible medium or that is stored in

an electronic or other medium and is retrievable in perceivable form.

(8) "Sign" means with present intent to authenticate or adopt a record:

(A) to execute or adopt a tangible symbol; or

(B) to attach to or logically associate with the record an electronic symbol, sound, or process.

(9) "State" means a state of the United States, the District of Columbia, Puerto Rico, the

United States Virgin Islands, or any territory or insular possession subject to the jurisdiction of the United States.

Legislative Note: If your state recognizes nonmarital relationships, such as civil unions and

domestic partnerships, consider whether these definitions need to be amended.

Comment

The definition of "amendment" includes "amendments" of agreements, narrowly understood, and also revocations.

The definitions of "premarital agreement" and "marital agreement" are part of the effort to clarify that this act is not intended to cover cohabitation agreements, separation agreements, or conventional day-to-day commercial transactions between spouses. Marital agreements and separation agreements (sometimes called "marital settlement agreements") are usually distinguished based on whether the couple at the time of the agreement intends for their marriage to continue, on the one hand, or whether a court-decreed separation, permanent physical separation or dissolution of the marriage is imminent or planned, on the other. To avoid deception of the other party or the court regarding intentions, one jurisdiction refuses to enforce a marital agreement if it is quickly followed by an action for legal separation or dissolution of the marriage. *See Minnesota Statutes* § 519.11, subd. 1a(d)(marital agreement presumed to be unenforceable if separation or dissolution sought within two years; in such a case, enforcement is allowed only if the spouse seeking enforcement proves that the agreement was fair and equitable).

While most premarital agreements and marital agreements will be stand-alone documents, a fragment of a writing that deals primarily with other topics could also constitute a premarital agreement or marital agreement for the purpose of this act.

With premarital agreements, the nature and timing of the agreement (between parties who are about to marry) reduces the danger that the act's language will accidentally include types of transactions that are not thought of as premarital agreements and should not be treated as premarital agreements (but see the discussion of *Mahr* agreements, below). There is a greater concern with marital agreements, since (a) spouses enter many otherwise enforceable financial transactions, most of which are not problematic and should not be made subject to special procedural or substantive constraints; and (b) there are significant questions about how to deal with agreements whose primary intention may not be to waive one spouse's rights at dissolution of the marriage or the other spouse's death, but where the agreement nonetheless has that effect.

In the terms of another uniform act, the purpose of the definition of "marital agreement" is to exclude from coverage "acts and events that have significance apart from their effect" upon rights at dissolution of the marriage or at the death of one of the spouses. *See Uniform Probate Code*, Section 2-512 ("Events of Independent Significance"). Such transactions might include the creation of joint and several liability through real estate mortgages, motor vehicle financing agreements, joint lines of credit, overdraft protection, loan guaranties, joint income tax returns, creation of joint property ownership with a right of survivorship, joint property with payment-on-death provisions or transfer-on-death provisions, durable power of attorney or medical power of attorney, buy-sell agreements, agreements regarding the valuation of property, the placing of marital property into an irrevocable trust for a child, etc.

The shorter definition of "premarital agreement" used by the Uniform Premarital

Agreement Act (in its Section 1(1): "an agreement between prospective spouses made in contemplation of marriage and to be effective upon marriage") had the disadvantage of encompassing agreements that were entered by couples about to marry but that were not intended to affect the parties' existing legal rights and obligations upon divorce or death, e.g., Islamic marriage contracts, with their deferred *Mahr* payment provisions. See Nathan B. Oman, "Bargaining in the Shadow of God's Law: Islamic *Mahr* Contracts and the Perils of Legal Specialization," 45 *Wake Forest Law Review* 579 (2010); Brian H. Bix, "*Mahr* Agreements: Contracting in the Shadow of Family Law (and Religious Law) – A Comment on Oman," *Wake Forest Law Review Online* 61 (2011), available at *http://wakeforestlawreview.com/*. The definition of "property" is adapted from the *Uniform Trust Code*, Section 103(12).

This act does not define "separation agreement," leaving this to the understanding, rules, and practices of the states, noting that the practices do vary from state to state (*e.g.*, that in many

states separation agreements require judicial approval while in other states they can be valid without judicial approval).

A premarital agreement or marital agreement may include terms not in violation of public policy of this state, including terms relating to: (1) rights of either or both spouses to interests in a trust, inheritance, devise, gift, and expectancy created by a third party; (2) appointment of fiduciary, guardian, conservator, personal representative, or agent for person or property; (3) a tax matter; (4) the method for resolving a dispute arising under the agreement; (5) choice of law governing validity, enforceability, interpretation, and construction of the agreement; or (6) formalities required to amend the agreement in addition to those required by this act.

SECTION 3. SCOPE.

(a)This [act] applies to a premarital agreement or marital agreement signed on or after

[the effective date of this [act]].

(b) This [act] does not affect any right, obligation, or liability arising under a premarital agreement or marital agreement signed before [the effective date of this [act]].

(c) This [act] does not apply to:

(1) an agreement between spouses which affirms, modifies, or waives a marital right or obligation and requires court approval to become effective; or

(2) an agreement between spouses who intend to obtain a marital dissolution or court-decreed separation which resolves their marital rights or obligations and is signed when a proceeding for

marital dissolution or court-decreed separation is anticipated or pending.

(d) This [act] does not affect adversely the rights of a bona fide purchaser for value to the extent that this [act] applies to a waiver of a marital right or obligation in a transfer or conveyance of property by a spouse to a third party.

Comment

This section distinguishes marital agreements, which are subject to this act, both from agreements that parties might enter at a time when they intend to obtain a divorce or legal separation or to live permanently apart, and also from the conventional transfers of property in which state law requires one or both spouses waive rights that would otherwise accrue at the death of the other spouse.

Subsection (c) is meant to exclude "separation agreements" and "marital settlement agreements" from the scope of the act. These tend to have their own established standards for enforcement. The reference to "a waiver of a marital right or obligation" in Subsection (d) would include the release of dower, curtesy, or homestead rights that often accompanies the conveyance of real property. In general, the enforceability of agreements in Subsections (b), (c) and (d) is left to other law in the state. This section is not meant to restrict third-party beneficiary standing where it would otherwise apply.

SECTION 4. GOVERNING LAW. The validity, enforceability, interpretation, and construction of a premarital agreement or marital agreement are determined:

(1) by the law of the jurisdiction designated in the agreement if the jurisdiction has a significant relationship to the agreement or either party and the designated law is not contrary to a fundamental public policy of this state; or

(2) absent an effective designation described in paragraph (1), by the law of this state, including the choice-of-law rules of this state.

Comment

This section is adapted from the *Uniform Trust Code*, Section 107. It is consistent with

Uniform Premarital Agreement Act, Section 3(a)(7), but is broader in scope. The section reflects traditional conflict of laws and choice of law principles relating to the enforcement of contracts.

See Restatement (Second) of Conflict of Laws, Sections 186-188 (1971). Section 187(2)(a) of that *Restatement* expressly states that the parties' choice of law is not to be enforced if "the chosen state has no substantial relationship to the parties or the transaction and there is no other reasonable basis for the parties' choice...." Section 187(2)(b) of the same *Restatement* holds that the parties' choice of law is not to be enforced if "application of the law of the chosen state would be contrary to a fundamental policy of a state which has a materially greater interest than the chosen state in the determination of the particular issue ...." The limitation of choice of law provisions to jurisdictions having some connection with the parties or the transaction tracks a similar restriction in the *Uniform Commercial Code*, which restricts choice of law provisions to states with a reasonable relation to the transaction (this was Section 1-105 under the UCC before the 2001 revisions; and Section 1-301 in the (2001) Revised UCC Article 1).

"Significant relation" and "fundamental public policy" are to be understood under existing state principles relating to conflict of laws, and "contrary to … fundamental public policy" means something more than that the law of the other jurisdiction differs from that of the forum state. *See, e.g.*, *International Hotels Corporation v. Golden*, 15 N.Y.2d 9, 14, 254 N.Y.S.2d 527, 530, 203 N.E.2d 210, 212-13 (1964); *Capital One Bank v. Fort*, 255 P.3d 508, 510-513 (Or. App. 2011) (court refused to apply law under choice of law provision because contrary to "fundamental public policy" of forum state); Russell J. Weintraub, *Commentary on the Conflict of Laws* 118-125 (6th ed., Foundation Press, 2010). For examples of choice of law and conflict of law principles operating in this area, see, *e.g.*, *Bradley v. Bradley*, 164 P.3d 537, 540-544 (Wyo. 2007) (premarital agreement had choice of law provision selecting Minnesota law; amendment to agreement held invalid because it did not comply with Minnesota law for modifying agreements); *Gamache v. Smurro*, 904 A.2d 91, 95-96 (Vt. 2006) (applying California law to prenuptial agreement signed in California); *Black v. Powers*, 628 S.E.2d 546, 553-556 (Va. App. 2006) (Virginia couple drafted agreement in Virginia, but signed it during short stay in the Virgin Islands before their wedding there; the agreement was held to be covered by Virgin Islands law because there was no clear party intention that

Virginia law apply and because Virgin Island law was not contrary to the forum state's public policy); *cf. Davis v. Miller*, 7 P.3d 1223, 1229-1230 (Kan. 2000) (parties can use choice of law provision to choose the state version of the Uniform Premarital Agreement Act to apply to a marital agreement, even though that Act would otherwise not apply).

SECTION 5. PRINCIPLES OF LAW AND EQUITY. Unless displaced by a provision of this [act], principles of law and equity supplement this [act].

Comment

This section is similar to Section 106 of the *Uniform Trust Code* and Section 1-103(b) of the *Uniform Commercial Code*, and incorporates the case-law that has developed to interpret and apply those provisions. Because this act contains broad, amorphous defenses to enforcement like "voluntariness" and "unconscionability" (Section 9), there is a significant risk that parties, and even some courts, might assume that other conventional doctrinal contract law defenses are not available because preempted. This section is intended to make clear that common law contract doctrines and principles of equity continue to apply where this act does not displace them. Thus, it is open to parties, e.g., to resist enforcement of premarital agreements and marital agreements based on legal incompetency, misrepresentation, duress, undue influence, unconscionability, abandonment, waiver, etc. For example, a premarital agreement presented to one of the parties for the first time hours before a marriage (where financial commitments have been made and guests have arrived from far away) clearly raises issues of duress, and might be voidable on that ground. *Cf.* In re *Marriage of Balcof*, 141 Cal.App.4th 1509, 1519-1527, 47 Cal.Rptr.3d 183, 190-196 (2006) (marital agreement held unenforceable on the basis of undue influence and duress); *Bakos v. Bakos*, 950 So.2d 1257, 1259 (Fla. App. 2007) (affirming trial court conclusion that premarital agreement was voidable for undue influence).

The application of doctrines like duress varies greatly from jurisdiction to jurisdiction: *e.g.*, on whether duress can be shown even in the absence of an illegal act, e.g. *Farm Credit Services of Michigan's Heartland v. Weldon*, 591 N.W.2d 438, 447 (Mich. App. 1998) (illegal act required for claim of duress under Michigan law), and whether the standard of duress should be applied differently in the context of domestic agreements compared to commercial agreements. This act is not intended to change state law and principles relating to these matters.

Rules of construction, including rules of severability of provisions, are also to be taken from state rules and principles. *Cf. Rivera v. Rivera*, 243 P.3d 1148, 1155 (N.M. App. 2010), *cert. denied*, 243 P.3d 1146 (N.M. 2010) (premarital agreement that improperly waived the right to alimony and that contained no severability clause deemed invalid in its entirety); *Sanford v. Sanford*, 694 N.W.2d 283, 291-294 (S.D. 2005) (applying state principles of severability to conclude that invalid alimony waiver in premarital agreement severable from valid provisions relating to property division); *Bratton v. Bratton*, 136 S.W.3d 595, 602 (Tenn. 2004) (property division provision in marital agreement not severable from provision waiving alimony).

Additionally, state rules and principles will govern the ability of parties to include elevated formalities for the revocation or amendment of their agreements.

SECTION 6. FORMATION REQUIREMENTS. A premarital agreement or marital agreement must be in a record and signed by both parties. The agreement is enforceable without consideration.

Comment

This section is adapted from *Uniform Premarital Agreement Act*, Section 2. Almost all jurisdictions currently require premarital agreements to be in writing. A small number of courts have indicated that an oral premarital agreement might be enforced based on partial performance, *e.g.*, In re *Marriage of Benson*, 7 Cal. Rptr. 3d 905 (App. 2003), *rev'd*, 36 Cal.4th 1096, 116 P.3d 1152 (Cal. 2005) (ultimately holding that the partial performance exception to statute of frauds did not apply to transmutation agreement), and at least one jurisdiction has held that a premarital agreement could be amended or rescinded by actions alone. *Marriage of Baxter*, 911 P.2d 343, 345-346 (Or. App. 1996), review denied, 918 P.2d 847 (Or. 1996). One court, in an unpublished opinion, enforced an oral agreement that a written premarital agreement would become void upon the birth of a child to the couple. *Ehlert v. Ehlert*, No. 354292, 1997 WL 53346 (Conn. Super. 1997). While this act affirms the traditional rule that formation, amendment, and revocation of premarital agreements and marital agreements need to be done through signed written documents, states may obviously construe their own equitable doctrines (application through Section 5) to warrant enforcement or modification without a writing in exceptional cases.

It is the consensus view of jurisdictions and commentators that premarital agreements are/or should be enforceable without (additional) consideration (the agreement to marry or the act of marrying is often treated as sufficient consideration). Additionally, most modern approaches to premarital agreements have by-passed the consideration requirement entirely: e.g., *Uniform Premarital Agreement Act*, Section 2; American Law Institute, *Principles of the Law of Family Dissolution*, Section 7.01(4) (2002); *Restatement (Third) of Property*, Section 9.4(a) (2003). In some states, courts have raised concerns relating to the consideration for marital agreements. The view of this act is that marital agreements, otherwise valid, should not be made unenforceable on the basis of lack of consideration. As the American Law Institute wrote on the distinction (not requiring additional consideration for enforcing premarital agreements, but requiring it for marital agreements): "This distinction is not persuasive in the context of a legal regime of no-fault divorce in which either spouse is legally entitled to end the marriage at any time." *Principles of the Law of Family Dissolution*, Section 7.01, Comment *c*, at 947-948 (2002).

The consideration doctrine is sometimes used as an indirect way to ensure minimal fairness in the agreement, and the seriousness of the parties. *See, e.g.*, Lon L. Fuller, "Consideration and Form," 41 *Columbia Law Review* 799 (1941). Those concerns for marital agreements are met in this act directly by other provisions. On the conclusion that consideration should not be required for marital agreements, see also *Restatement (Third) of Property*, Section 9.4(a) (2003), and

Model Marital Property Act, Section 10 (1983).

SECTION 7. WHEN AGREEMENT EFFECTIVE. A premarital agreement is effective on marriage. A marital agreement is effective on signing by both parties.

Comment

This section is adapted from *Uniform Premarital Agreement Act*, Section 4. The effective date of an agreement (premarital agreement at marriage, marital agreement at signing) does not foreclose the parties from agreeing that certain provisions within the agreement will not go into force until a later time, or will go out of force at that later time. For example, a premarital agreement may grant a spouse additional rights should the marriage last a specified number of years.

Parties sometimes enter agreements that are part cohabitation agreement and part premarital agreement. This act deals only with the provisions triggered by marriage, without undermining whatever enforceability the cohabitation agreement has during the period of cohabitation.

SECTION 8. VOID MARRIAGE. If a marriage is determined to be void, a premarital agreement or marital agreement is enforceable to the extent necessary to avoid an inequitable result.

Comment

This section is adapted from *Uniform Premarital Agreement Act*, Section 7. For example, if John and Joan went through a marriage ceremony, preceded by a premarital agreement, but, unknown to Joan, John was still legally married to Martha, the marriage between John and Joan would be void, and whether their premarital agreement should be enforced would be left to the discretion of the court, taking into account whether enforcement in whole or in part would be required to avoid an inequitable result.

This section is intended to apply primarily to cases where a marriage is void due to the pre-existing marriage of one of the partners. Situations where one partner is seeking a civil annulment (see Section 2(3)) relating to some claims of misrepresentation or mutual mistake would usually be better left to the main enforcement provisions of Sections 9 and 10.

SECTION 9. ENFORCEMENT.

(a) A premarital agreement or marital agreement is unenforceable if a party against whom enforcement is sought proves:

(1) the party's consent to the agreement was involuntary or the result of duress;

(2) the party did not have access to independent legal representation under

subsection (b);

(3) unless the party had independent legal representation at the time the agreement

was signed, the agreement did not include a notice of waiver of rights under subsection (c) or an

explanation in plain language of the marital rights or obligations being modified or waived by

the agreement; or

(4) before signing the agreement, the party did not receive adequate financial disclosure under subsection (d).

(b) A party has access to independent legal representation if:

(1) before signing a premarital or marital agreement, the party has a reasonable time to:

(A) decide whether to retain a lawyer to provide independent legal representation; and

(B) locate a lawyer to provide independent legal representation, obtain the lawyer's advice, and consider the advice provided; and

(2) the other party is represented by a lawyer and the party has the financial ability to retain a lawyer or the other party agrees to pay the reasonable fees and expenses of independent legal representation.

(c) A notice of waiver of rights under this section requires language, conspicuously

displayed, substantially similar to the following, as applicable to the premarital agreement or

marital agreement:

"If you sign this agreement, you may be:

Giving up your right to be supported by the person you are marrying or to whom you are married.

Giving up your right to ownership or control of money and property.

Agreeing to pay bills and debts of the person you are marrying or to whom you are married.

Giving up your right to money and property if your marriage ends or the person to whom you are married dies.

Giving up your right to have your legal fees paid."

(d) A party has adequate financial disclosure under this section if the party:

(1) receives a reasonably accurate description and good-faith estimate of value of the property, liabilities, and income of the other party;

(2) expressly waives, in a separate signed record, the right to financial disclosure beyond the disclosure provided; or

(3) has adequate knowledge or a reasonable basis for having adequate knowledge of the information described in paragraph (1).

(e) If a premarital agreement or marital agreement modifies or eliminates spousal support and the modification or elimination causes a party to the agreement to be eligible for support under a program of public assistance at the time of separation or marital dissolution, a court, on request of that party, may require the other party to provide support to the extent necessary to avoid that eligibility.

(f) A court may refuse to enforce a term of a premarital agreement or marital agreement if, in the context of the agreement taken as a whole[:]

[(1)] the term was unconscionable at the time of signing[; or

(2) enforcement of the term would result in substantial hardship for a party because of a material change in circumstances arising after the agreement was signed].

(g) The court shall decide a question of unconscionability [or substantial hardship] under subsection (f) as a matter of law.

Legislative Note: *Section 9(a) places the burden of proof on the party challenging a premarital agreement or a marital agreement. Amendments are required if your state wants to (1) differentiate between the two categories of agreements and place the burden of proof on a party seeking to enforce a marital agreement, or (2) place the burden of proof on a party seeking to enforce either a premarital agreement or marital agreement. If your state wants to permit review for "substantial hardship" caused by a premarital agreement or marital agreement at the time of enforcement, Section 9(f), including the bracketed language, should be enacted.*

Comment

This section is adapted from *Uniform Premarital Agreement Act*, Section 6. While this section gives a number of defenses to the enforcement of premarital agreements and marital agreements, other defenses grounded in the principles of law and equity also are available. See Section 5.

The use of the phrase "involuntary or the result of duress" in Subsection (a)(1) is not meant to change the law. There is significant and quite divergent case law that has developed under the "voluntariness" standard of the Uniform Premarital Agreement Act and related law –*e.g.*, *compare Marriage of Bernard*, 204 P.3d 907, 910-913 (Wash. 2009) (finding agreement "involuntary" when significantly revised version of premarital agreement was presented three days before the wedding) *and Peters-Riemers v. Riemers*, 644 N.W.2d 197, 205-207 (N.D. 2002) (agreement presented three days before wedding found to be "involuntary"; court also emphasized absence of independent counsel and adequate financial disclosure) *with Brown v. Brown*, No. 2050748, 19 So.3d 920 (Table) (Ala. App. 2007) (agreement presented day before wedding; court held assent to be "voluntary"), *aff'd sub. nom* Ex parte *Brown*, 26 So.3d 1222, 1225-1228 (Ala. 2009) *and Binek v. Binek*, 673 N.W.2d 594, 597-598 (N.D. 2004) (agreement sufficiently "voluntary" to be enforceable despite being presented two days before the wedding); *see also Mamot v. Mamot*, 813 N.W.2d 440, 447 (Neb. 2012) (summarizing five-factor test many courts use to evaluate "voluntariness" under the UPAA); *see generally* Judith T. Younger, "Lovers' Contracts in the Courts: Forsaking the Minimal Decencies," 13 *William & Mary Journal of Women and the Law* 349, 359-400 (2007) (summarizing the divergent interpretations of "voluntary" and related concepts under the UPAA); Oldham, "With All My Worldly Goods," *supra*, at 88-99 (same). This act is not intended either to endorse or override any of those decisions. One factor that courts should certainly consider: the presence of domestic violence would be of obvious relevance to any conclusion about whether a party's consent to an agreement was "involuntary or the result of duress."

The requirement of "access to independent counsel" in Subsections (a)(2) and (b) represents the view that representation by independent counsel is crucial for a party waiving important legal rights. The act stops short of requiring representation for an agreement to be enforceable, *cf. California Family Code* § 1612(c) (restrictions on spousal support allowed only if the party waiving rights consulted with independent counsel); *California Probate Code* §

143(a) (waiver of rights at death of other spouse unenforceable unless the party waiving was represented by independent counsel); *Ware v. Ware*, 687 S.E.2d 382, 387-391 (W. Va. 2009) (*access* to independent counsel required, and *presumption of validity* for premarital agreement available only where party challenging the agreement actually consulted with independent counsel). When a party has an obligation to make funds available for the other party to retain a lawyer, under Subsection (b)(2), this refers to the cost of a lawyer competent in this area of law, not necessarily the funds needed to retain as good or as many lawyers as the first party may have.

The notice of waiver of rights of Subsections (a)(3) and (c) is adapted from the

Restatement (Third) of Property, Section 9.4(c)(3) (2003), and it is also similar in purpose to

California Family Code §1615(c)(3). It creates a safe harbor when dealing with unrepresented parties by use of the applicable designated warning language of Subsection (c), or language substantially similar, but also allows enforcement where there has been an explanation in plain language of the rights and duties being modified or waived by the agreement.

The requirement of reasonable financial disclosure of Subsection (a)(4) and (d) pertains only to assets of which the party knows or reasonably should know. There will be occasions where the valuation of an asset can only be approximate, or may be entirely unknown, and this can and should be noted as part of a reasonable disclosure. Disclosure will qualify as "reasonably accurate" even if a value is approximate or difficult to determine, and even if there are minor inaccuracies. As the Connecticut Supreme Court stated, after reviewing cases from many jurisdictions on the comparable standard of "fair and reasonable disclosure," "[t]he overwhelming majority of jurisdictions that apply this standard do not require financial disclosure to be exact or precise. … [The standard] requires each contracting party to provide the other with a general approximation of their income, assets and liabilities…." *Friezo v. Friezo*, 914 A.2d 533, 549, 550 (Conn. 2007). Under Subsection (d)(1), an estimate of value of property, liabilities, and income made in good faith would satisfy this act even if it were later found to be inaccurate. Some commentators have urged that a waiver of the right of financial disclosure (or the right of financial disclosure beyond what has already been disclosed) be valid only if the waiver were signed after receiving legal advice. The argument is that it is too easy to persuade an unrepresented party to sign or initial a waiver provision, and that the party waiving that right would then likely be ignorant of the magnitude of what was being given up. Even when notified in the abstract of the rights being given up, it would make a great deal of difference if the party thinks that what was being given up was a claim to a portion of $80,000, when in fact what was being given up was a claim to a portion of $80,000,000. However, this act follows the current consensus among the states in not requiring legal representation for a waiver. One reason for not requiring legal advice is that this might effectively require legal representation for all premarital agreements and marital agreements. Under a requirement of legal representation, parties entering agreements might reasonably worry that even if there were significant disclosure, it would always be open to the other party at the time of enforcement to challenge the agreement on the basis that the disclosure was not sufficient, and that any waiver of disclosure beyond the amount given was invalid because of a lack of legal representation. In general, there was a concern that a requirement of legal representation would create an invitation to strategic behavior and unnecessary litigation.

"Conspicuously displayed" in Subsection (c) follows the language and standard of Uniform Commercial Code § 1-201(10), and incorporates the case-law regarding what counts as "conspicuous." Reference in Subsection (d)(3) to "adequate knowledge" includes at least approximate knowledge of the value of the property, liabilities, and income in question. Subsection (e) as adapted from the *Uniform Premarital Agreement Act*, Section 6(b). Other jurisdictions have in the past chosen even more significant protections for vulnerable parties. *See, e.g., N.M. Stat.* § 40-3A-4(B) (premarital agreement may not affect spouse's right to support); *Matter of Estate of Spurgeon*, 572 N.W.2d 595, 599 (Iowa 1998) (widow's spousal allowance could be awarded, even in the face of express provision in premarital agreement waiving that right); In re *Estate of Thompson*, No. 11-0940, 812 N.W.2d 726 (Table), 2012 WL 469985 (Iowa App. 2012) (same); *Hall v. Hall*, 4 So.3d 254, 256-257 (La. App. 2009), writ denied, 9 So.3d 166 (La. 2009) (waiver of interim support in premarital agreement unenforceable as contrary to public policy). This act attempts to give vulnerable parties significant procedural and substantive protections (protections far beyond what was given in the original *Uniform Premarital Agreement Act*), while maintaining an appropriate balance between such protection and freedom of contract. The reference in Subsection (f) to the unconscionability of (or substantial hardship caused by) a term is meant to allow a court to strike particular provisions of the agreement while enforcing the remainder of the agreement – consistent with the

238

normal principles of severability in that state (see Section 5 and its commentary). However, this language is not meant to prevent a court from concluding that the agreement was unconscionable as a whole, and to refuse enforcement to the entire agreement.

Subsection (f) includes a bracketed provision for states that wish to include a "second look," considering the fairness of enforcing an agreement relative to the time of enforcement. The suggested standard is one of whether "enforcement of the term would result in substantial hardship for a party because of a material change in circumstances arising after the agreement was signed." This language broadly reflects the standard applied in a number of states. *E.g.*, *Connecticut Code* § 46b-36g(2) (whether premarital agreement was "unconscionable . . . when enforcement is sought"); *New Jersey Statutes* § 37:2-38(b) (whether premarital agreements was "unconscionable at the time enforcement is sought"); *North Dakota Code* § 14-03.1-07 ("enforcement of a premarital agreement would be clearly unconscionable"); *Ansin v. Craven Ansin*, 929 N.E.2d 955, 964 (Mass. 2010) ("the terms of the [marital] agreement are fair and reasonable … at the time of divorce"); *Bedrick v. Bedrick*, 17 A.3d 17, 27 (Conn. 2011) ("the terms of the [marital] agreement are . . . not unconscionable at the time of dissolution"). However, it should be noted that even in such "second look" states, case law invalidating premarital agreements and marital agreements at the time of enforcement almost universally concerns rights at divorce. There is little case law invalidating waivers of rights arising at the death of the other

239

spouse grounded on the unfairness at the time of enforcement. Among the states that allow challenges based on the circumstances at the time of enforcement, the terminology and the application vary greatly from state to state. Courts characterize the inquiry differently, referring variously to "fairness," "hardship," "undue burden," "substantial injustice" (the term used by the American Law Institute's *Principles of the Law of Family Dissolution* § 7.05 (2002)), or just "unconscionability" at the time of enforcement. In determining whether to enforce the agreement or not under this sort of review, courts generally look to a variety of factors, including the duration of the marriage, the purpose of the agreement, the current income and earning capacity of the parties, the parties' current obligations to children of the marriage and children from prior marriages, the age and health of the parties, the parties' standard of living during the marriage, each party's financial and homemaking contributions during the marriage, and the disparity between what the parties would receive under the agreement and what they would likely have received under state law in the absence of an agreement. *See* Brett R. Turner & Laura W. Morgan, *Attacking and Defending Marital Agreements* (2nd ed., ABA Section of Family Law, 2012), p. 417. The American Law Institute argued that courts generally were (and should be) more receptive to claims when the marriage had lasted a long time, children had been born to or adopted by the couple, or there had been "a change of circumstances that has a substantial impact on the parties ... [and that] the parties probably

240

did not anticipate either the change, or its impact" at the time the agreement was signed. American Law Institute, *Principles of the Law of Family Dissolution* § 7.05(2) (2002).

One court listed the type of circumstances under which enforcement might be refused as including: "an extreme health problem requiring considerable care and expense; change in employability of the spouse; additional burdens placed upon a spouse by way of responsibility to children of the parties; marked changes in the cost of providing the necessary maintenance of the spouse; and changed circumstance of the standards of living occasioned by the marriage, where a return to the prior living standard would work a hardship upon a spouse." *Gross v. Gross*, 464 N.E.2d 500, 509-510 n.11 (Ohio 1984). Subsection (g) characterizes questions of unconscionability (or substantial hardship) as questions of law for the court. This follows the treatment of unconscionability in conventional commercial contracts. *See UCC* § 2-302(1) & Comment 3; *Restatement (Second) of Contracts* §208, comment f (1981). This subsection is not intended to establish or modify the standards of review under which such conclusions are considered on appeal under state law. Waiver or modification of claims relating to a spouse's pension is subject to the constraints of applicable state and federal law, including ERISA (Employee Retirement Income Security Act of 1974, 29 U.S.C. 1001 *et seq.*). *See, e.g., Robins v. Geisel*, 666 F.Supp.2d 463, 467-468 (D. N.J. 2009) (wife's premarital agreement waiving her right to any of her husband's separate property did not qualify as a waiver of her spousal rights as beneficiary under ERISA); *Strong v. Dubin*, 901 N.Y.S.2d 214, 217-220 (N.Y. App. Div. 2010) (waiver in premarital agreement conforms with ERISA waiver requirement and is enforceable). In contrast to the approach of the act, some jurisdictions put the burden of proof on the party seeking enforcement of an agreement. *See, e.g., Randolph v. Randolph*, 937 S.W.2d 815, 820-821 (Tenn. 1996) (party seeking to enforce premarital agreement had burden of showing, in general, that other party entered agreement "knowledgeably": in particular, that a full and fair disclosure of assets was given or that it was not necessary due to the other party's independent knowledge); *Stancil v. Stancil*, No. E2011-00099-COA-R3-CV, 2012 WL 112600 (Tenn. Ct. App., Jan. 13, 2012) (same); In re *Estate of Cassidy*, 356 S.W.3d 339, 345 (Mo. App. 2011)(parties seeking to enforce waivers of rights at the death of the other spouse have the burden of proving that procedural and substantive requirements were met). The Legislative Note directs a state to amend Subsection (a) appropriately if the state wants to place the burden of proof on the party seeking enforcement of a marital agreement, a premarital agreement, or both. In those jurisdictions, Subsection (a) should provide that the agreement is unenforceable unless the party seeking to enforce the agreement proves each of the required elements. Many jurisdictions impose greater scrutiny or higher procedural safeguards for marital agreements as compared to premarital agreements. *See, e.g., Ansin v. Craven-Ansin*, 929

N.E.2d 955, 961-964 (Mass. 2010); *Bedrick v. Bedrick*, 17 A.3d 17, 23-25 (Conn. 2011). Those jurisdictions view agreements in the midst of marriage as being especially at risk of coercion (the analogue of a "hold up" in a commercial arrangement) or overreaching. Additionally, these conclusions are sometimes based on the view that parties already married are in a fiduciary relationship in a way that parties about to marry, and considering a premarital agreement, are not. Linda J. Ravdin, *Premarital Agreements: Drafting and Negotiation* (American Bar Association, 2011), pp. 16-18. Also, some jurisdictions have distinguished "reconciliation agreements" entered during marriage with other marital agreements, giving more favorable treatment to reconciliation agreements. *See, e.g., Bratton v. Bratton*, 136 S.W.3d 595, 599-600 (Tenn. 2004) (summarizing the prior law in Tennessee under which reconciliation agreements were enforceable but other marital agreements were void). Many other jurisdictions and The American Law Institute (in its *Principles of the Law of Family Dissolution*, Section 7.01(3) & Comment *b* (2002)) treat marital agreements under the same standards as premarital agreements.

This is the approach adopted by this act.

SECTION 10. UNENFORCEABLE TERMS.

(a) In this section, "custodial responsibility" means physical or legal custody, parenting time, access, visitation, or other custodial right or duty with respect to a child.

(b) A term in a premarital agreement or marital agreement is not enforceable to the extent

that it:

(1) adversely affects a child's right to support;

(2) limits or restricts a remedy available to a victim of domestic violence under law of this state other than this [act];

(3) purports to modify the grounds for a court-decreed separation or marital dissolution available under law of this state other than this [act]; or

(4) penalizes a party for initiating a legal proceeding leading to a court-decreed separation or marital dissolution.

(c) A term in a premarital agreement or marital agreement which defines the rights or duties of the parties regarding custodial responsibility is not binding on the court.

Legislative Note: *A state may vary the terminology of "custodial responsibility" to reflect the terminology used in the law of this state other than this act.*

Comment

This section lists provisions that are not binding on a court (this contrasts with the agreements mentioned in Section 3, where the point was to distinguish agreements whose regulation fell outside this act). They include some provisions (*e.g.*, regarding the parents' preferences regarding custodial responsibility) that, even though not binding on a court, a court might consider by way of guidance.

There is a long-standing consensus that premarital agreements may not bind a court on matters relating to children: agreements cannot determine custody or visitation, and cannot limit
the amount of child support (though an agreed *increase* of child support may be enforceable). *E.g.*, In re *Marriage of Best*, 901 N.E.2d 967, 970 (Ill. App. 2009) ("Premarital agreements limiting child support are … improper"), appeal denied, 910 N.E.2d 1126 (Ill. 2009); *cf. Pursley v. Pursley*, 144 S.W.3d 820, 823-826 (Ky. 2004) (agreement by parties in a separation agreement to child support well in excess of guideline amounts is enforceable; it is not unconscionable or contrary to public policy). The basic point is that parents and prospective parents do not have the power to waive the rights of third parties (their current or future children), and do not have the power to remove the jurisdiction or duty of the courts to protect the best interests of minor children. Subsection (b)(1) applies also to step-children, to whatever extent the state imposes child-support obligation on step-parents. There is a general consensus in the case law that courts will not enforce premarital agreement provisions relating to topics beyond the parties' financial obligations *inter se*. And while some courts have refused to enforce provisions in premarital agreements and marital agreements that regulate (or attach financial penalties to) conduct during the marriage, *e.g.*, *Diosdado v. Diosdado*, 118 Cal. Rptr.2d 494, 496-497 (Cal. App. 2002) (refusing to enforce provision in agreement imposing financial penalty for infidelity); In re *Marriage of Mehren & Dargan*, 118 Cal.App.4th 1167, 13

Cal.Rptr.3d 522 (Cal. App. 2004) (refusing to enforce provision that penalized husband's drug use by transfer of property); *see also* Brett R. Turner and Laura W. Morgan, *Attacking and Defending Marital Agreements* 379 (2nd ed., ABA Section on Family Law, 2012) ("It has been generally held that antenuptial agreements attempting to set the terms of behavior during the marriage are not enforceable" (footnote omitted)), this act does not expressly deal with such provisions, in part because a few courts have chosen to enforce premarital agreements relating to one type of marital conduct: parties' cooperating in obtaining religious divorces or agreeing to appear before a religious arbitration board. *E.g.*, *Avitzur v. Avitzur*, 446 N.E.2d 136, 138-139 (N.Y. 1983) (holding enforceable religious premarital agreement term requiring parties to appear before religious tribunal and accept its decision regarding a religious divorce). Also, while there appear to be scattered cases in the distinctly different context of separation agreements where a court has enforced the parties' agreement to avoid fault grounds for divorce, e.g., *Massar v. Massar*, 652 A.2d 219, 221-223 (N.J. App. Div. 1994); *cf. Eason v. Eason*, 682 S.E.2d 804, 806-808 (S.C. 2009) (agreement not to use adultery as defense to alimony claim enforceable); see generally Linda J. Ravdin, *Premarital Agreements: Drafting and Negotiation* (ABA, 2011), p. 111 ("In some fault states, courts may enforce a provision [in a premarital agreement] that waives fault"), there appears to be no case law enforcing an agreement to avoid *no-fault* grounds. This act follows the position of the American Law Institute (*Principles of the Law of Family Dissolution*, Section 7.08(1) (2002)), that agreements affecting divorce grounds in any way should not be enforceable. It is common to include escalator clauses and sunset provision in premarital agreements and marital agreements, making parties' property rights vary with the length of the marriage. *Cf. Peterson v. Sykes-Peterson*, 37 A.3d 173, 177-178 (Conn. App. 2012), cert. denied, 42 A.3d 390 (Conn. 2012) (rejecting argument that sunset provision in premarital agreement is unenforceable because contrary to public policy). Subsection (b)(4), which makes provisions unenforceable that penalize one party's initiating an action that leads to the dissolution of a marriage, does not cover such escalator clauses. Additionally, nothing in this provision is intended to affect the rights of parties who enter valid covenant marriages in states that make that alternative form of marriage available. Section 10 does not purport to list all the types of provisions that are unenforceable.

Other provisions which are contrary to public policy would also be unenforceable. See Section

SECTION 11. LIMITATION OF ACTION. A statute of limitations applicable to an action asserting a claim for relief under a premarital agreement or marital agreement is tolled during the marriage of the parties to the agreement, but equitable defenses limiting the time for enforcement, including laches and estoppel, are available to either party.

Comment

This Section is adapted from *Uniform Premarital Agreement Act*, Section 8. As the

Comment to that Section stated: "In order to avoid the potentially disruptive effect of compelling litigation between the spouses in order to escape the running of an applicable statute of limitations, Section 8 tolls any applicable statute during the marriage of the parties ... .

However, a party is not completely free to sit on his or her rights because the section does preserve certain equitable defenses."

SECTION 12. UNIFORMITY OF APPLICATION AND CONSTRUCTION. In applying and construing this uniform act, consideration must be given to the need to promote uniformity of the law with respect to its subject matter among states that enact it.

SECTION 13. RELATION TO ELECTRONIC SIGNATURES IN GLOBAL AND

NATIONAL COMMERCE ACT. This [act] modifies, limits, or supersedes the Electronic

Signatures in Global and National Commerce Act, 15 U.S.C. Section 7001 et seq., but does not modify, limit, or supersede Section 101(c) of that act, 15 U.S.C. Section 7001(c), or authorize electronic delivery of any of the notices described in Section 103(b) of that act, 15 U.S.C.

Section 7003(b).

[SECTION 14. REPEALS; CONFORMING AMENDMENTS.

(a) [Uniform Premarital Agreement Act] is repealed.

(b) [Uniform Probate Code Section 2-213 (Waiver of Right to Elect and of Other Rights)] is repealed.

(c) [. . ..]

SECTION 15. EFFECTIVE DATE. This [act] takes effect ....

Appendix B

Utah's Uniform Premarital Agreement Act

30-8-1 Title.

This act shall be known as the "Uniform Premarital Agreement Act."

Enacted by Chapter 105, 1994 General Session

30-8-2 Definitions.

As used in this chapter:

(1) "Premarital agreement" means an agreement between prospective spouses made in contemplation of marriage and to be effective upon marriage.

(2) "Property" means an interest, present or future, legal or equitable, vested or contingent, in real or personal property, including income and earnings.

Enacted by Chapter 105, 1994 General Session

30-8-3 Writing -- Signature required.

A premarital agreement shall be in writing and signed by both parties. It is enforceable without consideration.

Amended by Chapter 297, 2011 General Session

30-8-4 Content.

(1) Parties to a premarital agreement may contract with respect to:

(a) the rights and obligations of each of the parties in any of the property of either or both of them whenever and wherever acquired or located;

(b) the right to buy, sell, use, transfer, exchange, abandon, lease, consume, expend, assign, create a security interest in, mortgage, encumber, dispose of, or otherwise manage and control property;

(c) the disposition of property upon separation, marital dissolution, death, or the occurrence or nonoccurrence of any other event;

(d) the modification or elimination of spousal support;

(e) the ownership rights in and disposition of the death benefit from a life insurance policy;

(f) the choice of law governing the construction of the agreement, except that a court of competent jurisdiction may apply the law of the legal domicile of either party, if it is fair and equitable; and

(g) any other matter, including their personal rights and obligations, not in violation of public policy or a statute imposing a criminal penalty.

(2) The right of a child to support, health and medical provider expenses, medical insurance, and child care coverage may not be affected by a premarital agreement.

Enacted by Chapter 105, 1994 General Session

30-8-5 Effect of marriage -- Amendment -- Revocation.

(1) A premarital agreement becomes effective upon marriage.

2) After marriage, a premarital agreement may be amended or revoked only by a written agreement signed by the parties. The amended agreement or the revocation is enforceable without consideration.

Enacted by Chapter 105, 1994 General Session

30-8-6 Enforcement.

(1) A premarital agreement is not enforceable if the party against whom enforcement is sought proves that:

(a) that party did not execute the agreement voluntarily; or

(b) the agreement was fraudulent when it was executed and, before execution of the agreement, that party:

(i) was not provided a reasonable disclosure of the property or financial obligations of the other party insofar as was possible;

(ii) did not voluntarily and expressly waive, in writing, any right to disclosure of the property or financial obligations of the other party beyond the disclosure provided; and

(iii) did not have, or reasonably could not have had, an adequate knowledge of the property or financial obligations of the other party.

(2) If a provision of a premarital agreement modifies or eliminates spousal support and that modification or elimination causes one party to the agreement to be eligible for support under a program of public assistance at the time of separation or marital dissolution, a court, notwithstanding the terms of the agreement, may require the other party to provide support to the extent necessary to avoid that eligibility.

(3) An issue of fraud of a premarital agreement shall be decided by the court as a matter of law.

Enacted by Chapter 105, 1994 General Session

30-8-7 Enforcement -- Void marriage.

If a marriage is determined to be void, an agreement that would otherwise have been a premarital agreement is enforceable only to the extent necessary to avoid an inequitable result.

Enacted by Chapter 105, 1994 General Session

30-8-8 Limitations of actions.

Any statute of limitations applicable to an action asserting a claim for relief under a premarital agreement is tolled during the marriage of the parties to the agreement.

Enacted by Chapter 105, 1994 General Session

30-8-9 Application and construction.

This act shall be applied and construed to effectuate its general purpose to make uniform the law with respect to the subject of this act among states enacting it.

Enacted by Chapter 105, 1994 General Session

Endnotes

[1] *Obergefell v. Hodges*, 135 S. Ct. 2071 (2015).

[2] Cott, Nancy, 2000, *Public Vows: A History of Marriage and the Nation*, Harvard University Press.

[3] *Windsor v. United States*, 133 S.Ct. 2675 (2013).

[4] *Obergefell v. Hodges*, *supra,* note 1.

[5] Barnett, Randy E., 2016, *Our Republican Constitution, Securing the Liberty and Sovereignty of We the People*, Harper Collins.

[6] *Dred Scott v. Sandford*, 60 U.S. 393 (1857).

[7] *Plessy v. Ferguson,* 163 U.S. 537 (1896).

[8] *Id* at 552-553 (Harlan, J., dissenting).

> According to the Constitutional Rights Foundation:
> "Jim Crow" was a derisive slang term for a black man. It came to mean any state law passed in the South that established different rules for blacks and whites. Jim Crow laws were based on the theory of white supremacy and were a reaction to Reconstruction. In the depression-racked 1890s, racism appealed to whites who feared losing their jobs to blacks. Politicians abused blacks to win the votes of poor white "crackers." Newspapers fed the bias of white readers by playing up (sometimes even making up) black crimes. Crf-usa.org.

[9] *Brown v. Board of Education*, 347 U.S. 483 (1954). Rather than taking the lead from Congress, the Court set an agenda for civil

rights to come resulting in the Civil Rights Act of 1957 that, according the United States' government's Civil Rights Digital Library, included voting rights protection, "established the Civil Rights Division in the Justice Department, and empowered federal officials to prosecute individuals that conspired to deny or abridge another citizen's right to vote. Moreover, it also created a six-member U.S. Civil Rights Commission charged with investigating allegations of voter infringement. But, perhaps most importantly, the Civil Rights Act of 1957 signaled a growing federal commitment to the cause of civil rights." www.crdl.usg.edu.

[10] Const. Amend. 13:

"Neither slavery nor involuntary servitude, except as a punishment for crime whereof the party shall have been duly convicted, shall exist within the United States, or any place subject to their jurisdiction." Formally abolishing slavery in the United States, the Thirteenth Amendment was passed by the Congress on January 31, 1865, and ratified by the states on December 6, 1865.

[11] Const.Amend.14:

"**Section 1.** All persons born or naturalized in the United States, and subject to the jurisdiction thereof, are citizens of the United States and of the State wherein they reside. No State shall make or enforce any law which shall abridge the privileges or immunities of citizens of the United States; nor shall any State deprive any person of life, liberty, or property, without due process of law; nor deny to any person within its jurisdiction the equal protection of the laws.

Section 2. Representatives shall be apportioned among the several States according to their respective numbers, counting the whole number of persons in each State, excluding Indians not taxed. But when the right to vote at any election for the choice of electors for President and Vice President of the United States, Representatives in Congress, the Executive and Judicial officers of a State, or the members of the Legislature thereof, is denied to any of the male inhabitants of such State, being twenty-one years of age, and citizens of the United States, or in any way abridged, except for participation in rebellion, or other crime, the basis of representation therein shall be reduced in the proportion which the number of such male citizens shall bear to the whole number of male citizens twenty-one years of age in such State.

Section 3. No person shall be a Senator or Representative in Congress, or elector of President and Vice President, or hold any office, civil or military, under the United States, or under any State, who, having previously taken an oath, as a member of Congress, or as an officer of the United States, or as a member of any State legislature, or as an executive or judicial officer of any State, to support the Constitution of the United States, shall have engaged in insurrection or rebellion against the same, or given aid or comfort to the enemies thereof. But Congress may, by a vote of two-thirds of each House, remove such disability.

Section 4. The validity of the public debt of the United States, authorized by law, including debts incurred for payment of pensions and bounties for services in suppressing insurrection or rebellion, shall not be questioned. But neither the United States nor any State shall assume or pay any debt or obligation incurred in aid of insurrection or rebellion against the United States, or any claim for the loss or emancipation of any slave; but all such debts, obligations and claims shall be held illegal and void.

Section 5. The Congress shall have power to enforce, by appropriate legislation, the provisions of this article.

[12] *Maynard v. Hill*, 125 U.S. 190 (1888).

[13] *Windsor v. United States, supra,* note 3.

[14] Maynard v. Hill, supra, note 12, at 205.

[15] *Obergefell v. Hodges, supra,* note 1, (Roberts, J., dissenting).

[16] *Windsor v. United States, supra,* note 3.

[17] *Id.*

[18] Barnett argues that the Eleventh Amendment does not bestow sovereignty on the individual states as others have claimed, as it simply prevents citizens of other states to sue in federal court.

[19] U.S. Const. Amend XI:

"The judicial power of the United States shall not be construed to extend to any suit in law or equity, commenced or prosecuted against one of the United States by citizens of another state, or by citizens or subjects of any foreign state."

[20] *Chisolm v. Georgia*, 2 U.S. 419 (1793).

[21] Doernberg, Donald L, "We the People: John Locke, Collective Constitutional Rights, and Standing to Challenge Government Action," 73 Cal. L. Rev. 52 (1985).

[22] *Chisolm v. Georgia, supra,* note 20, at. 435.

[23] According to Professor Doernberg:

"Locke's detailed discussion of trust demonstrates the existence of the trust and the collective nature of its creation. The legislature's supreme power is not, nor can possibly be absolutely Arbitrary over the Lives and Fortunes of the People. For it being but the *joynt* power of every Member of the Society given up to that Person, or Assembly, which is Legislator, it can be no more than those persons had in a State of Nature before they *enter'd* into Society, and gave up to the Community. Locke saw a two-step progression from the state of nature to civil society: first the combination of individuals into society, and second the vesting of power in the legislature as a trust. Because the legislature's power is only derived from "a positive voluntary Grant and Institution" by the people, it cannot be transferred by the legislature to any other hands. Thus, Locke's legislature functions within the trust metaphor. In emphasizing that the transfer of power from community to legislature is a delegation rather than an alienation, Locke explicitly makes the legislature's power subordinate to the people's "Supream Power to remove or alter the Legislative, when they find the Legislative act contrary to the trust reposed in them." Consequently, the legislature is responsible to the body politic in a far more direct way than to any individual member of it. " The legislative power is explicitly "limited to the publick good of the Society," and it is to the society that the legislature is responsible. Doernberg, "We the People," *supra*, note 21, at 62-63.

[24] *Adams v. Palmer,* 51 Me. 481, 483 (1818).

[25] E. Gregory Wallace, *Justifying Religious Freedom: The Western Tradition*, 114 Penn. St. L. Rev. 485 (2009).

[26] Henriques, H. S. Q. "Jewish Marriages and the English Law." *The Jewish Quarterly Review* 20, no. 3 (1908).

[27] U.S.Const. Amend 9.

The enumeration in the Constitution, of certain rights, shall not be construed to deny or disparage others retained by the people

[28] U.S. Const. Amend. 10

"The powers not delegated to the United States by the Constitution, nor prohibited by it to the States, are reserved to the States respectively, or to the people."

[29] According to History.com:

> The Kansas-Nebraska Act was an 1854 bill that mandated "popular sovereignty"–allowing settlers of a territory to decide whether slavery would be allowed within a new state's borders. Proposed by Stephen A. Douglas–Abraham Lincoln's opponent in the influential Lincoln-Douglas debates–the bill overturned the Missouri Compromise's use of latitude as the boundary between slave and free territory. The conflicts that arose between pro-slavery and anti-slavery settlers in the aftermath of the act's passage led to the period of violence known as Bleeding Kansas, and helped paved the way for the American Civil War (1861-65).
>
> On January 4, 1854, Stephen A. Douglas, wanting to ensure a northern transcontinental railroad route that

would benefit his Illinois constituents, introduced a bill to organize the territory of Nebraska in order to bring the area under civil control. But southern senators objected; the region lay north of latitude 36°30′ and so under the terms of the Missouri Compromise of 1820 would become a free state. To gain the southerners' support, Douglas proposed creating two territories in the area–Kansas and Nebraska–and repealing the Missouri Compromise line. The question of whether the territories would be slave or free would be left to the settlers under Douglas's principle of popular sovereignty. Presumably, the more northern territory would oppose slavery while the more southern one would permit it.

Although initially concerned about the political fallout, President Franklin Pierce gave Douglas and his southern allies his support. The "Appeal of the Independent Democrats," signed by such Free-Soilers as Salmon P. Chase and Charles Sumner and published in many northern newspapers, attacked Pierce, Douglas, and their supporters for breaking a sacred compact by repealing the Missouri Compromise.

The act passed Congress, but it failed in its purposes. By the time Kansas was admitted to statehood in 1861 after an internal civil war, southern states had begun to secede from the Union. The Independent Democrats and many northern Whigs abandoned their affiliations for the new antislavery Republican party, leaving southern Whigs without party links and creating an issue over which the already deeply divided Democrats would split even more. The railroad was eventually built but not along the route Douglas wanted and with funds voted by a Republican Congress during a Republican Civil War administration.

[30] *Lawrence v. Texas*, 539 U.S. 558, 571-572 (2003).

[31] Smith, George H., 2013, "Freedom, Rights and Political Philosophy, Part 5," libertarianism.org

[32] *Adamson v. California*, 332 U.S. 46, 70-71 (1946)(Black, J., dissenting).

[33] *Barron ex rel. Tiernan v. Mayor of Baltimore*, 32 U.S. 243 (1833).

[34] *McDonald v. City of Chicago, Ill.*, 130 S. Ct. 3020 (2010).

[35] *Marbury v. Madison*, 5 U.S. 137, 177-178 (1803).

[36] Smith, George H., "Freedom, Rights and Political Philosophy, Part 5," *supra*, note 31. .

[37] *Marbury v. Madison*, *supra*, note 35.

[38] Hammer, Christopher, "The Disaster of Innovation," www.teachingushistory.org.

[39] www.Historynet.com

[40] www.ushistory.org

[41] Kaplan, Fred, 2014, John Quincy Adams: American Visionary, Harper.

[42] *Ibid.*

[43] 30 U.S.1 (1831).

[44] Burke, Joseph C. "The Cherokee Cases: A Study in Law, Politics, and Morality." *Stanford Law Review*, vol. 21, no. 3, 1969, pp. 500–531.

[45] *Ibid.*

[46] Warren, Earl. "Chief Justice John Marshall: A Heritage of Freedom and Stability." *American Bar Association Journal*, vol. 41, no. 11, 1955, pp. 1008–1010.

[47] *Ibid.* at 1009.

[48] U.S.Const. Amend. 15.

Section 1. The right of citizens of the United States to vote shall not be denied or abridged by the United States or by any State on account of race, color, or previous condition of servitude. **Section 2.** The Congress shall have power to enforce this article by appropriate legislation.

[49] *Slaughter-House Cases*, 83 U.S. 36, 77 (1873).

[50] *Adamson v. California,* supra, note 32 at 71-72.

[51] *Id.* at 81.

[52] *Loving v. Virginia*, 388 U.S. 1 (1967).

[53] *Id.*

[54] 262 U.S. 390, 399 (1923).

[55] *Id.*

[56] *Id* at 401-402.

[57] 364 U.S. 339 (1960).

[58] *Id* at 347-348.

[59] *See generally, Planned Parenthood of Southeastern, Pa. v. Casey*, 505 U.S. 833 (1992).

[60] *Levy v. Louisiana*, 391 U.S. 68 (1968).

[61] *Griswold v. Connecticut*, 481 U.S. 479 (1965).

[62] See *Bowers* v. *Hardwicke*, 478 U.S. 186 (1986).

[63] *Planned Parenthood of Southeastern Pa. v. Casey supra*, note 59.

[64] *United States v. Guest*, 383 U.S. 745 (1966).

[65] *See Furman v. Georgia, infra*, note 243.

[66] *Gideon v. Wainwright*, 372 U.S. 335 (1963).

[67] *Miranda v. Arizona*, 384 U.S. 436 (1966).

[68] Const.Amend. 1:

"Congress shall make no law respecting an establishment of religion, or prohibiting the free exercise thereof; or abridging the freedom of speech, or of the press; or the right of the people peaceably to assemble, and to petition the Government for a redress of grievances."

[69] *District of Columbia v. Heller*, 128 S. Ct. 2783 (2008).

[70] 381 U.S. 479 (1965).

[71] *Id.* at 482.

[72] *Id.* at 488-489.

[73] *Id.* at 512.

[74] *Schenck v. United States*, 249 U.S. 47 (1919).

[75] *Id.* at 512-513

[76] *Troxel v. Granville*, 530 U.S. 57, 91-92 (2000)(*Scalia, J., dissenting*).

[77] *Id.* at 80 (Thomas, J., concurring in the judgment).

[78] Discussing free speech, Strauss says, "the text and original understandings of the First Amendment are essentially irrelevant to the American system of freedom of expression as it exists today." Strauss, David A., *The Living Constitution*, Oxford U. Press: 2010).

[79] *DeBoer v. Snyder*, 772 F. 3d 388, 416 (6th Cir. 2014).

[80] *McDonald v. City of Chicago, Ill., supra,* note 34. Rejecting Justice Black's desire for full incorporation of the Bill of Rights into the Fourteenth Amendment, the Court eventually moved in that direction by initiating what has been called a process of "selective incorporation," *i.e.,* the Court began to hold that the Due Process Clause fully incorporates particular rights contained in the first eight Amendments." *Id* at 3033-3034.

[81] 130 S. Ct. 876 (2010)

[82] No. 15-274 (2016).

[83] *Id.*

[84] 410 U.S. 113 (1973).

[85] *Shapiro v. Thompson,* 394 U.S. 618 (1969).

[86] *Stanley v. Illinois*, 405 U.S. 645 (1972)

[87] *District of Columbia v. Heller*, 128 S. Ct. 2783 (2008).

[88] *Loving v. Virginia, supra*, note 52.

[89] *Steffel v. Thompson*, 415 U.S. 452 (1974).

[90] *Valley Forge Christian College v. Americans United for Separation of Church and State, Inc.*, 454 U.S.464 (1982).

[91] As a district court explains: "The prudential component of the fitness prong considers "the extent to which resolution of the challenge depends upon facts that may not yet be sufficiently developed." Ernst & Young, F.3d at 535. Accordingly, cases "intrinsically legal nature" are likely to be found fit. *Riva v. Massachusetts*, 61 F.3d 1003, 1010 (1st Cir. 1995); *see Thomas v. Union Carbide Agr. Products Co.*, 473 U.S. 568, 581 (1985) (claim that a law violated Article III of the Constitution was fit for review because it was "purely legal, and [would] not be clarified by further factual development"). Courts are also likely to find cases fit when "all of the acts that are alleged to create liability have already occurred." *Verizon New England*, 651 F.3d at 189 (quotation marks and citation omitted); *see Roman Catholic Bishop of Springfield, 724 F.3d at 91-93*(dismissing claims that rely on a potential future application of an ordinance as unfit for review, but holding that the claims that "rest solely on the existence of the Ordinance" are fit for review because "no further factual development is necessary"); *Pustell v. Lynn Pub. Sch.,* 18 F.3d 50, 52 (1st Cir. 1994) (finding constitutional challenge fit where "[n]o further factual development [was] necessary for [the court] to resolve the question at issue")."

[92] *Roe v. Wade,* 410 U.S. 113, 126 (1973). Nothing is more illustrative of this prerequisite of standing and mootness than the abortion question. Prior to *Roe v. Wade*, the Court was able to

avoid the question because the human gestation period of 40 weeks would render a claim of a person seeking an abortion as moot before it could reach the Court. For the Court to consider abortion in *Roe*, the Court framed the issue with great delicacy:

> But when, as here, pregnancy is a significant fact in the litigation, the normal 266-day human gestation period is so short that the pregnancy will come to term before the usual appellate process is complete. If that termination makes a case moot, pregnancy litigation seldom will survive much beyond the trial stage, and appellate review will be effectively denied. Our law should not be that rigid. Pregnancy often comes more than once to the same woman, and in the general population, if man is to survive, it will always be with us. Pregnancy provides a classic justification for a conclusion of nonmootness. It truly could be "capable of repetition, yet evading review."

[93] *Brown v. Buhman, infra,* note 114.

[94] *Id.*

[95] 42 U.S.C. § 2000 *et seq.*

[96] 134 S.Ct. 2751 (2014).

[97] Recently, in the United State, a new vision of religious promises emerged: Covenant Marriage. However, as its website espouses, a covenant is not a contract. www.coveanantmarriage.com

[98] *Kitchen v. Herbert,* 755 F.3d 1193 (10th Cir. 2014), cert. denied, 135 S.Ct. 265 (2014**).**

Utah Code § 30-1-2(5) includes among the marriages that are "prohibited and declared void" those "between persons of the same sex." Id. In 2004, the Utah Legislature passed § 30-1-4.1, which provides: (1)(a) It is the policy of this state to recognize as marriage only the legal union of a man and a woman as provided in this chapter. (b) Except for the relationship of marriage between a man and a woman recognized pursuant to this chapter, this state will not recognize, enforce, or give legal effect to any law creating any legal status, rights, benefits, or duties that are substantially equivalent to those provided under Utah law to a man and a woman because they are married. (2) Nothing in Subsection (1) impairs any contract or other rights, benefits, or duties that are enforceable independently of this section. Id. The Legislature also referred a proposed constitutional amendment, known as Amendment 3, to Utah's voters. It states: (1) Marriage consists only of the legal union between a man and a woman. (2) No other domestic union, however denominated, may be recognized as a marriage or given the same or substantially equivalent legal effect. Utah Const. art. I, § 29; see Laws 2004, H.J.R. 25 § 1.

[99] *Id.*

[100] *Id.*

[101] 760 F.2d 1065 (1985).

[102] 98 U.S. 145 (1878).

[103] *Id.*

[104] Drakeman, Donald L., 2009, *Church, State and Original Intent*, Cambridge University Press.

[105] *Reynold v. United States, supra,* note 102, at 165-166.

[106] 25 U.S. 190 (1888).

[107] *Late Corp. of Church of Jesus Christ of Latter-day Saints v. United States,* 136 U.S. (1890).

[108] *Elia-Warnken v. Elia,* 463 Mass. 29 (Mass. 2012). The Massachusetts Supreme Court refused to honor a second marriage of a same-sex couple where one of the participants had a valid civil union in Vermont (and that under the law was treated as a marriage). While it is important to note that the Defendant was not espousing polygamy as a belief system, the Court did address the reasons why polygamy was forbidden in all 50 states.

[109] *Arcand v. Fleming,* 185 F.Supp. 22 (D. Conn. 1960)

[110] In *Our Republican Constitution, supra,* note 4, Barnett traces the theory of judicial restraint to the dissents of Justice Oliver Wendell Holmes and the writings of a law professor that became the majority view when President Franklin Delano Roosevelt packed the Court with his progress disciples in order to reverse decisions striking down his pet legislations like the NRA. According to Barnett, true judicial review was as espoused by Justice Chase in the 1798 decision of *Calder v. Bull* limited a state's authority to interfere with the private agreements of its citizens, and that any statute was not lawful unless it was within the state's power to do so under the Contracts Clause of the Constitution..

[111] *Vance v. Bradley,* 440 U.S. 93, 97 (1979)

[112] *Id.*

[113] *Miles v. United States*, 103 U.S. 304 (1881). "It is made clear by the record that polygamous marriages are so celebrated in Utah as to make the proof of polygamy very difficult. They are conducted in secret, and the persons by whom they are solemnized are under such obligations of secrecy that it is almost impossible to extract the facts from them when placed upon the witness stand. If both wives are excluded from testifying to the first marriage, as we think they should be under the existing rules of evidence, testimony sufficient to convict in a prosecution for polygamy in the Territory of Utah is hardly attainable. But this is not a consideration by which we can be influenced." *Id* at 315-316.

[114] *Brown v. Buhman*, 947 F.Supp.2d 1170 (2013).

[115] *Id*. at 1179-1180.

[116] *Kitchen v. Herbert, supra*, note 98 at 1214-1215.

[117] 74 Cal. App. 2d 41 (1946).

[118] The other states were Alabama, California, Indiana, Illinois, Michigan, New Jersey, Pennsylvania, Colorado and Massachusetts.

[119] www.About Catholics.com

[120] Anglican.org

[121] Judaism 101, "Divorce" www.jewfaq.org.

[122] According to Encyclopedia Britannica, an ecclesiastic court is a:

> Tribunal set up by religious authorities to deal with disputes among clerics or with spiritual matters involving either clerics or laymen. Although such courts

are found today among the Jews (*see bet din*) and among the Muslims (Sharīʿah) as well as the various Christian sects, their functions have become limited strictly to religious issues and to governance of church property. During earlier periods in history, the ecclesiastical courts often had a degree of temporal jurisdiction, and in the Middle Ages the courts of the Roman Catholic Church rivalled the temporal courts in power.

The range of spiritual matters dealt with often extended into the secular area. The ecclesiastical courts had jurisdiction over sacramental matters that included anything having to do with marriage, such as separation and legitimacy. They also had exclusive jurisdiction over cases involving wills; in England, the ecclesiastical courts, which became Anglican in the 16th century, had complete jurisdiction in matters of succession to personal property until the 16th century and then, in competition with the courts of chancery, until 1857. The courts also claimed jurisdiction over clergy accused of most types of crimes.

[123] *Barber v. Barber*, 62 U.S. 582, 590-591 (1859).

[124] Henriques, H. S. Q. "Jewish Marriages and the English Law," *supra*, note 26, at 391-449.

[125] Everitt, Lauren, "Ten Key Moments in the History of Marriage," BBC News Magazine, March 14, 2012.

[126] Henriques, H. S. Q., *supra*, note 26 at 391-449.

[127] The etymology of the word is evident in the dictionary definition. See e.g., Dictionary.com.

[128] Everitt, Laura, "Ten Key Moments," *supra*, note 125.

[129] Henriques, H. S. Q., "Jewish Marriages and the English Law." *supra*, note 26 at 391-449.

[130] Blackstone, in his Commentaries, says, "The right of trial by jury, or the country, is a trial by the peers of every Englishman, and is the grand bulwark of his liberties, and is secured to him by the Great Charter." *Strauder v. West Virginia*, 100 U.S. 303, 308-309 (1880).

[131] Collingwood, R.G., 2015, *The Idea of History*, Revised Edition, (originally published 1946).

[132] E. Gregory Wallace, *Justifying Religious Freedom: The Western Tradition, supra*, note 25.

[133] Randall, Willard Sterne, *Alexander Hamilton: A Life*, 2010, Harper Collins.

[134] *Everson v. Board of Education*, 330 U.S. 1 (1947), *citing,* A Bill for Establishing Religious Freedom, enacted by the General Assembly of Virginia, January 19, 1786. See 1 Randall, "The Life of Thomas Jefferson" (1858) 219-220; XII Hening's Statutes of Virginia (1823) 84. "That no man shall be compelled to frequent or support any religious worship, place, or ministry whatsoever, nor shall be enforced, restrained, molested, or burthened in his body or goods, nor shall otherwise suffer on account of his religious opinions or belief. . . ."

Test provisions in *Everson* forbade officeholders to "deny . . . the truth of the Protestant religion," *e.g.* Constitution of North Carolina (1776) § XXXII, II Poore, *supra,* 1413. Maryland permitted taxation for support of the Christian religion and limited civil office to Christians until 1818, *id.,* I, 819, 820, 832.

See also, Drakeman, Donald L., *Church, State and Original Intent*, 2009, *supra*, note 104, discussing *Reynolds v. United States, supra*, note 102. In his first chapter, Drakeman tells us that one group of scholars focusing on the language of the Establishment Clause claimed it was intended to prevent the federal government from involving itself in the states' power to establish a religion.

[135] 83 U.S. 130 (1872).

[136] Ushistory.org

[137] Sachar, Howard M., 1992, *A History of the Jews in America*, Vintage Books.

Article VII of the Constitution declares: "No religious Test shall ever be required as a qualification to any Office or Public Trust under the United States."

See also, Drakeman, Donald L., *Church, State and Original Intent*, supra, note 104. In Chapter 2, Drakeman notes that Massachusetts declared Christianity as its state religion shortly after the Revolution.

[138] *Updegraph v. Commonwealth*, 11 Serg. & Rawle 394 (Pa. 1824).

[139] 44 U.S. 589 (1845).

[140] *Barber v. Barber, supra,* note 123.

[141] *Adams v. Palmer,* 51 Me. 481, 483 (1818).

[142] *Cantwell v. Connecticut,* 310 U.S. 296, 310 (1940).

[143] Chapter CXXVI – An Act to punish and prevent the Practice of Polygamy in the Territories of the United States and other Places, and disapproving and annulling certain Acts of the Legislative Assembly of the Territory of Utah.

Be it enacted by the Senate and House of Representatives of the United States of America in Congress assembled, That every person having a husband or wife living, who shall marry any other person, whether married or single, in a Territory of the United States, or other place over which the United States have exclusive jurisdiction, shall, except in the cases specified in the proviso to this section, be adjudged guilty of bigamy, and, upon conviction thereof, shall be punished by a fine not exceeding five hundred dollars, and by imprisonment for a term not exceeding five years: Provided, nevertheless, That this section shall not extend to any person by reason of any former marriage whose husband or wife by such marriage shall have been absent for five successive years without being known to such person within that time to be living; nor to any person by reason of any former marriage which shall have been dissolved by the decree of a competent court; nor to any person by reason of any former marriage which shall have been annulled or pronounced void by the sentence or decree of a competent court on the ground of the nullity of the marriage contract.

Sec. 2. And be it further enacted, That the following ordinance of the provisional government of the State of Deseret, so called, namely: "An ordinance incorporating the Church of Jesus Christ of Latter Day Saints," passed February eight, in the year eighteen hundred and fifty-one, and adopted, reenacted, and made valid by the governor and legislative assembly of the Territory of Utah by an act passed January nineteen, in the year eighteen hundred and fifty-five, entitled "An act in relation to the compilation and revision of the laws and resolutions in force in Utah Territory, their publication, and distribution," and all other acts and parts of acts heretofore passed by the said legislative assembly of the Territory of Utah, which establish, support, maintain, shield, or countenance polygamy, be, and the same hereby are, disapproved and annulled: Provided, That this act shall be so limited and construed as not to affect or interfere with the right of property legally acquired under the ordinance heretofore mentioned, nor with the right "to worship God according to the dictates of conscience," but only to annul all acts and laws which establish, maintain, protect, or countenance the practice of polygamy, evasively called spiritual marriage, however disguised by legal or ecclesiastical solemnities, sacraments, ceremonies, consecrations, or other contrivances.

Sec. 3. And be it further enacted, That it shall not be lawful for any corporation or association for religious or charitable purposes to acquire or hold real estate in any Territory of the United States during the existence of the territorial government of greater value than fifty thousand dollars; and all real estate acquired or held by any such corporation or association contrary to the provisions of this act shall be forfeited and escheat to the United States: Provided, That existing vested rights in real estate not be impaired by the provisions of this section.

APPROVED, July 1, 1862

[144] Drakeman, Donald L., *Church, State and Original Intent, supra,* note 104. In Chapter 2, Drakeman explains that the defense counsel in *Reynolds* barely raised the constitutional issue in his brief, choosing to rely instead on English Common Law. Rather, the counsel for the government raised it as an opportunity to seize upon the slippery slope of harrowing acts and gruesome murders in the name of religion. He further explains that the Chief Justice Waite was able to achieve a near unanimous vote for conviction in raising, but not discussing or answering how to define "religion", even though he could have sought to define religion was in 1789, thus eliminating the 50-year old Mormon faith from the definition. Rather, Waite's decision to use the "history of our times' argument, one consistent with the Democratic Constitution as Barnett defines in *Our Republican Constitution, supra.* Drakeman explains in detail the verbal gymnastics in Waite's decision, even to go as far as to ignore Jefferson's role by claiming that the author the Declaration was in France in 1789 and played no part in the drafting of the Constitution, and to rather turn to the morals of society argument to conclude: "we think it may safely be said there never has been a time in any State of the Union when

polygamy has not been an offence against society ..." *Reynold v. United States, supra*, note 74, at 165-166. Drakeman also explains that Justice Waite relied heavily on "the greatest historian of his day", George Bancroft, who a contemporary described as "redolent of the ideas of the new Jacksonion democracy ..."

See also, Cott, Nancy, *Private Vows, supra* note 2 In *Public Vows*, Dr. Cott explains that federal government control over the family began with the Freedman's Bureau, an agency created after the Civil War to assist, and to dictate to the newly free how to morph into roles of traditional marriage and the Christian Family model. After all, marriage between slaves was simply a personal agreement to cohabit. The state would not recognize it. These people were not naturally Christian. Rather, they came from a culture that did not recognize marriage as between husband and wife, but, similar to Mormons, believed a man could have multiple wives.

[145] *Brown v. Buhman, supra*, note 114.

[146] *Kitchen v. Herbert, supra*, note 98, at 1193.

[147] *Bowers v. Hardwicke, supra*, note 40, at 196-197

[148] Raico, Ralph, 1975, "Gay Rights: A Libertarian Approach," libertarianism.org.

[149] The Weinstein Co., 2014.

[150] It is theorized that our only bachelor President, James Buchanan, was gay. Prior to his election in 1856, he spent his time with what was known as the Washington Dandies, a group of

bachelors who took no interest in women. *See, e.g.,* historynewsnetwork.org.

[151] *Nemetz v. Immigration and Naturalization Service*, 647 F. 2d 432 (4th Cir. 1981).

[152] *Skinner v. Oklahoma ex rel. Williamson*, 316 U.S. 535 (1942).

[153] 478 U.S. 186, 190-191 (1986).

[154] *Id.* at 186.

[155] *Lawrence v. Texas, supra,* note 28.

[156] Cott, Nancy, *Public Vows, supra,* note 2.

[157] *Obergefell v. Hodges, supra,* note 1.

[158] *Kitchen v. Herbert, supra,* note 98.

[159] Spaht, Katherine Shaw, "The Last One Hundred Years: The Incredible Retreat of Law from the Regulation of Marriage" *La. L. Rev.* 63: 243 (2003).

[160] In one Pennsylvania case, the court reported the divorce was 1600 days in the process, accumulating a record of more than a million words, and 16 volumes before the magistrate entered an order refusing the divorce. *Boyer v. Boyer*, 183 Pa. Superior Ct. 260 (1957)

[161] Whitehead, Barbara D., 1998, *The Divorce Culture: Rethinking Our Commitments to Marriage and Family*, Knopf Publishing Group.

[162] *Ibid.*

As psychologists suggest, a person cannot rely on others to be happy. Surveys five years after divorce concluded that those that

277

divorced because they were unhappy were just, if not more, unhappy five years later, showing the emotional damage to their children from the divorce was unnecessary. *See also*, Shaw, Katherine (n/k/a "Spaht"), "Revolution and Counter-Revolution: The Future of Marriage in the Law," *Loy. L. Rev.*, 49: 1 (Spring 2003).

[163] Mead, Margaret. 1962, *Male and Female*, New American Library.

[164] Weitzman, Lenore, 1985, *The Divorce Revolution*, Free Press.

[165] Census.gov/, cdc.gov/.

[166] *Gomez v. Perez,* 409 U.S. 535 (1973). The beginning of the end of traditional marriage began in 1968 with the Supreme Court decision of *Levy v. Louisiana, supra,* note 60, and in 1972, with its decision in *Gomez.* In *Levy*, the issue was, whether a child born outside of marriage could recover not from her father, but her mother. 391 U.S. 68 (1968). Under the Christian Family model a mother had the primary duty to support any child born out of wedlock, and thus a child could adopt from her mother. But Louisiana took it a step further, as Louisiana adopted French law, not English Common Law. In *Levy*, the Louisiana statute denied the right of a child born to an unwed mother her right to recover from the death of her mother. Nevertheless, in their brief before the Supreme Court, the mother and child argued what would become the mantra for all future support cases: The status of a child at birth should not deprive her of her rights. It is important to note here that this mantra will be repeated in cases, even where

adult women quenched their lust and raped boys as young as 13, causing their pregnancy, to justify why the biological father should have to pay child support to his rapist.

In his brief before the Supreme Court, Louisiana's Attorney General warned that giving "illegitimate" children equal protection would support a deviation in sexual behavior that is "costly to society," and that it is right for the state to deny equal treatment to children born outside of marriage, something that will "endanger the stability of marriage and family by abolishing distinctions between legitimates and illegitimates." 1968 WL 112828 (1968).The Attorney General justified giving superior rights to children born during lawful wedlock. "Since marriage as an institution is fundamental to our existence as a free nation, it is the duty of the [state] to encourage it." He decried the impact of giving government benefits to children born outside of marriage as the reason for the recent increase in out of wedlock births. The Attorney General's argument relied on the 19th Century Supreme Court cases on the subject of marriage:

> Tradition supports the power of Louisiana, rather than the federal government, to regulate the institution of marriage within the state's borders, and to prescribe all the effects of marriage, including status of offspring and property rights derived from marriage.
>
> Recognition of marriage as a civil contract in English Common law was transferred to the American colonies where it provided the legal structure of the American

family. The acceptance of marriage as a contract carried with it the power of the colonial legislatures to determine the obligations and rights of marriage. The state was considered the third party to every marriage ceremony, presenting the public interest imposing its legal and ethical standards upon as otherwise private undertaking.

The year before *Levy* was argued, Illinois law professor Harry Krause published what would be the foundation for the Uniform Parentage Act, a law review article arguing that legal "bastards" were entitled to the same support as children born during the marriage.[166] Krause ignored the impact on marriage, and found the only purpose of establishing paternity was to provide the child with financial relief. In *Levy*, the Court struck a knife into the Christian Family model, with the Court voting 9-0 in favor of the child, finding that the aforementioned bastards (or illegitimates) were entitled to Equal Protection and would receive the same level of scrutiny as that of gender discrimination.

[167] At common law, the child born during the marriage was presumed to be of the marriage, absent a showing of lack of access. Although rebutting the presumption required clear and convincing evidence, in today's world, DNA testing is so exact as to exclude the husband as the child's father and thus meet the standard. *K.E.M. v. P.C.S.,* 38 A.3d 798 (Pa. 2012). Of course, as the facts of that case indicate, the wife who agrees to divorce her husband and agrees that her husband is the father of the child in a

judgment might not be allowed to proceed against the natural father.

[168] Personal Responsibility and Work Opportunity Reconciliation Act of 1996 required that states permit paternity to be established via a paternity affidavit in place of a judicial proceeding, Pub. L. No. 104-193, § 101-116, 110 Stat. 2105, 2110-85 (1996 Personal Responsibility and Work Opportunity Reconciliation Act of 1996, Pub. L. No. 104-193, § 101-116, 110 Stat. 2105, 2110-85 (1996).

The Indiana provides an example of this change, as explained in *In re the Paternity of E.M.L.G.*, 863 N.E.2d 867 (Ind. App. 2007):

[P]rior to 2001, Indiana Code section 31-14-7-1 stated that "a man is presumed to be a child's biological father if . . . (3) the man executed a paternity affidavit in accordance with IC XX-XX-X-X.1." Relying on this statute, our court held that Indiana Code section 31-14-7-1 provided that the "execution of a 'paternity affidavit' operat[ed] to create a legal presumption that the man is the child's biological father," and that such presumption could be rebutted. *In re Paternity of M.H.*, slip op. at 4. However, since then, Public Law 138-2001, sec. 6, amended this section by deleting subsection three regarding the presumption for a man who has executed a paternity affidavit.

In addition, our General Assembly contemporaneously inserted the following language: "[a] man is a child's legal father if the man executed a paternity affidavit in accordance with IC XX-XX-X-X.1 and the paternity affidavit has not been rescinded or set aside under IC XX-XX-X-X.1." Ind. Code § 31-14-7-3 (2001). The General Assembly specifically chose to remove the language merely creating a "presumption" that a man who executed a paternity affidavit was the biological father of the child, and instead it inserted language providing that such a man became the "legal father" upon execution of such an affidavit unless he rescinded the affidavit within the sixty-day time frame provided for under Indiana Code section 16-37-2-2.1. "

[169] *Obergefell v. Hodges, supra*, note 1.

[170] *Burns v. Burns*, 224 P.2d 178 (Wyo. 1950).

[171] *Id.*

[172] *Foley v. Interactive Data Corp.*, 765 P.2d 373 (1988).

[173] According the Second Restatement of Conflicts:

"s 187. LAW OF THE STATE CHOSEN BY THE PARTIES

(1) The law of the state chosen by the parties to govern their contractual rights and duties will be applied if the particular issue is one which the parties could have resolved by an explicit provision in their agreement directed to that issue.

(2) The law of the state chosen by the parties to govern their contractual rights and duties will be applied, even if the particular issue is one which the parties could not have resolved by an explicit provision in their agreement directed to that issue, unless either

(a) the chosen state has no substantial relationship to the parties or the transaction and there is no other reasonable basis for the parties' choice, or

(b) application of the law of the chosen state would be contrary to a fundamental policy of a state which has a materially greater interest than the chosen state in the determination of the particular issue and which, under the rule of s 188, would be the state of the applicable law in the absence of an effective choice of law by the parties.

(3) In the absence of a contrary indication of intention, the reference is to the local law of the state of the chosen law."

[174] *Bustamante v. Bustamante*, 645 P. 2d 40, 41 (Utah 1982). As stated therein:

> Section 30-3-1 confers jurisdiction on the district court to dissolve a marriage when plaintiff or defendant is an "actual and bona fide resident" of this state and of the county where the action is brought for three months immediately preceding the commencement of the action. The term "bona fide" resident connotes a good faith intention to reside in a particular place, a "home feeling" for that place ... an intention to live elsewhere permanently ... "Actual" residence requires physical presence. ... To establish an actual and bona fide residence, "... one must have some abode in the county to which he intends to return and where, in doing so, he would be no trespasser." Factors that may reflect the

requisite intent to return or remain in a jurisdiction include voting, owning property, paying taxes, having family in the area, maintaining a mailing address, being born or raised in the area, working or operating a business, and having children attend school in the forum. (*Citations omitted.*)

[175] *Id.*

[176] *Maynard v. Hill*, supra, note 12.

[177] *Auten v. Auten*, 308 N.Y. 155 (1954).

[178] Barbara Brudno Gardner, Marital Property and the Conflict of Laws: The Constitutionality of the Quasi-Community Property Legislation, 54 Cal. L. Rev. 252 (1966).

[179] 28 U.S.C.A. §1738 reads as follows:

The Acts of the legislature of any State, Territory, or Possession of the United States, or copies thereof, shall be authenticated by affixing the seal of such State, Territory or Possession thereto.

The records and judicial proceedings of any court of any such State, Territory or Possession, or copies thereof, shall be proved or admitted in other courts within the United States and its Territories and Possessions by the attestation of the clerk and seal of the court annexed, if a seal exists, together with a certificate of a judge of the court that the said attestation is in proper form.

Such Acts, records and judicial proceedings or copies thereof, so authenticated, shall have the same full faith and credit in every court within the United States and its Territories and Possessions as they have by law or usage in the courts of such State, Territory or Possession from which they are taken.

(Passed June 25, 1948)

In addition, the Fourteenth Amendment requires that all judgments for money, including support must meet the Supreme Court standards for Due Process. As the Supreme Court of Pennsylvania explains:

This test of "minimum contacts" announced in *International Shoe Co. v. Washington, supra,* is not susceptible of mechanical application; rather the facts of each case must be weighed to determine whether the requisite affiliating circumstances are present. *Kulko v. Superior Court of California,* 436 U.S. 84, 98 S.Ct. 1690, 56 L.Ed.2d 132 (1978). The Court recognized in [Kulko] that "this determination is one in which few answers will be written 'in black and white. The greys are dominant and even among them the shades are innumerable.'" [*Quoting Kulko*] The nature of the required "minimum contacts" has generally been given broad interpretation and emphasis has been placed upon the aspect of fair play and substantial justice. However, the United States Supreme Court, in *Hanson v. Denckla,* 357 U.S. 235, 78 S.Ct. 1228, 2 L.Ed.2d 518*518 1283 (1958), warned that "it is a mistake to assume that this trend heralds the eventual demise of all restrictions on the personal jurisdiction of state courts." *Scoggins v. Scoggins,* 555 A. 2d 1314 (Pa. 1989).

[180] The Parental Kidnaping Prevention Act (PKPA or Act) imposes a duty on the States to enforce a child custody determination entered by a court of a sister State if the determination is consistent with the provisions of the Act. In order for a state court's custody decree to be consistent with the provisions of the Act, the State must have jurisdiction under its own local law and one of five conditions set out in § 1738A(c)(2) must be met. Briefly put, these conditions authorize the state court to enter a custody decree if the child's home is or recently has been in the State, if the child has no home State and it would be in the child's best interest for the State to assume jurisdiction, or if the child is present in the State and has been abandoned or abused. Once a State exercises jurisdiction consistently with the provisions of the Act, no other State may exercise concurrent jurisdiction over the custody dispute, § 1738A(g), even if it would have been empowered to take jurisdiction in the first instance, and all States must accord full faith and credit to the first State's ensuing custody decree. *Thompson v. Thompson*, 484 U.S. 174 (1988)

With regard to support judgments, §1738(B) provides jurisdictional guidelines for entering and modifying child support orders:

a)GENERAL RULE.—The appropriate authorities of each State—

(1) shall enforce according to its terms a child support order made consistently with this section by a court of another State; and

(2) shall not seek or make a modification of such an order except in accordance with subsections (e), (f), and (i).

(b)DEFINITIONS.—In this section:

(1) The term "child" means—

(A) a person under 18 years of age; and

(B) a person 18 or more years of age with respect to whom a child support order has been issued pursuant to the laws of a State.

(2) The term "child's State" means the State in which a child resides.

(3) The term "child's home State" means the State in which a child lived with a parent or a person acting as parent for at least 6 consecutive months immediately preceding the time of filing of a petition or comparable pleading for support and, if a child is less than 6 months old, the State in which the child lived from birth with any of them. A period of temporary absence of any of them is counted as part of the 6-month period.

(4) The term "child support" means a payment of money, continuing support, or arrearages or the provision of a benefit (including payment of health insurance, child care, and educational expenses) for the support of a child.

(5) The term "child support order"—

(A) means a judgment, decree, or order of a court requiring the payment of child support in periodic amounts or in a lump sum; and

(B)includes—

(i) a permanent or temporary order; and

(ii) an initial order or a modification of an order.

(6) The term "contestant" means—

(A) a person (including a parent) who—

(i) claims a right to receive child support;

(ii) is a party to a proceeding that may result in the issuance of a child support order; or

(iii) is under a child support order; and

(B) a State or political subdivision of a State to which the right to obtain child support has been assigned.

(7) The term "court" means a court or administrative agency of a State that is authorized by State law to establish the amount of child support payable by a contestant or make a modification of a child support order.

(8) The term "modification" means a change in a child support order that affects the amount, scope, or duration of the order and modifies, replaces, supersedes, or otherwise is made subsequent to the child support order.

(9) The term "State" means a State of the United States, the District of Columbia, the Commonwealth of Puerto Rico, the territories and possessions of the United States, and Indian country (as defined in section 1151 of title 18).

(c)REQUIREMENTS OF CHILD SUPPORT ORDERS.—A child support order made by a court of a State is made consistently with this section if—

(1) a court that makes the order, pursuant to the laws of the State in which the court is located and subsections (e), (f), and (g)—

(A) has subject matter jurisdiction to hear the matter and enter such an order; and

(B) has personal jurisdiction over the contestants; and

(2) reasonable notice and opportunity to be heard is given to the contestants.

(d)CONTINUING JURISDICTION.—

A court of a State that has made a child support order consistently with this section has continuing, exclusive jurisdiction over the order if the State is the child's State or the residence of any individual contestant unless the court of another State, acting in accordance with subsections (e) and (f), has made a modification of the order.

(e)AUTHORITY TO MODIFY ORDERS.—A court of a State may modify a child support order issued by a court of another State if—

(1) the court has jurisdiction to make such a child support order pursuant to subsection (i); and

(2) (A) the court of the other State no longer has continuing, exclusive jurisdiction of the child support order because that State no longer is the child's State or the residence of any individual contestant; or

(B) each individual contestant has filed written consent with the State of continuing, exclusive jurisdiction for a court of another State to modify the order and assume continuing, exclusive jurisdiction over the order.

(f)RECOGNITION OF CHILD SUPPORT ORDERS.—If 1 or more child support orders have been issued with regard to an obligor and a child, a court shall apply the following rules in determining which order to recognize for purposes of continuing, exclusive jurisdiction and enforcement:

(1) If only 1 court has issued a child support order, the order of that court must be recognized.

(2) If 2 or more courts have issued child support orders for the same obligor and child, and only 1 of the courts would have continuing, exclusive jurisdiction under this section, the order of that court must be recognized.

(3) If 2 or more courts have issued child support orders for the same obligor and child, and more than 1 of the courts would have continuing, exclusive jurisdiction under this section, an order issued by a court in the current home State of the child must be recognized, but if an order has not been issued in the current home State of the child, the order most recently issued must be recognized.

(4) If 2 or more courts have issued child support orders for the same obligor and child, and none of the courts would have continuing, exclusive jurisdiction under this section, a court having jurisdiction over the parties shall issue a child support order, which must be recognized.

(5) The court that has issued an order recognized under this subsection is the court having continuing, exclusive jurisdiction under subsection (d).

(g)ENFORCEMENT OF MODIFIED ORDERS.—

A court of a State that no longer has continuing, exclusive jurisdiction of a child support order may enforce the order with respect to nonmodifiable obligations and unsatisfied obligations that accrued before the date on which a modification of the order is made under subsections (e) and (f).

(h)CHOICE OF LAW.—

(1)IN GENERAL.—

In a proceeding to establish, modify, or enforce a child support order, the forum State's law shall apply except as provided in paragraphs (2) and (3).

(2)LAW OF STATE OF ISSUANCE OF ORDER.—

In interpreting a child support order including the duration of current payments and other obligations of support, a court shall apply the law of the State of the court that issued the order.

(3)PERIOD OF LIMITATION.—

In an action to enforce arrears under a child support order, a court shall apply the statute of limitation of the forum State or the State of the court that issued the order, whichever statute provides the longer period of limitation.

(i)REGISTRATION FOR MODIFICATION.—

If there is no individual contestant or child residing in the issuing State, the party or support enforcement agency seeking to modify, or to modify and enforce, a child support order issued in another State shall register that order in a State with jurisdiction over the nonmovant for the purpose of modification.

291

(Added Pub. L. 103–383, § 3(a), Oct. 20, 1994, 108 Stat. 4064; amended Pub. L. 104–193, title III, § 322, Aug. 22, 1996, 110 Stat. 2221; Pub. L. 105–33, title V, § 5554, Aug. 5, 1997, 111 Stat. 636; Pub. L. 113–183, title III, § 301(f)(2), Sept. 29, 2014, 128 Stat. 1944.)

The Uniform Interstate Family Support Act (9 1B West's U.Law Ann. (1999) § 101 et seq. (UIFSA)), which has been adopted by all states, governs, inter alia, the procedures for establishing, enforcing and modifying child support orders in cases in which more than one state is involved. The 1996 version of the UIFSA took effect in California on August 4, 1997. (See Fam.Code, § 4900 et seq.) Together with the Federal Full Faith and Credit for Child Support Orders Act (FFCCSOA) (28 U.S.C. 1738B, the UIFSA ensures that in every case only one state exercises jurisdiction over child support at any given time. (See UIFSA, § 201, com. at pp. 275-277. Hogoboom & King, Cal. Practice Guide: Family Law (The Rutter Group 2003) ¶ 18:725, p. 18-190.) *In re Marriage of Crosby & Grooms*, 10 Cal. Rptr. 3d 146 (2004).

[181] (N.H. Stat. §457:39).

[182] *Hesington v. Estate of Hesington*, 640 S.W. 2d 824 (Mo. App. 1982).

[183] *"No State shall...pass any...Law impairing the Obligation of Con-tracts...."*

ARTICLE I, SECTION 10, CLAUSE 1.

[184] *United States Trust Co. of NY v. New Jersey*, 431 U.S. 1, 5 (1977)(Burger, C.J., concurring)

[185] *In re Marriage of Franks*, 542 P. 2d 845, 850 (Col. 1975).

[186] *U.S. Trust Co. of New York v. New Jersey*, 431 U.S. U.S.1, 25 (1977).

[187] *Buffalo Teachers Fed. v. Tobe*, 464 F.3d 362, 368 (2d Cir. 2016) *citing Energy Reserves Group v. Kansas Power & Light*, 459 U.S. 400, 411-13 (1993).

[188] Meyer v. Nebraska, supra, note 54.

[189] Barnett, Our Republican Constitution, *supra* at note 4. Barnett devotes his last chapter to the case of *United States v. Carolene Products, Co.*, where he complains that the Supreme Court actually invented a legislative purpose not presented to the trial or appellate court in order to justify the constitutionality of a state regulation. 304 U.S. 144 (1938). Barnett begins his book with his disgust of a Chief Justice Roberts' opinion accepting a statutory purpose to the Affordable Care Act that it was clear that Congress never considered in order to render the law constitutional, that it was a tax.

[190] *See* Utah Code Ann. § 30-8-6(1)(b) attached as Appendix B

[191] Re*ese v. Reese*, 984 P. 2d 987, 994 (Utah 1999), *quoting, Mathie v.Mathie*, 12 Utah 2d 116, 120-121, 363 P.2d 779, 782-73 (1961).

[192] *Irving Trust Co. v. Day*, 314 U.S. 556 (1942).

[193] *Volid v. Volid*, 286 NE 2d 42 (Ill. App. 1972).

[194] *Id.*

[195]   *In re Marriage of Franks*, 542 P. 2d 845 (Col. 1975).

[196] *Casto v. Casto*, 508 So. 2d 330, 334 (Fla. 1987).

[197] *Bratton v. Bratton*, 136 SW 3d 595 (Tenn. 2004), *Pierce v. Pierce,* 994 P. 2d 193 (Utah 2000).

[198] *Id.*

[199] *Avitzur v. Avitzur*, 58 NY 2d 108 (N.Y. 1983).

[200] *Keyes v. Keyes,* 351 P. 3d 90 (Utah App.2015).

[201] *Neilson v. Neilson*, 780 P. 2d 1264, 1269 (Utah App. 1988).

[202] *Potter v. Murray City*, 760 F.2d 1065 (1985).

[203] Henriques, H. S. Q. "Jewish Marriages and the English Law," *supra*, note 26, at 391-449.

[204] *Barber v. Barber*, *supra*, note 123, at 600-601

[205] 83 U.S. 139 (1873)(Bradley, J., concurring).

[206] *Id* at 141-142. Ironically, in 1872, the Court refused to interfere in the inner workings of religious societies, claiming that the United States, unlike England, believed in religious freedom. *Watson v. Jones*, 80 U.S. 679, 728 (1872).

[207]   Randall, Willard Sterne, *Alexander Hamilton: A Life, supra*, note 133.

[208] *Barber v. Barber*, *supra*, note 123, at 603.

[209] Estin v. Estin, 334 U.S. 541, 547 (1948).

[210]   *Orr v. Orr*, 440 U.S. 268 (1979), striking down an Alabama law that only men could be required to pay spousal support.

[211] *Id.*

[212]   *Boyer v. Boyer*, *supra*, note 160,

[213] As Dr. Cott described the 19th Century free love movement in *Public Vows,* author, Christina Hoff Sommers, explains the source of these views. Sommers, Christina H., 2013, *Freedom Feminism, It's Surprising History and Why it Matters Today,* American Enterprise Institute for the Public.

In this book, Sommers says that the feminist movement consisted of two distinct groups, the "egalitarian school" and the more conservative "maternal school." Disparaging the Christian Family model, the progressive "egalitarian school":

> [R]egarded women as independent agents rather than wives and mothers, and aimed to liberate them through appeals to universal rights. ... Maternal feminism, by contrast, was traditionalist and family-centered. It embraced rather than rejected women's established roles as homemakers, caregivers and providers of domestic tranquility.

According to Sommers, in the 19th Century, the maternal school had great appeal to the majority of women. These women were principally involved in achieving the vote, as well as female issues regarding the preservation of the Christian Family model, such as Prohibition with its relief from the alcoholism that besieged their families, and pushing out of society any sign of prostitution, securing for them the sexual attention of present and future husbands. Yet, while Sommers acknowledges that western women now have the same rights and opportunities as men, she rejects the egalitarian belief that women aspire to be just like men:

The major battles of American women for equality and opportunity have been fought and won. Women in the United States have their freedom; they have achieved or exceeded parity with men in most ways.

Yet, speaking of America and Western Civilization, Sommers writes:

Women, far more than men, struggle with the challenge of combining work and family ... The negotiation of the social and sexual relations between males and females is a constant feature of human existence. The unique circumstances of women require special attention and protection.

Sommers goes on to describe the frustrations of the more conservative feminists who want to continue their Victorian roles as was part of the Christian Family model. It is that conflict that continues to rage, the reason why there is confusion among women, and disillusionment among men, on what it really means to have equal rights.

[214] Mead, Margaret, *Male and Female, supra,* note 163.

[215] Krauskopf, Joan M., Thomas, Rhonda C., "Partnership Marriage: The Solution to an Ineffective and Inequitable Law of Support," *Ohio St. L.J.* 35: 558 (1974).

[216] The duties of the marital contract, other than the sexual component, are increasingly vague. Perry, Twila L., "The 'Essentials of Marriage': Reconsidering the Duty of Support and Services," *Yale J.L. & Feminism* 15: 1 (2003).

In the mid-70s up to the early 80s, many feminist writers, including University of California-Berkeley professor Marjorie Maguire Shultz, and Lenore Weitzman sought to eliminate the outdated definitions of parenting through a proposal of contract marriage. Weitzman believed contract marriage was necessary to permit women to leave their maternal roles so they can achieve what had been a man's world of business and industry, and eliminate age-old prejudice. She also suggested that it was unfair to men to place them in the perpetual role of provider, and contract marriage would permit the participants to determine their own roles.

[217] www.trumanlibrary.org.

[218] *Estin v. Estin, supra*, note 209.

[219] *Stanton v. Stanton*, 421 U.S. 7 (1975), finding that mothers and fathers are equally responsible for providing for their children. *See Webb v. Hillsboro Co. Hosp. Auth.*, 521 So.2d 199 (Fla. Dist. Ct. 1988), holding that Equal Protection requires that husband and wives owe a reciprocal duty to provide for the necessary support of each other.

[220] *Elia-Warnken v. Elia, supra*, note 108.

[221] *Noble v. Noble* 761 P.2d 1369 (1988).

[222] DeLorean v. DeLorean, 511 A. 2d 1257 (N.J. Sup. Ct. 1986).

[223] According to www.churchofengland.org, the ceremony is: Standing before the minister, a hymn may be sung. The couple is then asked to join hands and make their vows in the presence of God. Facing each other, the groom says his vow:

to have and to hold,

from this day forward;

for better, for worse,

for richer, for poorer,

in sickness and in health,

to love and to cherish,

till death us do part;

according to God's holy law.

In the presence of God I make this vow.

The bride then says her vow:

to have and to hold,

from this day forward;

for better, for worse,

for richer, for poorer,

in sickness and in health,

to love and to cherish, *and obey*

till death us do part;

according to God's holy law.

In the presence of God I make this vow.

In the Anglican ceremony, the maid of honor and best man hand the rings to the minister, who blesses the "symbol of unending love and faithfulness, to remind them of the vow and covenant which they have made this day through Jesus Christ our Lord." The groom then the bride place the bands on each other's fourth finger of the left hand. While holding the ring, they individually pledge:

I give you this ring

as a sign of our marriage.

With my body I honour you,

all that I am I give to you,

and all that I have I share with you,

within the love of God,

Father, Son and Holy Spirit.

Now officially joined in matrimony in the eyes of God, the priest makes a Proclamation to the congregation, announcing the couple as husband and wife as he joins their hands and says, "Those whom God has joined together let no one put asunder."

[224] *Volid v. Volid, supra,* note 193

[225] *Karchner v. Mumie*, 398 Pa. 13, 15 (Pa. 1959).

[226] *Norton v. MacFarlane*, 818 P. 2d 8, 16 (Utah 1991).

[227] *McQuarters v. Ducote*, 234 S.W. 2d 433 (Tex. App. 1950). To establish this character of action the plaintiff must prove: (1) that the defendant intentionally or purposely enticed away the spouse, (2) that there has been loss of affection or consortium, and (3) that defendant's conduct was the controlling cause of the loss.

[228] *Karchner v. Mumie, supra*, note 225, at 15.

[229] *Id.*

[230] *Norton v. MacFarlane, supra*, note 226, at 12.

[231] *See, e.g., Helsel v. Noellsch*, 107 S.W.3d 231 (Mo. 2003).

[232] *Norton v. MacFarlane, supra*, note 226, at 12. *See also Fitch v. Valentine*, 959 So. 2d 1012 (Miss. 2007).

[233] *Thomas v. Siddiqui*, 869 S.W. 2d 740 (Mo. 1994).

[234] As a New York's highest court explained in 1884 in *Todd v. Weber:*

> In our opinion there is in the record, as above quoted, evidence of an agreement made upon valuable consideration, and, therefore, also binding in law upon him and consequently upon his estate. It is true that by the common law the child that is born before marriage is so far *nullius filius* that he cannot inherit; but he may acquire rights. Nor is his putative father under any legal liability at common law to support him [*citation omitted*] yet it is said he may take him out of the parish (*Sherman's Case,* 1 Ventris, 210) and maintain him, or by will leave any of his property to him, or in his life-time make other provision for

300

his support. So if he acknowledges or adopts the child as his own, and at his request it is cared for by others, he becomes liable in favor of the party providing for it [citations omitted] and remains so until he renounces the child or otherwise notifies the persons who have it, that he will no longer be bound to them. From these or like circumstances a promise to make compensation may be implied, and of course such a promise may also be expressed by him. In either case the natural obligation arising out of the relation of the putative father to his child will uphold a contract upon which an action may be sustained. 50 Sickels 181 (N.Y. 1884).

[235] Posner, Eric A., 2000, *Law and Social Norms*, Harvard University Press.

[236] A girl must be unmarried and chaste in order to bring a cause of action for seduction. *See, Davis v. Stroud*, 52 Cal. App.2d 308 (Cal. App. 1942). In the 20th Century, Congress double downed on that theme with the passage of the Mann Act, making it a crime for a man to take a woman not his wife across state lines for the purpose of debauchery or prostitution. *Bell v. United States*, 349 U.S. 81 (1955).

[237] Posner, Eric, *Law and Social Norms*, *supra*, note 235, *Chapter 6.*

[238] Krist, Gary, 2014, *Empire of Sing: A Story of Sex, Jazz, Murder, and the Battle for Modern New Orleans*, Broadway Books.

[239] *Slaughter-House Cases*, supra, note 49.

[240] Weitzman, Lenore, 1985, *The Divorce Revolution*, Free Press.

[241] Scott, Elizabeth S. and Robert E Scott, "Marriage as Relational Contract," *Va. L. Rev.*, 84:1225 (1998).

[242] *Gomez v. Perez, supra,* note 166.

[243] At common law, the child born during the marriage was presumed to be of the marriage, absent a showing of lack of access. Although rebutting the presumption required clear and convincing evidence, in today's world, DNA testing is so exact as to exclude the husband as the child's father and thus meet the standard. *K.E.M. v. P.C.S.,* 38 A.3d 798 (Pa. 2012). Of course, as the facts of that case indicate, the wife who agrees to divorce her husband and agrees that her husband is the father of the child in a judgment might not be allowed to proceed against the natural father under the doctrines of res judicata and collateral estoppel.

[244] Jeffrey, Terrance P., "Census: 49% of Americans Get Gov't Benefits; 82M in Households on Medicaid," CSNnews.com, (October 23, 2013):

In total, the Census Bureau estimated, 151,014,000 Americans out of a population then estimated to be 306,804,000 received benefits from one or more government programs during the last three months of 2011. Those 151,014,000 beneficiaries equaled 49.2 percent of the population. This included 82,457,000 people--or 26.9 percent of the population--who lived in households in which one or more people received

Medicaid benefits. Also among the 151,014,000 who received benefits from one or more government programs during that period: 49,901,000 who collected Social Security; 49,073,000 who got food stamps; 46,440,000 on Medicare; 23,228,000 in the Women, Infants and Children program, 20,223,000 getting Supplemental Security Income; 13,433,000 who lived in public or subsidized rental housing; 5,098,000 who got unemployment; 3,178,000 who got veterans' benefits; and 364,000 who got railroad retirement benefits.

[245] *See* Appendix B, *infra.*

[246] Krauskopf, Joan M. "Rehabilitative Alimony: Uses and Abuses of Limited Duration Alimony." *Family Law Quarterly*, vol. 21, no. 4, 1988, pp. 573–589.

[247] www.eeoc.gov. According to the U.S. Equal Employment Opportunity Commission, the Equal Pay Act of 1963 (Pub. L. 88-38) (*EPA*), as amended, "as it appears in volume 29 of the United States Code, at section 206(d). The *EPA*, which is part of the Fair Labor Standards Act of 1938, as amended (*FLSA*), and which is administered and enforced by the *EEOC*, prohibits sex-based wage discrimination between men and women in the same establishment who perform jobs that require substantially equal skill, effort and responsibility under similar working conditions."

[248] *Volid v. Volid, supra,* note 193, at 391.

[249] Census.gov/, cdc.gov/.

[250] Sowell, Thomas, 2006, *The Vision of the Anointed: Self-Congratulations as the Basis for of Social Policy,* Basic Books.

[251] Census.gov/, cdc.gov/.

[252] Census.gov/, cdc.gov/.

[253] Smith, Helen, 2013, *Men on Strike, Why Men are Boycotting Marriage, Fatherhood, and the American Dream,* Encounter Books.

See also, Eberstadt, Nicholas, 2016, *Men Without Work: America's Invisible Crisis,* Templeton Press. According to Eberstadt, the number of prime-age men outside the workforce exploded in the time period between 1965 and 2015 to more than 7 million, 6.5 times higher than a half a century before, growing at a rate of three times those inside the workforce or those looking for work.

[254] Hall v. Hall, 858 P.

2d 1018 (Utah App.

1993).

[255] *Id.*

[256] *Neilson v. Neilson, supra,* note 201, at 1268-1269:

> The public limitation imposed by the trial court in this case has been applied in several other jurisdictions as a limit on the enforceability of prenuptial agreements, even though they are not *per se* contrary to public policy because they were made in contemplation of divorce. For example, in a case apparently relied upon heavily by the trial court here, the California Supreme

Court held that a prenuptial agreement violates the public policy favoring and protecting marriage only insofar as its terms, evaluated objectively, "encourage or promote dissolution." [*Citations omitted.*] [A]agreements that "provided for or tended to induce divorce or separation" would be contrary to public policy; [*Citations omitted.*] (prenuptial agreement enforceable as long as it does not encourage divorce); [*Citations omitted.*] (prenuptial agreement providing for disposition of property is enforceable if, among other things, the terms do not "promote or encourage divorce or profiteering by divorce"). [*Citations omitted.*]

[257] Scott, Elizabeth S. and Robert E Scott, "Marriage as Relational Contract," *Va. L. Rev.*, 84:1225 (1998).

[258] *Lassiter v. Department of Social Services*, 452 U.S. 18, 27 (1981), *quoting Stanley v. Illinois*, 405 U.S. 645, 651 (1972).

[259] Bruce, Andrew Alexander. "The Beveridge Child Labor Bill and the United States as Parens Patriæ." *Michigan Law Review*, vol. 5, no. 8, 1907, pp. 627–638

[260] Rendleman, Douglas R., "Parens Patriae: From Chancery to the Juvenile Court," 23 S.C.L. Rev. 205 (1971).

[261] *Pierce v. Society of Sisters*, 268 U.S. 510, 535 (1925).

[262] *Prince v. Massachusetts*, 321 U.S. 158 (1944).

[263] *Id* at 165.

[264] *Santosky v. Kramer*, 455 U.S. 745, 753 (1982).

[265] *Parham v. JR*, 442 U.S. 584, 602 (1979).

[266] *Troxel v. Granville, supra,* note 76.

[267] *Jones v. Barlow*, 154 P. 3d 808 (2007).

[268] www.uniformlaws.org/

[269] www.uniformlaws.org/

[270] As an attorney practicing for more than 25 years in family law, I have hundreds of stories of absurd results from trial court judges, and if you ask any other family law attorney with like experience, they would tell you hundreds more.

[271] *See Delorean v. Delorean, supra,* note 222

[272] *Ex Parte. Devine*, 398 So.2d 686 (Ala. 1981).

[273] Cott, Nancy, *Public Vows, supra* note 2.

[274] *Ex parte Devine, supra,* note 272, at 688.

[275] Blacklaws v. Milne, 82 Ill. 505, 506 (1876).

[276] *Ex Parte Devine, supra,* note 272, *quoting Hibbette v. Bains,* 29 So. 80 (Miss. 1900).

[277] *Id* at 688-689.

[278] *Id* at 689.

[279] *Id, quoting, Helms v. Franiscus*, 2 Bland Ch (Md) 544 (1830).

[280] *Id.*

[281] *Id, quoting,* Thomas *v. Thomas*, 101 So. 738 (Ala. 1924).

[282] *Id.*

[283] *Id., quoting, Frontiero v. Richardson*, 411 U.S. 677 (1973).

[284] Grall, Timothy, "Custodial Mothers and Fathers and Their Child Support: 2011," *U.S. Census Bureau* (October 2013).

[285] In re Marriage of Hansen, 733 NW 2d 683, 691 (Iowa 2007), *quoting, In re Marriage of Burham,* 283 N.W.2d 269 (1979).

[286] *Id, quoting, In re Marriage of Muell,* 408 N.W.2d 774, 775 (Iowa App. 1987).

[287] Cases involving the use of a mental health professional to make custody determination include: *KEITH R. v. Superior Court,* 174 Cal. App. 4th 1047 (Cal. App. 2009), *Leard v. Schenker,* 931 So. 2d 355 (La. 2006), *In re Marriage of Martin,* 42 P. 3d 75 (Colo. App. 2002), *Dranko v. Dranko,* 824 A.2d 1215 (Pa. 2003).

Cases involving the use of a Guardian ad Litem, a family law attorney, making a representation to the court as well as acting as the attorney for the child include: *Hensarling v. Hensarling,* 824 So. 2d 583 (Miss. 2002), *In re CF,* 113 Ohio St. 3d 73 (Ohio 2007), *In re Marriage of Bates,* 918 N.E.2d 714 (Ill. 2004).

[288] *Id* at 693.

[289] In *Rosen v. Celebrezze,* the Ohio Supreme Court discusses the inception of the Uniform Child Custody Jurisdiction Act and its methodology for resolving interjurisdictional disputes, as well as its replacement, The Uniform Child Custody Jurisdiction and Enforcement Act. 117 Ohio St. 3d 241 (Ohio 2008).

[290] *United States v. Booker,* 543 U.S. 220 (2005).

[291] *Id* at 233. "If the Guidelines as currently written could be read as merely advisory provisions that recommended, rather than required, the selection of particular sentences in response to differing sets of facts, their use would not implicate the Sixth Amendment. We have never doubted the authority of a judge to

exercise broad discretion in imposing a sentence within a statutory range." *Id.*

[292] 391 U.S. 68 (1968). In his brief before the Supreme Court, Louisiana's Attorney General warned that giving "illegitimate" children equal protection would support a deviation in sexual behavior that is "costly to society," and that it is right for the state to deny equal treatment to children born outside of marriage, something that will "endanger the stability of marriage and family by abolishing distinctions between legitimates and illegitimates." 1968 WL 112828 (1968). The Attorney General justified giving superior rights to children born during lawful wedlock. "Since marriage as an institution is fundamental to our existence as a free nation, it is the duty of the [state] to encourage it." He decried the impact of giving government benefits to children born outside of marriage as the reason for the recent increase in out of wedlock births. The Attorney General's argument relied on the 19th Century Supreme Court cases on the subject of marriage:

> Tradition supports the power of Louisiana, rather than the federal government, to regulate the institution of marriage within the state's borders, and to prescribe all the effects of marriage, including status of offspring and property rights derived from marriage.
>
> Recognition of marriage as a civil contract in English Common law was transferred to the American colonies where it provided the legal structure of the American family. The acceptance of marriage as a contract carried

with it the power of the colonial legislatures to determine the obligations and rights of marriage. The state was considered the third party to every marriage ceremony, presenting the public interest imposing its legal and ethical standards upon as otherwise private undertaking.

[293] *Id* at 692.

[294] Henriques, H. S. Q., "Jewish Marriages and the English Law," *supra,* note 26.

[295] *In re Burrus*, 136 U.S. 586, 593-594 (1890).

[296] *Ankenbrandt v. Richards*, 504 U.S. 689 (1992).

[297] As explained in *Rose v. Rose*, 481 U.S. 619 (1979): "On the rare occasion when state family law has come into conflict with a federal statute, this Court has limited review under the Supremacy Clause to a determination whether Congress has 'positively required by direct enactment' that state law be pre-empted." [*Citations omitted.*]. Before a state law governing domestic relations will be overridden, it "must do 'major damage' to 'clear and substantial' federal interests." [*Citations omitted.*]." *Id* at 625.

[298] *Rosado v. Wyman*, 397 U.S. 397 (1970).

[299] Wisconsin Law Professor Tonya L. Brito explains that "As part of the Social Security Act of 1935, Congress established the federal welfare system, Aid to Dependent Children (later renamed Aid to Families with Dependent Children, or AFDC), a means-tested cash assistance program. AFDC was modelled on the then existing Mothers' Pension welfare programs, which states

established between 1910 and 1920. At that time, advocates for government aid for poor mothers and children championed the value of mothering and argued that mothers would best serve their children's well-being by caring for them in their own homes. These advocates urged that without government aid to poor mothers and children, family destitution would result, causing institutionalization of children in orphanages, child neglect due to maternal employment outside the home, or the children themselves working long hours in factories alongside their mothers. Like Mothers' Pensions, AFDC provided small cash benefits to poor single mothers. However, eligibility was broadened under AFDC. While Mothers' Pensions were primarily reserved for widows, mothers qualified for AFDC assistance if the family lacked a male wage earner because of death, desertion, or incapacity." Brito, Tonya L., "Fathers Behind Bars: Rethinking Child Support Policy Toward Low Income Noncustodial Fathers and Their Families," *Journal of Gender, Race and Justice*, 15: 617 (Spring 2012).

See U. S. Advisory Commission Report on Intergovernmental Relations, Statutory and Administrative Controls Associated with Federal Grants for Public Assistance 5-7 (1964) (hereafter cited as Advisory Commission Report). The category singled out for welfare assistance by AFDC is the "dependent child," who is defined in § 406 of the Act, 49 Stat. 629, as amended, 42 U. S. C. § 606 (a) (1964 ed., Supp. II), as an age-qualified "needy child . . . who has been deprived of parental support or care by reason of the death, continued absence from the home, or physical or mental incapacity of a parent, and who is living with" any one of several listed relatives.

[300] *King v. Smith*, 392 U.S. 309 (1968).

[301] Social Services Amendments of 1974, Pub. L. No. 93-647, § 101(a), 1974 U.S.C.C.A.N. (88 Stat. 2337) 2716, 2732-40. The Federal Child Support Act of 1984 required all states to allow children to sue for paternity up until their 18th birthday. 42 U.S.C.A. § 666(a)(5) (Supp. 1985).

[302] Recently, a New Jersey teenager, Rachel Canning, made national news by suing her parents for child support after she voluntarily left the home. After the trial court refused her request, however, she moved back in with her parents. Horowitz, Ben, March 14, 2015, "NJ teen Rachel Canning agrees to dismiss lawsuit against her parents," www.NJ.com.

[303] Brito, Tonya L., "Fathers Behind Bars," *supra,* note 299.

The 11th Circuit Court of Appeals explained the reasoning in in 1989 in *Wehunt v. Ledbetter*, 875 F.2d 1558 (1989):

> Title IV-D does not create any enforceable right: it was not enacted for the "especial benefit" of AFDC families. A Title IV-D program operates under a separate legislative and regulatory framework than that of a Title IV-A program. Title IV-A provides funds from the public treasure to support children in need. Title IV-D seeks to recover those funds and restore the Treasury balance by enforcement of support obligations owed by

311

the absent parents of these children. The driving force behind the program is recovery of welfare payments and a parallel commitment to remove and keep families from the necessity of welfare dependence by establishing and enforcing support obligations. The legislative history indicates that in enacting Title IV-D Congress was primarily concerned with collecting child support in order to reduce the welfare rolls.

The **problem of welfare** in the United States is, to a considerable extent, a problem of the **non-support of children by their absent parents**. Of the 11 million recipients who are now receiving Aid to Families With Dependent Children (AFDC), **4 out of every 5** are on the rolls because they **have been deprived** of the support of **a parent who has absented himself from the home.** [*Emphasis added.*]

The Committee believes that all children have the right to receive support from their fathers. The Committee bill, like the identical provision passed by the Senate (H.R. 3153) last year, is designed to help children attain this right, including the right to have their fathers identified so that support can be obtained. The immediate result will be a lower welfare cost to the taxpayer but, more importantly, as an effective support collection system is established fathers will be deterred from deserting their families to welfare and children will be spared the effects of family breakup. S.Rep. No. 93-1356, 93rd Cong., 2d Sess., *reprinted in* [1974] *U.S.Code Cong. & Admin. News* 8133, 8145-46 (beginning paragraphs of "Section IV. Child Support").

The above-quoted language indicates the concern Congress felt over the welfare problem. Its reading indicates the goal of Title IV-D was to immediately lower the cost to the taxpayer as well as to lessen the number of families enrolling in welfare in the future — benefits to society as a whole rather than specific individuals. This reading is consistent with the concern evidenced by Congress in "Section II. Social Services" entitled *"Rapid rise in Federal funds for social services,"* and *"Federal funds for social services limited in 1972."* which precedes the section on child support.

[304] 45 CFR § 303.5.

[305] The Moynihan Report, a/k/a Office of Policy Planning and Research, United States Department of Labor, "The Negro Family: The Case for National Action." (March 1965).

[306] Maldonado, Solangel, "Deadbeat or Deadbroke: Redefining Child Support for Poor Fathers," *U.C. Dav. L. Rev.* 39: 991 (March 2006).

[307] The Moynihan Report, supra, note 305.

[308] Cott, Nancy, *Public Vows, supra*, note 2.

[309] Collingwood, R.G., *The Idea of History, supra,* note 131.

[310] Posner, Eric, *Law and Social Norms, supra,* note 235, at 149.

[311] Cdc.gov.

[312] Eberstadt, Nicholas, *Men Without Work: America's Invisible Crisis, supra,* note 253.

[313] Patterson, Elizabeth G., "Civil Contempt and the Indigent Child Support Obligor: The Silent Return to Debtor's Prison," Cornell Journal of Law and Public Policy, 18:1 (Fall 2008).

[314] *Ibid.*

[315] Henry, Ronald K., "The Innocent Third Party: Victims of Paternity Fraud," *Family Law Quarterly*, 40:1 (Spring 2006).

[316] 45 CFR § 303.5.

[317] At common law, the child born during the marriage was presumed to be of the marriage, absent a showing of lack of access. Although rebutting the presumption required clear and convincing evidence, in today's world, DNA testing is so exact as to exclude the husband as the child's father and thus meet the standard. *K.E.M. v. P.C.S.,* 38 A.3d 798 (Pa. 2012). Of course, as the facts of that case indicate, the wife who agrees to divorce her husband and agrees that her husband is the father of the child in a judgment might not be allowed to proceed against the natural father.

[318] Prior to the Uniform Parentage Act, states generally required the appointment of a guardian ad litem, or other representative, of the child when paternity was challenged during a divorce proceeding. *See, e.g., S. v. S.,* 595 S.W.2d 357 (Mo. App. 1980).

[319] The 1973 version of the UPA was consistent with trial courts that refused to terminate the husband's parental rights to a child born during a lawful marriage unless, as in a step-parent adoption, there was another man to take his place as the provider for the child.

See. e.g., Adoption of R.A.B. v. R.A.B., 562 S.W.2d 356 (Mo. 1978).

[320] www.uniformlaws.org. The 1973 version of the Act reads as follows:

> "§ 11. [Blood Tests] (a) The court **may**, and upon request of a party shall, require the child, mother, or alleged father to submit to blood tests. The tests shall be performed by an expert qualified as an examiner of blood types, appointed by the court. "

[321] www.uniformlaws.org. The 2002 version of the Act reads as follows:

> "SECTION 502. ORDER FOR TESTING. (a) Except as otherwise provided in this [article] and [Article] 6, the court **shall** order the child and other designated individuals to submit to genetic testing if the request for testing is supported by the sworn statement of a party to the proceeding: (1) alleging paternity and stating facts establishing a reasonable probability of the requisite sexual contact between the individuals; or (2) denying paternity and stating facts establishing a possibility that

sexual contact between the individuals, if any, did not result in the conception of the child."

While the comments to the Act do permit trial courts to use equitable principals to deny a request, the unambiguous language of the statute do not.

[322] *See e.g., Callender v. Skiles*, 591 N.W.2d 182 (Iowa 1999).

[323] The North Carolina Supreme Court spelled out the reason for the change in 1953:

"At common law the father of a bastard child is under no legal obligation to support it. [*Citation omitted*]. However, the father of a bastard is under a natural and moral duty to support his bastard. [*Citations omitted*]. Recognizing that the common law rule is not adapted to the public opinion of **a modern [C]hristian state** and that a poor innocent child should not be suffered to famish as a victim of his father's lust, unless supported at the public charge or by charity, statutes in most states impose on the father the legal duty to support his bastard child. 10 C.J.S., Bastards, § 18, page 86. G.S. § 49-2 **makes this moral obligation of the father, legal and enforceable**, and we see no good reason why our courts should not enforce it in this case, where the father is subject to our jurisdiction. [*Citation omitted*]. [*Emphasis added*]." *State v. Tickle*, 77 S.E.2d 632 (N.C. 1953).

[324] *See Sanchez v. LDS Social Services*, 680 P. 2d 753 (Utah 1984). The Uniform Laws Commission provides a history of the changes in parentage law in its prelude to its 2000 version of the UPA:

"The National Conference of Commissioners on Uniform State Laws has addressed the subject of parentage throughout the 20th Century. In 1922, the Conference promulgated the "Uniform Illegitimacy Act," followed by the "Uniform Blood Tests To Determine Paternity Act" in 1952, the "Uniform Paternity Act" in 1960, and certain provisions in the "Uniform Probate Code" in 1969. The "Uniform Illegitimacy Act" was withdrawn by the Conference and none of the other Acts were widely adopted. As of June 1973, the Blood Tests to Determine Paternity Act had been enacted in nine states, the "Uniform Paternity Act" in four, and the "Uniform Probate Code" in five. The most important uniform act addressing the status of the nonmarital child was the Uniform Parentage Act approved in 1973 [hereinafter referred to as UPA (1973)]. As of December, 2000, UPA (1973) was in effect in 19 states stretching from Delaware to California; in addition, many other states have enacted significant portions of it. Among the many notable features of this landmark Act was the declaration that all children should be treated equally without regard to marital status of the parents. In addition, the Act established a set of rules for presumptions of parentage, shunned the term "illegitimate," and chose instead to employ the term "child with no presumed father." UPA (1973) had its genesis in a law review article, Harry D. Krause, A Proposed Uniform Act on Legitimacy, 44 TEX. L.

317

REV. 829 (1966); see also Krause, Equal Protection for the Illegitimate, 65 MICH. L. REV. 477 (1967). Professor Krause followed with a pathfinding book, ILLEGITIMACY: LAW AND SOCIAL POLICY (1971), and then went on to serve as the reporter for UPA (1973). When work on the Act began, the notion of substantive legal equality of children regardless of the marital status of their parents seemed revolutionary. Even though the Conference had put itself on record in favor of equal rights of support and inheritance in the Paternity Act and the Probate Code, the law of many states continued to differentiate very significantly in the legal treatment of marital and nonmarital children. A series of United States Supreme Court decisions invalidating state inheritance, custody, and tort laws that disadvantaged out-of-wedlock children provided the both the impetus and a receptive climate for the Conference to promulgate UPA (1973). Case law has not always reached consistent results in construing UPA (1973)."

[325] *See e.g., Estate of Cornelious*, 674 P. 2d 245 (Cal. 1984).

[326] Personal Responsibility and Work Opportunity Reconciliation Act of 1996, Pub. L. No. 104-193, § 101-116, 110 Stat. 2105, 2110-85 (1996 Personal Responsibility and Work Opportunity Reconciliation Act of 1996, Pub. L. No. 104-193, § 101-116, 110 Stat. 2105, 2110-85 (1996). The 1996 federal law required states to create statutes that would legally bind a man to parenthood by executing an affidavit (along with the natural mother), attesting to his parentage. The Indiana provides an example of this change, as

318

explained in *In re the Paternity of E.M.L.G.*, 863 N.E.2d 867 (Ind. App. 2007) :

> "[P]rior to 2001, Indiana Code section 31-14-7-1 stated that "a man is presumed to be a child's biological father if . . . (3) the man executed a paternity affidavit in accordance with IC XX-XX-X-X.1." Relying on this statute, our court held that Indiana Code section 31-14-7-1 provided that the "execution of a 'paternity affidavit' operat[ed] to create a legal presumption that the man is the child's biological father," and that such presumption could be rebutted. *In re Paternity of M.H.*, slip op. at 4. However, since then, Public Law 138-2001, sec. 6, amended this section by deleting subsection three regarding the presumption for a man who has executed a paternity affidavit.
>
> In addition, our General Assembly contemporaneously inserted the following language: "[a] man is a child's legal father if the man executed a paternity affidavit in accordance with IC XX-XX-X-X.1 and the paternity affidavit has not been rescinded or set aside under IC XX-XX-X-X.1." Ind. Code § 31-14-7-3 (2001). The General Assembly specifically chose to remove the language merely creating a "presumption" that a man who executed a paternity affidavit was the biological father of the child, and instead it inserted language providing that such a man became the "legal father" upon execution of such an affidavit unless he rescinded the affidavit within the sixty-

day time frame provided for under Indiana Code section 16-37-2-2.1. "

[327] Henry, Ronald K., "The Innocent Third Party: Victims of Paternity Fraud," *supra,* note 315.

[328] 45 CFR § 303.5(g). Apparently, there was no requirement that hospitals hire attorneys to provide this legal information. Rather, as set form in subsection 5:

> The State must provide to all hospitals, State birth record agencies, and other entities designated by the State and participating in the State's voluntary paternity establishment program:
>
> **(i)** Written materials about paternity establishment,
>
> **(ii)** Form necessary to voluntarily acknowledge paternity, and
>
> **(iii)** Copies of a written description of the alternatives to, the legal consequences of, and the rights (including any rights, if a parent is a minor, due to minority status) and responsibilities of acknowledging paternity.

[329] 45 CFR § 303.5(g)(ii)(F).

[330]American Association of Blood Banks, Annual Report Summary 4 (2010). According to the report, this does not mean that 30 percent of the men who signed the affidavit were excluded, as such a statistic is not available as, logically, as many men who signed the affidavit might never gotten the test to find out. *See,* Greenwood, Anne, Comment, "Predatory Paternity Establishment: A Critical Analysis of the Acknowledgment of

Paternity Process in Texas," *35 St. Mary's L.J.* 421, 425 (2004).

[331] *See, e.g., Decanay v. Menoza*, 573 F 2d. 1075 (9th Cir. 1978)(finding that it was the duty of the court to determine whether a financial settlement was in the minor's best interests.)

[332] *See, e.g., S.J.V. by Blank v. Voshage*, 860 S.W.2d 802, 804 (Mo. App. 1993):

> This procedural difference is used to determine whether a guardian ad litem or a next friend is to be appointed to represent the interests of the minor party. "The next friend normally prosecutes action and a guardian ad litem defends actions." It has been stated, however, "they are both officers of the court and their rights and duties are basically the same." (*Citations omitted.*).

[333] www.marriage.uslegal.com.

[334] In the most egregious case in my career, a man was incarcerated for a violation of his probation from a plea of guilty for a child who was not his, but that the mother had convinced him he was and to sign the paternity affidavit. The Missouri Division of Child Support Enforcement (n/k/a the Family Support Division) had entered a child support order that was based on an income ten times his highest ever salary. The man had never received the notice, and I was able to prove sewer service -- the false return of service of process. After the family court obtained a genetic test excluding him, it voided the child support order. After six months of incarceration, the judge in the criminal case finally let him out. If it wasn't for his mother's ability to pay for my services, he

would have served out his full term in jail, and like so many men, be in a perpetual trap.

335 Cohen, Alan W., 2015, *America Solved: A New Family for the 21st Century,* Elliot Publishing.

336 Collingwood, R.G., *The Idea of History, supra,* note 131.

337 *Stanley v. Illinois*, 405 U.S. 645 (1972).

338 www.dictionary.com

339 *Reynolds v. United States*, *supra*, note 102.

340 Cott, Nancy, *Public Vows*, *supra*, note 2.

341 Einstein, Albert, "The Negro Question," 1946.

342 *Mattox v. United States*, 156 U.S. 237 (1895).

343 *Brown v. Buhman, supra,* note 114.

344 *Wisconsin v. Yoder*, 406 U.S. 205 (1972).

345 *Id* at 209.

346 *Id* at 218. The Supreme Court's reference to *Braunfeld v. Brown* is significant because it was the last Supreme Court decision to permit the Christian state to control the daily workings of non-Christians who don't want to follow its tenets, particularly the Sabbath. *Braunfeld v. Brown*, 361 U.S. 599, 605 (1961). The statute in question forbade any citizens from doing business on Sunday, and the Plaintiff was an orthodox Jew who celebrated his Sabbath on Saturday, and wished to do business on Sunday. Citing *Reynolds v. United States*, *supra*, note 102, the Court found the impact of the statute as a "secular' one, and not directly preventing the Plaintiff from practicing his faith. Rather the Court found the

matter an infringement on commerce, and applied the rational basis test:

> [W]e cannot find a State without power to provide a weekly respite from all labor and, at the same time, to set one day of the week apart from the others as a day of rest, repose, recreation and tranquility—a day when the hectic tempo of everyday existence ceases and a more pleasant atmosphere is created, a day which all members of the family and community have the opportunity to spend and enjoy together, a day on which people may visit friends and relatives who are not available during working days, a day when the weekly laborer may best regenerate himself. This is particularly true in this day and age of increasing state concern with public welfare legislation. *Id* at 607.

In his dissent, Mr. Justice Brennan rejected the rational basis test when it involved the ability of a citizen to exercise his faith, proposing that strict scrutiny that would require a compelling state interest. Brennan found the state interest is not compelling. Rather, he found Pennsylvania's justification that the majority so willing accepted, to be "almost chimerical" – meaning it was so outlandish that it qualified as science fiction. *Id* at 614.

[347] 494 U.S. 872 (1990).

[348] 42 U.S.C. § 2000 *et seq.*

[349] *City of Boerne v. Flores*, 521 U.S. 507 (1997).

[350] 134 S.Ct. 2751 (2014).

[351] *Wisconsin v. Yoder*, *supra*, note 344.

[352] Donald Sterling not only was stripped of his ownership, but the NBA gave him a lifetime ban. Espn.com

[353] Posner, Eric, *Law and Social Norms*, *supra*, note 235, at 95.

[354] *See generally*, *Furman v. Georgia*, 408 U.S. 238 (1972).

[355] *BMW of North America, Inc. v. Gore*, 617 U.S. 559, 568 (1996).

[356] *Gertz v. Robert Welch, Inc.*, 418 U.S. 323 (1974).

[357] Posner, Eric, Law and Social Norms, *supra*, note 235, at 149.

[358] *Pilot Life Ins. Co. v. Dedeaux*, 481 U.S. 41 (1987).

[359] Posner, *Eric, Law and Social Norms*, *supra* note 235, at 150

[360] Collingwood explains in *The Idea of History* that Plato was arguing against the existing beliefs of the Sophists that the individual Collingwood, R.G., *The Idea of History*, *supra*, note 131.

[361] *Id*.

[362] Mead, Margaret, *Male and Female*, *supra*, note 163.

[363] Posner, Eric, Law and Social Norms, *supra,* note 235, at Chapter 5.

See also State ex Rel. Div. of Fam. S. v. Standridge, 676 S.W. 2d 513 (Mo. 1984), finding that at common law, husbands were not responsible to third parties for the support of his wife and children if the wife left the household with their children without his assent or good cause.

[364] *Levy v. Louisiana, supra,* note 60.

[365] Cohen, Alan W., *America Solved, supra,* note 335.

[366] *In re Estate of Hollett*, 150 N.H. 39 (S.Ct. 2003).

[367] *See, e.g., Peters v. Narick*, 270 S.E. 2d 760 (W. Va. 1980).

[368] *Unander v. Unander*, 506 P. 2d 719 (Or. 1973).

[369] See *DeLorean v. DeLorean, supra,* note 222.

[370] *See Hulse v. Criger*, 247 SW 2d 855 (Mo.1952).

[371] *Mallen v. Mallen*, 622 S.E.2d 812, 815 (Ga. 2005).

[372] Spaht, Katherine, "The Last One Hundred Years," *supra,* note 159.

[373] *Marvin v. Marvin,* 557 P. 2d 106 (Cal.1976).

[374] Brinig, Margaret F., "The Influence of Marvin v. Marvin on Housework During the Marriage," 76 Notre Dame L. Rev. 1311 (2000-2001).

[375] *See Brown v. Buhman, supra,* note 114.

[376] *See Ellsworth v. American Arbitration Ass'n,* 148 P.3d 983 (Utah 2006).

[377] Knapp, Charles L., "Taking Contracts Private: The Quiet Revolution in Contract Law," 71 Fordham L. Rev. 761 (2002).

[378] *See DeLorean v. DeLorean, supra,* note 222.

[379] Collingwood, R.G., *The Idea of History, supra,* note 131.

[380] Kaplan, Fred, *John Quincy Adams: American Visionary, supra,* note 41.

[381] Gladwell, Malcolm, 2000, *The Tipping Point,* Little Brown and Company.

[382] Moore, Stephen, May 31, 1999, "Speed Doesn't Kill: The Repeal of the 55-MPH Speed Limit," Cato Institute. www.cato.org.

[383] McWhorter, John, 2005, *Winning the Race, Beyond the Crisis in Black America,* Gotham Books.

[384] Smith, Helen, *Men on Strike, Why Men are Boycotting Marriage, Fatherhood, and the American Dream, supra,* note 253.

[385] Eberstadt, Nicholas, *Men Without Work: America's Invisible Crisis, supra,* note 253.

[386] Mead, Margaret, *Male and Female, supra,* note 163.

[387] Kaplan, Fred, *John Quincy Adams: American Visionary, supra,* note 41.

Made in the USA
San Bernardino, CA
26 February 2017